JOB EVALUATION

JOB
EVALUATION

BY

JOHN A. PATTON
President
John A. Patton Management Engineers, Inc.

AND

REYNOLD S. SMITH, JR.
Assistant to the President
Unistrut Products Company

1955

RICHARD D. IRWIN, INC.
HOMEWOOD, ILLINOIS

———

First Printing, May 1949
Second Printing, January 1950
Third Printing, June 1952
Fourth Printing, June 1954
Fifth Printing, June 1955

PREFACE

IF THE reader, after studying this volume, realizes that the elimination of wage rate inequities involves substantially more than the evaluation of jobs and the subsequent assignment of money rates to jobs, the efforts of the authors will have been well rewarded.

Job evaluation has afforded both management and labor with techniques whereby, in a systematic manner, problems of wage rate determination can be solved with a reasonable degree of accuracy. Unfortunately, many job evaluation applications have failed to gain their legitimate objectives. In the opinion of the authors, the failures result, to a large extent, from a lack of knowledge of job evaluation practicalities. Therefore, in the preparation of this text an effort has been made to emphasize the practicalities involved in applying job evaluation principles and to enable the reader to share in the experiences of the authors in installing numerous job evaluation systems in manufacturing and merchandising companies, hospitals, restaurants, newspapers, social institutions, and service organizations.

During the early period of development of job evaluation methods, the prerogative of setting wage rates was vested in management. Today, however, this prerogative is shared in most instances with organized labor. Refusal to be practical in facing this social change has been a frequent cause of failure of job evaluation projects. Because of the absolute necessity of securing labor's acceptance of job evaluation as a technique of wage rate determination, considerable stress has been placed by the authors on the matter of dealing with the union.

The reader is introduced to the subject of job evaluation by a discussion in Chapter 1 of such matters as the origin and historical development of job evaluation and the scope, advantages, and objectives of formal programs of eliminating wage rate inequities. Such discussions enable the reader to understand better the more technical subjects that follow. Of the four generally recognized methods of job evaluation, the three less widely applied—namely, ranking, predetermined grading, and factor comparison—are explained in Chapter 2. Point rating, the most widely accepted of the four methods, is treated in the third chapter. In Chapter 4 the analysis of jobs, the gathering and recording of job data, and the preparation of written job descriptions are described; while Chapter 5 is devoted to the actual procedure of determining the relative worth of jobs. The process of gathering, assembling, interpreting, and applying locality and industry wage survey data is discussed in Chapter 6, while the application of money rates to jobs and the many ramifications involved in such applications are made the subject matter of Chapter 7.

One of the most common reasons for the failure of job evaluation is management's failure to sell the idea to those who may be affected. While selling the idea is the first step—and one of the most important steps—in a program, a clear understanding of the technical aspects of plans and procedures will help the reader to understand better what must be sold. Therefore, this problem is discussed in Chapter 8, after the reader has become acquainted with the technicalities of job evaluation. The composition of job evaluation committees and the qualifications of the job analyst are discussed in Chapter 9. Chapter 10 treats the subject of problems and procedures of job evaluation administration; and Chapter 11 sets forth the opinions of the authors (resulting from their experiences) as to why job evaluation programs fail.

The consensus among many authorities is that a job evaluation installation will be only partially effective if it is not complemented with a method of measuring the worth of the individual on a particular job. For this reason the last chapter involves a discussion of merit rating.

The authors wish to express their sincere appreciation to their many friends in the labor, management, and consulting fields whose suggestions and criticisms aided materially in the presentation of the text. Special acknowledgement is due Professors John F. Mee and Thomas J. Luck, of Indiana University, Professor Michael J. Jucius, of Ohio State University, and Mr. Ralph H. Landes, for their assistance in reviewing the manuscript and offering constructive suggestions for the improvement of the subject matter. A debt of gratitude is acknowledged to Eleanor Pestka and Georgia Andros for their help in the typing of the manuscript.

JOHN A. PATTON
REYNOLD S. SMITH, JR.

CHICAGO, ILLINOIS
April 1949

TABLE OF CONTENTS

LIST OF ILLUSTRATIONS

Chapter 1

INTRODUCTION

W AGES, simply stated, are the compensation paid for the performance of a task or a group of tasks. Inasmuch as labor has some direct or indirect bearing on the ability of an organization to produce an income, it is a problem of management to distribute the payroll in such manner that each employee will receive an equitable share of the income produced. The complete wage formula should provide such equitable distribution. Job evaluation is the foundation of the complete formula upon which are erected such increments as wage incentives and profit-sharing bonuses. To job evaluation is assigned the problem of establishing and maintaining proper relationships between the rates paid for all occupations.

The purpose of this text is to present an analysis of methods of preventing and eliminating inequities in wage rates and to discuss, not only the procedures involved in job evaluation, but the steps to be taken prior to and after the installation of a plan for job evaluation. There should be a background of understanding of the origin, present status, uses, scope, and objectives of job evaluation against which to project a knowledge of the principles of technique and procedure. This chapter is devoted to providing such a background.

Before proceeding, however, it should be understood that job evaluation is not a science. As the following discussion unfolds, it will be realized that human judgment is too variable to allow for claims of scientific accuracy in the application of job evaluation.

For the most part, the accuracy of job evaluation is attained from a systematic approach. Job evaluation concerns itself not with the general wage level but with the objective establishment of the relative worth of one job to another; it thereby provides the differential over and above the minimum wage to remunerate the worker for skill, effort, responsibility, and conditions under which work is performed. (See Figs. 1–1 and 1–2.) While

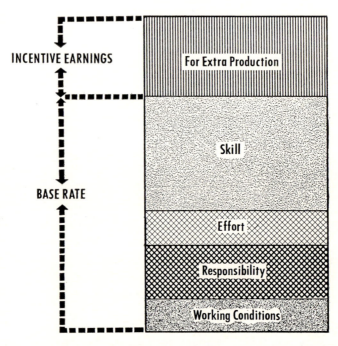

Fig. 1–1.—Composition of earnings and evaluated base rates under a wage incentive system.

not scientific, job evaluation is the most acceptable present-day method of determining, through a refinement of our opinions, equitable wage relationships.

Origin and History of Job Evaluation

The Middle Ages.—Informal job evaluation was strongly entrenched in industry in the Middle Ages, when the historical differentials between apprentice, helper, journeyman, and master had already been established. The maintenance of

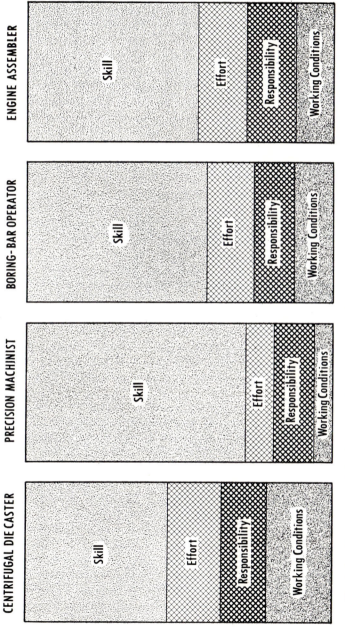

FIG 1-2.—Comparison of the four general characteristics of job content in each of four jobs carrying the same base rate. Taken from an actual evaluation.

such differentials has since clashed in many instances with the requirements of mass production and is responsible, to a considerable extent, for the resistance of many craft unions to job evaluation. It is well to consider the effect the impact of job evaluation will have against traditional wage differentials. Some industries have advisedly refrained from radical disturbances of inequitable traditional wage differentials, for to completely erase established inequities would not overcome prejudices of long standing.

The Machine Age.—The most powerful influence on job content and, therefore, on wage differentials was the advent of mass production which resulted in the Machine Age. The original metalsmith was a combination of foundry worker, blacksmith, and machinist. However, as industrial growth took place and operating units expanded, increased production necessitated specialization on the part of the worker. The metalsmith first became a machinist, blacksmith, or foundry worker and later perhaps a specialist in horizontal turret lathe operations or coremaking. Each successive step toward complete specialization narrowed the scope of skill required of the worker. Throughout this period of change in skill requirements, working conditions improved, laborsaving devices reduced physical effort, and more costly materials and equipment were handled; however, little was done to systematically recognize these changes by adjusting the wage rates to reflect widening or narrowing differences in job content.

Modern Concept of Job Evaluation.—The United States Civil Service Commission in 1871 made one of the first attempts at job evaluation. But it was nearly forty years later, in 1909, that the modern concept of job evaluation originated, as a result of a requirement of the Civil Service Commission of Chicago. Shortly thereafter the Commonwealth Edison Company of Chicago pioneered the field. At that time, however, modern business management was, for the most part, too awe-stricken with the possibilities of wage incentives to realize that superimposing incentive earnings on maladjusted base rates would multiply the inequalities. Consequently, job evaluation remained almost wholly on a flat basis. In 1924 Merrill R. Lott introduced one of the present-day methods of formal job evaluation (Fig. 1–3). His plan incorporated fifteen factors or work

GENERAL CHARACTERISTIC	ORIGINAL FIFTEEN JOB CHARACTERISTICS
Skill	Time usually required to become highly skilled in an occupation. Time usually required for the skilled person in the occupation to become adapted to the employer's needs. Educational requirements of an occupation. Degree of skill, manual dexterity, and accuracy required.
Effort	Necessity of constantly facing new problems, variety of work. Physical effort required. Monotony of work.
Responsibility	Money value of parts worked on—possible loss to company through personal errors, unintentional. Dependence that must be placed upon the integrity and honesty of effort of the employee.
Working Conditions	Cleanliness of working conditions. Exposure to health hazard. Exposure to accident hazard.
Factors Considered Extraneous	Number of men employed in an occupation in the locality—the labor supply. Possibility of an employee locating with another company with a similar earning capacity. Prevailing rate of pay in locality.

Fig. 1–3.—The grouping under general characteristics of the fifteen characteristics proposed by Merrill R. Lott, showing segregation of those considered unnecessary.

characteristics, some unnecessary, others unrelated; but, amateurish as it was by present standards, it did lay the foundation for meeting future needs.[1]

Because of continued specialization and individualization, job nomenclature became exceedingly complex. Occupations

[1] M. R. Lott, *Wage Scales and Job Evaluation* (New York: Ronald Press Co., 1926), p. 52.

having identical titles varied as to skill, effort, and responsibility requirements and as to working conditions; while many similar occupations were referred to by various titles. Not knowing what constituted the job, the going rate was not obtainable for informal rate setting. Minimum wage laws were enacted under the Fair Labor Standards Act of 1938, which lifted the lower end of the wage scale, but the Act failed to adjust the upper end of the scale and resulted in further inequities.

In the thirties, however, the scope of collective bargaining widened considerably, particularly as the result of the organization of millions of skilled and semiskilled workers. Collective bargaining forced wage levels upward, but with little thought given to the existent misalignment of rates. The result was such a hodgepodge of rates that management and unions alike were without a sound defensible system of wage determination as a device for collective bargaining. Only a few companies had foreseen the probable impact of social legislation and the attempts at labor organization on wage structures and had systematically established their wage rates.

The popularity of job evaluation swelled during World War II. This occurred partly because many new occupations were originated as a result of changes in or the introduction of new production methods and partly as a means of justifying wage increases under the Wage and Salary Stabilization Law of 1942. Executive Order 9250 of the law states in part: "The National War Labor Board shall not approve any increase in the wage rates prevailing on September 15, 1942 unless such increase is necessary to correct maladjustments or inequalities or to aid in the effective prosecution of the war." A system of establishing rates was necessary, primarily because management was faced with a labor shortage and was forced to secure a means of measuring relative worth of jobs so that intelligent bids could be made for the workers' services.

Thus, for the most part, widespread acceptance of job analysis has taken place during such periods of increasing wages. What the attitude toward the matter will be during periods of declining wages is not known. Where labor and management have already accepted job evaluation, the problems attendant to downward rate adjustment should be eased.

While job evaluation resulted primarily from a need on the part of management for a method of determining equitable wage rate differentials, sight should not be lost of the other worth-while results that accrued to those who adopted formal methods. Properly applied, job evaluation resulted, in many instances, in a reduced number of grievances, simplified wage negotiations, and elimination of many misunderstandings through clarification of the lines of authority. Further, many managements found that, because they had accurate job data and impartial techniques to work with, supervision became less subjective and policies of fairness were implemented.

Present Status of Job Evaluation

A Period of Adjustment.—Despite the broad acceptance of job evaluation, it is still an open field for research, development, and readjustment. The formal systems conceived less than a quarter of a century ago were hardly born when the demand for them became urgent. Time was too limited to permit natural development of job evaluation. The need for systematic wage patterns was realized *after* management was actually confronted with problems that only job evaluation could aid in solving. Many companies rushed into their projects without sufficient prior planning; plans were poorly selected; frequently, employees were not informed of the job evaluation program, with a resulting lack of co-operation; and many companies failed to revise their programs to meet changing conditions. If management had used foresight, plans could have been available that would have permitted a trial stage for job evaluation. This was not done, however, and many concerns are suffering the consequences. The deficiencies and weaknesses of their job evaluation programs are evident, and efforts are now being made to overcome these difficulties.

Problems to Be Solved.—The immature status of job evaluation is reflected, partially at least, in problems it has yet not solved. There are certain factors, not as yet included in job evaluation plans, which make certain jobs more or less attractive than other jobs and which have an influence on wage rates for this reason. The demand for certain skills can influence rates to the extent of forcing them beyond the limits of any plan. How can a supply-and-demand factor be incorporated into a plan? Prospects of future advancement may be an attractive feature of one job but may be entirely unimportant in another. Can such a factor be logically included as a measure of relative job worth? Men are attracted to occupations characterized by steady rather than by seasonal employment. Should plans include a factor to measure such a characteristic? What about pressure from organized groups? Are we to incorporate a sex factor to distinguish a male from a female occupation, or are we ready to consider a job as a job regardless of whether a man or woman performs it? What are we to do about the relatively few traditional inequalities that have existed for years? These are but a few of the problems which must be solved before we can consider job evaluation to have become of age. Many of these are human relations problems, and as yet no systematic method has been devised to solve them.

A Field for Research.—Solutions to the problems cited above afford the student a vast field for research. Before a widely acknowledged belief in the value of job evaluation can be expected, however, improvement in available methods and elimination of the causes of criticism must be attempted. That room exists for considerable fact-finding and study is indicated by the fact that there are four distinct techniques used in determining relative job content. These techniques are referred to collectively as "job evaluation," and each is discussed in later chapters. Exponents of each technique frequently argue relentlessly and disagree violently over the relative advantages that their method may have over all the others. Unions criticize job evaluation primarily because they feel that it tends to reduce their effectiveness at the bargaining table. They also feel strongly on the matters of re-evaluation of jobs and subsequent downgrading of employees as a result of technological changes. In short, job evaluation is one of the most controversial questions in current wage administration. Effecting a meeting of the minds of all parties in this wage administration controversy will be hastened through research into methods of eliminating the basic causes of disagreement.

Job Evaluation Not Universally Accepted.—While the use of job evaluation as an aid to wage setting is rather widespread, its acceptance is by no means universal. Numerous companies are without job evaluation programs for various reasons. They fail to appreciate its advantages, are reluctant to disturb long-established rate differentials, have not overcome union objections, do not understand its application, or in many instances their management is lethargic. Many unions have, up to this time, refused or resisted job evaluation, feeling that it partially destroys one of their prerogatives, i.e., the drawing-up of a wage scale which they consider a principle function of collective bargaining. Traditional differentials are problems which many unions must face if they are to accept methods of wage setting other than those effected through collective bargaining; and such differentials may prove difficult hurdles to negotiate, particularly by some of the strongly entrenched craft unions. There are also those who are intolerant of the efforts of the exponents of job evaluation. Such an attitude today is as logical as the attitude toward the efforts of the Wright brothers to fly a half-century ago.

Despite these adverse attitudes, however, job evaluation has made substantial advances in the last ten years and is still in a state of partial development. Because we know where its deficiencies lie, our efforts toward improvement should be in the right direction, and, as a result, the next decade should witness broader acceptance on the part of both labor and management. To date job evaluation is the best-known method of establishing equitable wage rates.

Uses for Job Evaluation

Improved Industrial Relations.—While job evaluation serves numerous purposes, one of the fundamental reasons for its existence is its widespread acceptance as a management and union tool for improving industrial relations. The state of these relations is a measure of the workers' satisfaction with their jobs. Two generally recognized sources of dissatisfaction among labor are the wage level and the relationship of income of one worker to another; the latter is the primary concern of job evaluation. Because defensible wage rates can be arrived at on a logical basis, unions and management have a factual, rather than an arbitrary basis for collective bargaining which should aid in eliminating constant renegotiation of wage rates. The ability of unions and management to substantiate rate differentials reduces to a minimum wage rate grievances resulting from workers' misconceptions of the worth of their jobs. Personalized rates are abolished under properly administered plans. Job evaluation does not recognize as measurements of relative worth such factors as religion, political affiliations, color, sex, or relationship to the boss; and, therefore, it eliminates personal favoritism. Job evaluation also assists management in maintaining a position in the labor market and in conforming to industry and community wage rates, since closer comparison of jobs can be made through use of properly written descriptions of job content.

Aid to Hiring.—Industrial psychologists frequently attribute excessive labor turnover to the worker's dissatisfaction with his job because of management's failure to match aptitudes and vocational interests with assigned tasks. An occupation cannot be evaluated systematically without first determining its requirements. It follows that, once requirements are known, personnel departments are better equipped to fit the right man to the right job; recruitment, selection, placement, and training of applicants is aided; and turnover and training costs are reduced. Because workers are placed in occupations they are best suited for and interested in, their morale level is raised and their productivity is increased.

Other Advantages of Job Evaluation.—Job evaluation provides certain advantages to unions and their members. Such advantages lie in the union's ability, through an evaluation plan, to maintain proper rates for jobs which are made more complex or more fatiguing by the addition of new duties. Here unions are not working to the detriment of the company but, by demanding rate revisions for modified jobs, are merely helping management to tread the straight and narrow. That some unions realize the advantages of job evaluation was demonstrated by the extent to which the United Steel Workers of America (C.I.O.) actively participated in the formulation and installation of the job evaluation plan of the Carnegie-Illinois Steel Corporation. This large union constantly campaigns for the adoption of the same plan by companies whose employees are organized under the union's direction. The plan is usually referred to by the union officers and members as the "steelworker's plan."

It has been said that all of the real advantages of job evaluation accrue to the union. Wages are never decreased as the result of the program, but the overpaid man retains his old rate while the underpaid worker gets a raise. To a certain extent this is true, and it accounts for much of the union's willingness to participate in evaluation programs. But it represents a shortsighted management viewpoint; for the basic purpose of job evaluation is to eliminate wage inequities, and that is as advantageous to management as it is to the union.

To say that the union and its members receive all the benefits of an equitable wage rate schedule is to ignore a great many possible advantages to management as well as the basic purpose of job evaluation. The benefits which management receives from the existence of such a schedule are substantial and sufficient to justify the installation of a sound plan. Another benefit of job evaluation, which is certainly not confined to an occasional application, is that job evaluation is essential to the installation of a wage incentive. Whenever production under an incentive plan is measured on a time basis, base rates determine the employees' earnings; and if there are inequities in those base rates, they will be magnified by the production and earning increases, and the incentive plan will likely fail. Further, in some cases the pattern of job description and job analysis can be and has been employed as a basis for training employees in the duties of their jobs, or in the activities of their own or related departments. In many instances the study of jobs prior to evaluation has uncovered method improvements.

It may be concluded from this review of the advantages and benefits of job evaluation that management and employee, or union where one is involved, can both receive substantial benefits from a properly applied and installed job evaluation program. Most of the advantages directly enjoyed by one also accrue to the other. For example, the worker cannot help but benefit by the elimination of inequities, by working under a better-trained supervisor, or by having the opportunity to attain a better position which is afforded by well-defined job requirements. Yet these advantages or benefits are usually thought of as belonging to management. The same, however, is true of the benefits which unions consider most important to them.

Why Inequities between Wage Rates?

Job evaluation is no patented formula for the cure of all industrial relations and wage administration ills. It does provide a solution for many problems; and, if applied now, as it should have been in the past, it can be a strong preventive. Wage rate inequities cannot be laid at the door of any particular individual or group of individuals, for management, labor, and government have all had their hands in the shaping of wage structures. The Industrial Revolution and the Machine Age have been pointed out as important contributing factors, just as future phases in our economic history will have disturbing effects on wage differentials unless means are available to quiet these disturbances.

Effect of World War II Economy.—Present-day inequities stem from many causes. The rapid expansion of our industrial activity during the war and the draining of millions of men from the labor market for service in the armed forces resulted in an unprecedented bidding-up of wage rates with little regard for the maintenance of rate relationships. Certain occupations were in excessively high demand, while the demand for some remained practically unchanged despite equality of skill, responsibility, and other characteristics. New, untrained employees began to take home larger pay checks than those with many years' experience. Changes in methods simplified operations, thus reducing the amount of skill required; but the stress of a tight labor market precluded downward adjustments of hiring rates. Many companies took advantage of the National War Labor Board's policy of wage stabilization by using infinitesimal changes in job content to substantiate disproportionate rate increases. Transfers between jobs of similar worth were used as excuses for upward rate revisions. Standard hiring rates were disregarded by many. After the war, the monetary gains of labor were stabilized; but it will be years before many wage inequities will be erased.

Effect of the Depression Economy.—Just as the war-boom economy had a disturbing effect on differentials, so, too, did the depression economy of the thirties. Wages sank to levels low enough to make working unattractive as compared to joining the relief ranks. Twenty and twenty-five cent hourly rates were not unusual; but when they sank below that level, pride was discarded and charity patronized. Meanwhile, the highly skilled worker's wages dropped, and the spread between the skilled and unskilled rates narrowed both percentagewise and in terms of money. Government added its influence by enacting minimum wage laws. This had the effect of raising the rates paid the unskilled workers, while the highly skilled workers received little attention. Some shortsighted managements could not resist the temptation of reducing higher rates to make up for the increases in lower rates forced on them by law.

Internal Causes of Inequities.—The reasons for inequities in one company or industry are not the same as those in other concerns, for rarely will the same set of circumstances prevail. Most managements and unions have, at one time or another, been guilty of certain abuses. One common grievance of employees is that they are hired for work requiring a minimum of experience and carrying a corresponding rate, but that, when they have gained experience and skill, they are given more difficult tasks to perform without a rate increase to compensate them for the increased worth of the job. Whether such a condition is incurred deliberately or by oversight, it cannot help but have an effect on employee relations. Favoritism toward individuals or to a type of work can also warp a wage structure just as can the arbitrary judgment of foremen and other supervisors.

Likewise, an unbalanced viewpoint toward the worth of a task can result in many inequities. The foreman who came up through the ranks as a lathe hand may, in his own mind, inflate the value of the lathe job and undervalue the position of shipping clerk. Top management is often guilty of the same error, with the result that clerical positions in the sales department may receive a higher rate of pay than those in the production department, or vice versa, when the general requirements of the jobs are the same. It will be seen in later discussions that percentage wage increases have disturbed wage structures by destroying the balance of differentials and, in many instances, by magnifying the inequities.

The Unions' Responsibility.—Unions, also, must bear their share of criticism. They have had unlimited opportunities for correcting many inequalities which plague their officials, grievance comitteemen, and stewards and which, at times, are causes for dissension among the members. Demanding and accepting blanket rate increases, regardless of the relative worth of individual jobs, only serves to continue overpayment in some occupations and to deny others additional, justifiable increases. Arbitrators have handed down decisions that gave no evidence whatever of a desire to maintain equity between rates. An example is the decision of an arbitrator who awarded a group of lathe operators a pay adjustment for making setups they were not making, were not required to make, and for which the company furnished setup men. The reasoning behind the decision was based on the fact that other operators had formerly been paid for making these setups and that to deny the present operators payment for the work, whether performed or not, would eliminate a portion of their potential wages.

The foregoing statements mention some, but by no means all, of the reasons for rate inequities. Before programming a job evaluation project, it is well for one to consider the reasons why rates are out of line; for success of the program may be affected if it does not fit into the surrounding circumstances.

Scope of Job Evaluation

Whenever the jobs of an organized body of men can be defined, it is possible to devise a plan of job evaluation. Plants, offices, government bodies, and armies can derive benefits from a sound program. The scope of any undertaking, then, would not be limited by the plan but by the capabilities of those charged with its installation and administration, assuming, of course, that the proper plan had been applied. Job evaluation programs are usually confined to a company-wide or plant-wide basis, for as a general rule the object is to solve a problem confronting a single company, plant, or office rather than an entire industry or community. Too great an undertaking, such as the evaluation of the occupations within one industry, may result in considerable loss of accuracy in establishing the differentials. While required skills within an industry may be identical, other characteristics which measure relative job worth, such as responsibility requirements and working conditions, may differ between plans owing to company policy, aggressiveness in reducing hazards, or funds expended in the improvement of work surroundings.

Ordinarily the attention of labor and management is focused on the problems within their own plants and locals. Such being the case, the problems are simplified because the interested parties are familiar with the occupations and job requirements and are not confronted with unreliable job nomenclature and lack of standard titles.

Inequalities are not confined to factory occupational rates. Clerical employees, supervisors, technical personnel, and executives are as interested in the reasons for rate differentials as are

the shop personnel, and they are entitled to as much consideration. They, too, are interested in the bases of compensation,
the mechanics of promotion and demotion, the qualifications
for higher paid jobs, and the amount and method of wage rate
changes. Because the characteristics of clerical and supervisory
occupations are not the same as for shop jobs, there has been
little success in using one plan to cover both types of work.

Job evaluation, then, is not confined to any particular type
of work, but its scope is limited in any one installation to those
jobs affected by operation methods and policies of the same
management.

Objectives of Job Evaluation

Analysis of Wage Administration Weaknesses.—Prior to establishing a job evaluation program, it is well to consider its objectives. To install a plan without objective may well prove to be
a waste of effort and funds and may be a disturbing influence
on labor relations. Labor has certain fundamental general
desires, namely: continued employment at wages that permit a
few of life's luxuries; opportunities for advancement; a feeling of
responsibility; and a desire to be treated with a measure of equality. The worker's specific desires are not necessarily common
to all companies, and what these desires are management must
determine for itself. A check on the list of advantages that can
result from a program to eliminate wage rate inequities may
bring to light certain weaknesses in a wage administration plan.
Analysis of the gains secured by other organizations can produce similar results. A review of wage rate grievances, past
and present, should also reveal weaknesses in wage administration practices. When the list of grievances are known, the
objectives of the program automatically evidence themselves.

Some of the more commonly known objectives of job evaluation projects are:

1. To determine whether or not wage and salary rate inequalities
   exist.

2. To reduce the number of grievances resulting from a mal-adjusted wage rate structure.
3. To provide accurate job data for use in—
   a) Hiring new employees
   b) Determining promotional qualities
   c) Determining lines of promotion
   d) Maintaining consistency in promotion
   e) Rehiring old employees after a layoff or a leave of absence
   f) Determining whether or not employees are qualified for their jobs
   g) Placing men in the best jobs available
   h) Conserving skill through a revamping of jobs
   i) Training supervisors
   j) Revealing opportunities for technological improvement
   k) Improving working conditions
   l) Eliminating hazards
   m) Delineating lines of authority and promotion.
4. To provide a sound wage rate foundation prior to applying a system of wage incentives.
5. To eliminate undue stress on seniority where seniority alone does not qualify an employee for a particular job.
6. To assist management in maintaining a wage policy of either leadership, average position, or low wage scale.

Fulfillment of Some Employee Desires.—Full employment and the general wage level are not problems that can be solved by job evaluation, if they can be solved at all. Therefore, job evaluation can hardly claim to enable the employee to attain the few luxuries desired. While the program may not create opportunities for advancement, it points out where they lie, and that is an aid to the employee in directing his or her efforts. The mere fact that a job analyst reviews the employees' jobs and secures the employees' approval of the job descriptions tends to create in employees a feeling of importance and responsibility. Knowing that their occupations are all receiving the same consideration, employees are more likely to feel that a condition of equality exists. Thus, job evaluation, partially at least, satisfies some of the fundamental wants of all employees. Whether it satisfies the more specific desires can be determined only by an analysis of the desires and by matching them with the advantages gained through job evaluation.

Ultimate Objective.—What management's desires are is made known when the requirements of the employees are known. It is the co-operation resulting from mutually satisfactory industrial relations that is the ultimate objective of a job evaluation project.

Policies Affecting a Job Evaluation Program

The first major step in a program of job evaluation is to sell the idea to the employees or their representatives, the foremen, supervisors, department heads, and others who may be interested in or affected by the project. In order for the idea to be sold, however, certain policies having a direct bearing on the acceptance or rejection of the program must be formulated.

Participation Policy.—Management's decision as to who is to participate in the program will have a definite effect on the success of the project. Whether or not there is a union to be considered, it will be to the best advantage of all concerned if the employees are invited to be a part of the entire project. Some unions have a definite policy of nonparticipation, feeling that to take part sanctions the work of management and that it is more desirable to accept or reject the evaluation after completion when results can be seen[2]. On the other hand, some union authorities believe that if there is a refusal to participate the union will have no arguments with which to challenge the position of management.[3] The second position seems to be more sound, and adherence to it should not only enhance the value of the program to both union and management but also fortify the union with answers to the questions of members regarding job evaluation practices and procedures. Those employees who are respected by the general force should be invited to

[2]United Electrical, Radio, and Machine Workers of America, *U. E. Guide to Wage Payment Plan, Time Study and Job Evaluation*, Topic No. 49 (1947), p. 77.

[3]William Gomberg, *A Labor Union Manual on Job Evaluation*, (Chicago: Roosevelt College, Labor Education Division, 1947), p. 48.

join in the discussions, even though they may lend little or nothing to such discussions. There is an advantage in pursuing such a policy, however, for employees will have more confidence in the program knowing that they were represented. Then, too, such representatives may prove of considerable value in bringing to light details concerning working conditions, hazards, and physical effort that are occasionally overlooked.

The participation policy must be tempered to fit the circumstances. For instance, large numbers of employees who are distributed between many plant or office locations make participation in the entire job evaluation project far less feasible. Justifying the expense of such an undertaking would be difficult. In some cases there will not be employees who are mentally capable of participating in the program.

Training Policy.—A policy outlining the methods to be applied in training personnel in job evaluation practices and procedures must be formulated at an early date. Will foremen and other supervisors be trained to understand the meaning and advantages of the program or will just those who will do the actual work be trained? Will union stewards, grievance committeemen, and union officials receive training, and, if so, will they attend the same classes with the management representatives? What and how much publicity will precede the installation of the program? These are all questions which must be answered. It must also be borne in mind that the laissez-faire concept of employee relations will reduce substantially the probabilities of employee acceptance of a plan if acceptance is not entirely precluded.

Union Policies.—The policies governing an evaluation program must take into consideration what the union has decreed regarding job evaluation. If an international union has laid down principles designed to guide the locals in the development, acceptance, and application of a job evaluation plan, it is advisable to consider the effect that such principles may have on the ultimate success of the program.

Use of Consultant.—Another policy question to be reckoned with is whether or not an outside consultant will be retained. When management has on its staff a well-trained person, capable of handling the job, the necessity for outside aid is lessened. The greatest advantage to be secured from outside help emanates from the fact that the properly qualified consultant is trained, can do the job more expeditiously because of the knowledge and experience at his disposal, and is not hampered by internal red tape. On the other hand, management must eventually handle the problem itself, and to rely too much on outside aid may not be feasible. In any event, the consultant retained should be acceptable to both labor and management, and he must be absolutely impartial in his relations with either party. The retention of a professional management engineer as a nonparticipating adviser may be the most satisfactory approach.

Policies Embodied in Union Agreements.—Many policies will be covered in agreements with the union and will eventually become parts of the contract between the union and management. Such matters as preparation and approval of job descriptions, the plan to be used, rate ranges, merit rating, or single rate are usually covered in such agreements. Whether embodied in a formal written document or not, out-of-line rates or those in excess of evaluated rates must be given considerable attention and thought when policies are being established. How are out-of-line rates treated in instances where a worker returns to his old job after quitting voluntarily; where he has been upgraded to a higher classified job; where downgrading for cause occurs; where there is a temporary layoff due to lack of work; where there is a transfer to avoid layoff, a transfer at the employee's request, or at the option of the company? These and other questions on out-of-line rates must be answered. Other points to be covered may include the employee's jobs that are to be evaluated, the review of employees' occupations as a step toward reclassification, and the handling of disagreements on evaluation.

There is no set of policies applicable to all job evaluation projects. Policy will be dictated by the objectives of management in installing the program, the objectives of the union in accepting it, the policies of the union itself, and the bearing that such a program will have on future industrial relations.

Time Limits for a Job Evaluation Program

A job evaluation program can be a long drawn-out undertaking unless it is well organized. In large plants, having an excess of 2,000 employees, the evaluation committee often finds its job a never-ending one because of the frequency of job content changes. This frequently results in the bogging-down and loss of interest in the project. It is important, therefore, that schedules be set up, work be definitely assigned, and those to whom the work is assigned be held responsible for the maintenance of schedules.

A complete job evaluation program can generally be accomplished in a period of time equal to four hours times the number of jobs studied and evaluated. Thus, if there are four hundred job descriptions to be written, the complete program will require approximately 1,600 hours, or forty weeks. This figure can obviously fluctuate, for no two sets of circumstances are alike. The complexity of jobs, the attitudes of supervision and workers toward accepting the program, the additional training and selling time necessary, the capabilities and number of personnel involved in executing the program, and the decisions on the retention of a consultant are all factors that influence the time required for completion of a project. Once a time estimate is made, deadlines should be set for each phase of the installation of the job evaluation program, and responsible persons should be held to them.

A complete program of job evaluation embraces six general phases. In the order of their treatment in this text, they are:

1. Selecting the method of evaluation to be used and the plan to be employed.

2. Securing job facts as a basis for job analysis and the preparation of descriptions.

3. Determining relative values for jobs and classifying employees.

4. Applying money values to relative job worth.

5. Selling the idea of job evaluation to supervisors, employees, and union in order to gain the co-operation and understanding so vital to a successful program.

6. Administering the system.

As will be discussed later, the first steps to be taken in establishing a job evaluation project are the selling of the program to participants and the selecting of personnel who will constitute the various committees responsible for carrying out the program. However, many of the problems involved in these steps are more fully realized if the technicalities of job evaluation are known. Accordingly, the two chapters immediately following are concerned with the selection of job evaluation methods and plans.

QUESTIONS

1. Is job evaluation scientific? Explain.
2. What do you believe to be the primary reason for the existence of rate inequities? What other reasons can you state?
3. The advent of mass production resulted in many wage rate inequities. How could such inequities have been prevented?
4. What will be the result of superimposing a wage incentive on a base rate structure in which rate inequities exist?
5. Do you know of an industry in which a program of job evaluation would not be advisable? Explain.
6. What are some of the factors influencing wage rates which are not included in job evaluation plans?
7. Has there been universal acceptance of job evaluation on the part of labor? Management? Explain.
8. What favorable effects does job evaluation have on industrial relations? What may be some unfavorable effects?

9. How does a union benefit from a program of job evaluation?

10. Is job evaluation limited to a particular group of employees or type of occupation? Explain.

11. What are some of the fundamental desires of employees which job evaluation assists in fulfilling?

12. What is the first major step in the job evaluation program? Why is it so important that this step be taken at the beginning of the program?

13. What are some of the policies management should formulate prior to undertaking a job evaluation program?

14. How many weeks are required to complete an evaluation program involving two hundred jobs? If possible, check your answer with a number of companies that have instituted job evaluation programs.

Chapter 2

SELECTING THE PLAN

A COMMON error in job evaluation is applying indiscriminately a method or plan that has been used elsewhere. The mistake lies not in the fact that the plan has been used previously but in assuming that the particular plan chosen was used under similar circumstances. Job evaluation measures the worth of one job in relation to another by determining, either individually or collectively, the relative presence of certain job characteristics. The same yardstick cannot be applied in all cases because job characteristics may be evident to a greater or lesser degree in one company than in another. Certain characteristics may be entirely absent from some vocations. The time and effort required by a system in use in a large organization would be unwarranted in a smaller business. It should not, however, be assumed that different companies have not used, with a measure of success, identical systems or plans. Where this is possible, an advantage may likely accrue to both union and management alike in that closer comparison of wage rates is facilitated and the experiences of other companies and unions with the plan can be checked.

Whatever the method and plan selected, it must be borne in mind that, once applied, the plan will be the foundation of wage and salary determination and administration. Therefore, before a choice is made, all methods, techniques, and available plans should be carefully appraised to determine which one best suits the requirements of the company.

One of the first phases of the program, then, will be to study plans which appear to be most applicable, to determine the time required and the cost of installation and administration, and to learn how other organizations have approached the problem of selecting a job evaluation plan.

Evaluation Plans of Other Companies

Through consultation with other companies, management and the union acquire an insight into the advisability of using or disregarding certain plans. They become acquainted with the practical problems to be encountered during an installation. Because systematic job evaluation has been seriously applied for the past two decades, many companies have installed plans; and, as a result, older methods, techniques, and systems have been subjected to either discard, considerable alteration and refinement, or replacement by newly developed ideas. It seems logical that all concerned can benefit from these experiences. In making a survey, efforts should be confined, if possible, to companies of approximately the same size and having similar operations and working conditions.

Despite an abundance of literature enumerating the advantages and disadvantages of various systems, there is, unfortunately, little unbiased, practical information that would be beneficial to management in selecting a plan to meet its particular requirements. Consequently, the system used will, in most instances, be the one agreed upon as a result of judgment, preference, and negotiation. Most systems and plans have some claim of advantage over other plans, and it is possible to work out combinations of plans to better meet the needs of a particular organization. However, before a plan can be selected those charged with making the selection should know the advantages, disadvantages, and method of applying each of the commonly used systems of job evaluation. Such knowledge will enable them to determine which system is most qualified to meet their requirements.

Four Methods of Job Evaluation

Among practical students of job evaluation there are four general methods of evaluating jobs: predetermined grading or classification, job ranking, factor comparison, and point rating. The first three of these methods are described in this chapter, and the fourth is examined in the next chapter.

Predetermined Grading Method

This system or method involves arbitrarily established job levels or classifications. All jobs to be evaluated are analyzed and the broad job characteristics determined. Classifications are then made, and each job is placed in its respective classification or grade. Carefully prepared job descriptions are advisable so that job content can be compared with the written grade requirements.

The best-known example of predetermined grading is that employed by the Westinghouse Electric Corporation for the grading of salaried (not hourly paid) employees. This plan includes seven grades of salaried positions, ranging from office boy, included in the first grade, up to and including senior elected policy-making officers in the seventh grade. The grades and their definitions used in the Westinghouse plan are as follows:

GRADE 1. UNSKILLED

The positions of this group, mostly clerical in character, require accuracy and dependability but no extended training. Office boy, record clerk, and file clerk.

GRADE 2. SKILLED

The positions of this group, mostly clerical in character, require training of hand or mind. The group includes such positions as stenographer, production clerk, detail draftsman, and ledgerman. Among the nonclerical positions of this group are laboratory assistant, power-plant operator, and demonstrator.

GRADE 3. INTERPRETIVE

The positions of this group call for ability to classify work and apply established procedures to its accomplishment. Many of the positions are clerical, such as correspondents; but others are nonclerical, such as foremen, laboratory assistants, and layout draftsmen.

In most positions of this group the work is nonsupervisory in character. In the highest positions the work is supervisory and involves little or no substantial amount of work of the same kind as that done by those supervised. Illustrations are chief clerk, office manager, foreman.

GRADE 4. CREATIVE

The positions of this group are those of a creative character such as engineer, salesman, staff supervisor, attorney, system designer, and working group leader and section supervisor within these fields of activity.

GRADE 5. EXECUTIVE

The positions of this group are those of department manager, local sales manager, superintendent, general foreman, and the assistant managers and superintendents of large departments. The function is that of departmental management in a broad sense.

GRADE 6. ADMINISTRATIVE

The positions of this group involve responsibilities of large magnitude or over-all character or for mixed functional division, such as division manager, district sales manager of high-order functional character, such as accounting director, chief or consulting engineer, director of research, treasurer, general manager of purchases and traffic, and general works manager.

GRADE 7. POLICY

The positions of this group are those of the senior elected policy officers of the company.[1]

The United States Civil Service Commission and many state civil service bodies commonly use the predetermined grading method. This system can also be used in conjunction with point rating as a means of reducing the number of jobs to be evaluated, and it can be implemented by the ranking method as a means of refining the relationships of jobs within predetermined grades.

Where there are a large number of similar or identical machines or operations that require varying degrees of operational skill, the practice of evaluating each operator's job has often resulted in an unnecessarily large number of jobs being evaluated and a consequent increase in the time, effort, and expense of installation. By setting up broad job classifications covering similar operations and then slotting the operator's job into the appropriate classification or grade, the amount of

---

[1]Westinghouse Electric Corporation, *Industrial Relations Manual*, January 10, 1940, Part I, sec. 1, p. 4.

work involved is substantially reduced. Figure 2–1 shows written classification definititions that might be applied to all vertical turret lathe occupations in a single plant. It will be noted that the definitions contain nothing in the way of informa-

---

LATHE, TURRET, VERTICAL A

Consists of diversified types of vertical type turret lathe operations. Duties are: to drill, ream, bore, turn, face, chamfer, and groove to tolerances of plus 0.000 or minus 0.0006 on bore diameters using a single tool. Requires adjustment of speeds, feeds, and sequence of suboperations and making difficult setups requiring aligning, blocking, and clamping. Operator grinds ordinary cutting tools. (Carbide tipped tools, reamers, radii, and grooving tools are ground in the toolroom.) Work is from complicated blueprints and verbal instructions and requires use of necessary instruments for measuring and a general knowledge of materials.

LATHE, TURRET, VERTICAL B

Consists of ordinary types of vertical turret lathe operations. Duties are: to drill, ream, bore, turn, face, chamfer, and groove to tolerances of plus or minus 0.001; where "sized" tools are provided for some bores or reamed holes, the tolerances are to plus or minus 0.0005. Requires adjustment of speeds and feeds and making ordinary setups. Operator grinds standard tools. (Carbide tipped tools, special forming tools, and reamers are ground in the toolroom.) Work is from detailed blueprints and verbal instructions and requires the use of necessary instruments for measuring.

LATHE, TURRET, VERTICAL C

Consists of simple types of vertical turret lathe operations. Duties are: to rough bore, turn, and face to tolerances of plus or minus 0.005; where "sized" tools are provided for some bores or reamed holes, the tolerances are to plus or minus 0.001 or less. Requires adjustment of speeds and feeds and making simple setups. Operator grinds standard tools. (All special tools, carbide tipped tools, and reamers are ground in the toolroom.) Work is from simple detailed blueprints and verbal instructions and requires the use of necessary instruments for measuring.

Fig. 2–1.—An example of predetermined grade level definitions of the three grades of vertical turret lathe operations of a single plant.

tion as to effort, responsibility, or working conditions; therefore, for there to be an accurate comparison of job content, there must be the same degree of prevalence of these characteristics all three grades.

Advantages and Disadvantages.—The advantages of the predetermined grading method lie in its simplicity and the speed with which jobs can be evaluated. Being simple, the method lends itself well to explanation to employees and, therefore, makes the problem of selling the plan easier. Little time and effort are involved, and direct cost of installation and maintenance is at a minimum. It is an improvement over rate setting by fiat in that it has some semblance of system and can eliminate the consideration of personalities.

The disadvantages of the method outweigh the advantages, however. The wide range of job characteristics within a given plan makes the defining of grades a problem unless broad generalities are used, in which case negotiation of assignment of jobs to grades often bogs down. Blanket judgment is passed on jobs, and an error in slotting a job into a grade may set a precedent that may result in severe distortion of the wage structure. The appraisal of jobs as a whole precludes analysis and, therefore, accurate worth determination. Experience has also shown that there is a strong tendency for this method to perpetuate existing inequities, for in many cases the grade into which a job is placed is determined by the rate of the person on the job.

Job Ranking Method

This method of evaluation requires that an individual or committee rank all jobs in the order of their relative worth. The first step is the selection of a group of key jobs, the duties and responsibilities of which are well known and whose going rates are in alignment with those for similar jobs in the community. Then the jobs are ranked. Ranking by a committee is obviously more accurate than ranking by an individual, and even greater accuracy is assured if rankings are made at a few days' or weeks' interval and if the averages of each individual's ranking are used. The ranking process is made easier by the use of small cards upon which the name of one key job is written. This permits stacking the cards in their rank order and thus facilitates rearrangement of the cards when the rank order of the jobs is changed. Figure 2–2 shows the results of a job rank-

TABLE OF JOB RANKINGS — KEY JOBS

JOB TITLE	CONSULTANT	UNION MEMBER A	UNION MEMBER B	MGT. MEMBER A	MGT. MEMBER B	AVG.* RANK	RATE
ASSEMBLER, BENCH	9	9	10	10	10	9.6	1.00
AUTOMATIC SCREW MACHINE SETUP MAN	4	4	5	3	2	3.6	1.40
CARPENTER A	5	5	4	5	5	4.8	1.40
CRANEMAN	6	7	6	8	7	6.8	1.33
DRILL–PRESS OPERATOR	7	6	8	7	8	7.2	1.10
ELECTRICIAN A	3	3	2	4	3	3.0	1.45
HELPER, TRADES	11	11	11	12	11	11.2	0.95
INSPECTOR–TESTER	10	10	9	9	9	9.4	1.02
JANITOR	13	13	14	14	13	13.4	0.93
LABORER	14	14	13	13	14	13.6	0.95
MACHINIST A	2	2	3	2	4	2.6	1.48
PLATER	8	8	7	6	6	7.0	1.25
TOOL AND DIE MAKER	1	1	1	1	1	1.0	1.68
TRUCKER, ELECTRIC	12	12	12	11	12	11.8	1.04

*AVERAGE RANKING OF EACH MEMBER. AVERAGE OF 5 WEEKLY RANKINGS.

W.R. Prada
Chairman, Ranking Committee
June 12, 1948

FIG. 2–2.—Form used for recording job rankings by individual members of a job ranking committee.

ing completed by a committee of five, consisting of two union members, two management members, and a consultant.

When the rankings have been completed, the jobs will fall in the order shown in Figure 2–3. The asterisks indicate the rates which are out of line and which must be adjusted either

\multicolumn{3}{c}{TABLE OF FINAL JOB RANKINGS– KEY JOBS}
NO.	JOB TITLE	RATE
1	TOOL AND DIE MAKER	1.68
2	MACHINIST A	1.48
3	ELECTRICIAN A	1.45
4	AUTOMATIC SCREW MACHINE SETUP MAN	1.40
5	CARPENTER A	1.40
6	CRANEMAN	1.33
7	PLATER	1.25
8	DRILL-PRESS OPERATOR	1.10
9	INSPECTOR –TESTER	1.02 *
10	ASSEMBLER, BENCH	1.00 *
11	HELPER, TRADES	0.95 *
12	TRUCKER, ELECTRIC	1.04 *
13	JANITOR	0.93 *
14	LABORER	0.95 *

*RATE NOT IN RANK ORDER

W. R. Prada
Chairman, Ranking Committee
June 12, 1948

Fig. 2–3.—Form used for recording final rankings agreed to by members of a job ranking committee.

through negotiation, when a union is involved, or through group judgment.

After the key jobs have been ranked, the remaining jobs to be evaluated are compared with the key jobs and their relative position on the list determined. For example, the committee may decide that lathe operator A should be listed somewhere between the craneman and carpenter A. The rate for lathe operator A would therefore fall somewhere between $1.33 and $1.40 per hour and would be subject to negotiation.

Advantages and Disadvantages.—Simplicity and speed are the advantages of the ranking method over the predetermined grading method. Such simplicity lends itself well to explanation of the system to employees.

One of the disadvantages of the ranking method is that, for practical reasons, it is confined to companies having relatively few jobs to be evaluated. It is unlikely that in large organizations there will be enough key personnel sufficiently acquainted with all jobs to form a committee capable of intelligent ranking. Another disadvantage lies in the necessity of either assuming equal spacing between jobs and, therefore, equal rate differences, or of assigning arbitrary rates. Neither method can be considered a sound practice.

The job ranking method is also weak in its assumption that an individual can look at a job in its entirety and make an appraisal of the composite worth of the factors involved. One individual may be unbalanced in his attitude toward one characteristic and unconsciously misrank the other characteristics as a result. Frequently, the ranking will be done without recourse to job descriptions; and, consequently, there will be a tendency to allow existing rates to sway judgments. One of the most serious shortcomings of the ranking method is the lack of records defending the relative rank of jobs; a reranking of a job because of a change in job content would be difficult to defend. At best, job ranking, while better than no job evaluation at all, is hardly defendable in the light of other available methods.

Factor Comparison Method

This method was originated in 1926 by Eugene J. Benge, its present and foremost exponent. Fundamentally, the method introduces a monetary scale into a system of ranking which recognizes a number of job characteristics rather than composite factors.[2] The procedure followed in this method involves:

[2]For a more extensive treatment of the factor comparison method, refer to E. J. Benge, *Job Evaluation Manual*, National Foremen's Conference, and Benge, Burke, and Hay, *Manual of Job Evaluation* (New York: Harper & Bros., 1941).

1. Selecting the representative key jobs as in the job ranking method.

2. Selecting the critical factors to be used in the plan.

3. Ranking the selected jobs under each factor.

4. Apportioning the going money rates among factors.

5. Ranking the jobs according to money value and establishing a monetary scale by comparing job ranking with money ranking.

6. Evaluating the remaining jobs by interpolation and negotiation.

Selecting Key Jobs.—The first step in determining the scales to be used in evaluation is to select the key jobs. These jobs should be a representative cross section of all the jobs in the plant or office. They should include, if possible, the jobs characterized by maximum and minimum skill, effort, responsibility, and working condition requirements and carrying maximum and minimum going rates. Rates for key jobs should be comparable to those within the immediate competitive area, and any disagreement on an existing rate should be cause for eliminating the job from the group. It is also important that the definition of each job be clearly understood. The number of jobs selected should range from ten to twenty-five depending on the size of the company and the scope of its operations and activities.

Selecting Critical Factors.—Following the selection of key jobs, the critical factors to be utilized must be agreed upon. While it is possible to use as many as thirty factors, that number is highly impracticable. Generally, four to seven factors are employed, with the majority of plans using five, namely: skill, mental effort, physical effort, responsibility, and working conditions.[3] Each factor should be clearly defined to facilitate agreement on the job requirements. Most often, failure by a committee to reach a meeting of minds on the requirements of a job can be attributed to a lack of mutual understanding of terminology rather than to a lack of mutual understanding of what factors constitute a particular job. As soon as the critical factors are chosen, the committee should compose its own

---

[3] Benge, Burke, and Hay, *op. cit.*, p. 99.

definitions, for with all members having a voice in defining the factors there will be greater assurance of accuracy and agreement on terminology.

Agreement of Factor Definition and Key Job Content.—After these factors have been chosen and the committee has reached an agreement as to their meaning, each member should be given a complete description of each key job. If necessary, jobs may be observed. This will help to remove any disagreement as to job content as set forth in the description and to assure uniformity of interpretation among members. The committee chairman is responsible for agreement among members as to factor definitions and key job content. When the chairman is satisfied that agreements have been reached, the process of job ranking can begin.

Ranking Selected Jobs.—There are a number of methods for recording rankings; however, the method is unimportant, provided correct results are gained with a minimum of time and effort. To help clarify the explanation of rankings, the fourteen key jobs used to explain the job ranking method will be used.

For purposes of illustration it can be assumed that each committee member—two from the union, two from management, and a consultant—is furnished with fourteen cards, the name of a key job appearing on each card. The members are asked to rank the jobs by arranging the cards in the order of relative importance of a single factor—skill, for example. Thus, if in the opinion of a committee member, the tool and die maker requires the greatest amount of skill and the laborer the least, the tool and die maker card is placed on top of the stack and the laborer job card on the bottom. When all members have completed their rankings, each member reads the names of the jobs from the cards, starting with the job given the highest skill ranking and ending with the job given the lowest ranking.

The committee chairman should be prepared with a form similar to the one shown in Figure 2–4; and, as the rankings are called off, he should enter them on the proper line and in the appropriate column. Thus, if a member reads "carpenter A" from the fifth card the chairman enters a "5" on the line opposite carpenter A in the column headed by the name of the

JOB FACTOR RANKING TABLE —
FACTOR: Skill

KEY JOB TITLE	UNION MEMBER A	UNION MEMBER B	MGT. MEMBER A	MGT. MEMBER B	CONSULTANT	AVG.
TOOL AND DIE MAKER	1	1	1	1	1	1.0
ELECTRICIAN A	3	2	4	3	3	3.0
MACHINIST A	2	3	2	4	2	2.6
AUTOMATIC SCREW MACHINE SETUP MAN	4	5	3	2	4	3.6
CARPENTER A	5	4	5	5	5	4.8
CRANEMAN	7	6	8	7	6	6.8
PLATER	8	7	6	6	8	7.0
DRILL-PRESS OPERATOR	6	8	7	8	7	7.2
ASSEMBLY, BENCH	7	10	10	10	9	9.6
INSPECTOR-TESTER	10	9	9	9	10	9.4
TRUCKER, ELECTRIC	12	12	11	12	12	11.8
HELPER, TRADES	11	11	12	11	11	11.2
JANITOR	13	14	14	13	13	13.4
LABORER	14	13	13	14	14	13.6

COMMITTEE CHAIRMAN: _W. R. Bader_
DATE: _July 15, 1948_

Fig. 2–4.—A form suitable for recording committee members' job ranking for a certain factor.   Used in the factor comparison method.

member announcing his rankings. When all rankings have been announced by the five members of the committee and recorded, the rankings for each job are cross-totaled and divided by five; the average ranking is then entered in the "average" column.

This ranking procedure is repeated for each of the remaining job factors, and the averages are entered on a summary form similar to Figure 2–5. All forms are then studied to determine what, if any, inconsistencies may prevail in the rankings. If misunderstandings are indicated, the committee members should iron out these differences at that time. The key jobs should be reranked at least once, preferably twice, allowing one to two weeks between rankings. When all rankings have been completed, the results should be averaged and the rankings in terms of whole numbers entered on a form similar to Figure 2–6. This form should be retained for future reference.

Apportioning Money Rates.—The next step is to apportion the average going money rates among the job factors. This is accomplished by asking each committee member to allot so much of the rate for each job among the job factors in the proportions which he believes to be proper. Each member fills in a form similar to Figure 2–7; then the money values for each factor are averaged. Just as jobs were reranked for each factor, one or more rerankings and reapportionments of money values may be necessary. The money apportionments and rankings shown in Figure 2–7 represent the composite opinions of all committee members.

Comparing Job and Money Rankings.—A comparison between the job rankings and the money rankings is now made. This is done by the chairman of the committee, who may use a form similar to Figure 2–8. Where the job ranking and money ranking are the same, no adjustment is required; but where there are differences between the money and job rankings, the committee members are asked to rerank and to reapportion the money values in an attempt to arrive at a common figure. Whenever there is such a wide difference in thought among the members that money apportionments cannot be brought

AVERAGE JOB RANKINGS BY FACTOR

KEY JOB TITLE	SKILL	MENTAL DEMAND	PHYSICAL DEMAND	RESPONSIBILITY	WORKING CONDITIONS
TOOL AND DIE MAKER	1.0	1.0	9.4	1.8	11.0
ELECTRICIAN A	3.0	4.2	7.2	3.4	3.8
MACHINIST A	2.6	2.8	11.8	3.6	7.0
AUTOMATIC SCREW MACHINE SETUP MAN	3.6	2.2	7.8	5.2	6.8
CARPENTER A	4.8	6.2	3.6	7.1	7.6
CRANEMAN	6.8	4.6	5.6	1.2	4.0
PLATER	7.0	10.9	5.4	7.8	1.8
DRILL-PRESS OPERATOR	7.2	9.0	9.6	9.2	12.0
ASSEMBLER, BENCH	9.6	6.8	13.0	13.8	12.8
INSPECTOR-TESTER	9.4	8.0	14.0	13.2	13.6
TRUCKER, ELECTRIC	11.8	10.4	11.2	5.8	10.6
HELPER, TRADES	11.2	12.2	1.8	9.8	8.6
JANITOR	13.4	13.2	3.4	11.4	4.2
LABORER	13.6	13.8	1.2	11.6	1.2

COMMITTEE CHAIRMAN: W. R. Prada

DATE July 15 1978

Fig. 2-5.—Form used for recording the average of all committee members' rankings for each factor. Used in the factor comparison method.

FINAL AVERAGE JOB RANKINGS BY FACTOR

KEY JOB TITLE	SKILL	MENTAL DEMAND	PHYSICAL DEMAND	RESPONSIBILITY	WORKING CONDITIONS
TOOL AND DIE MAKER	1	1	9	2	1
ELECTRICIAN A	3	4	7	3	3
MACHINIST A	2	3	12	4	7
AUTOMATIC SCREW MACHINE SETUP MAN	4	2	8	5	6
CARPENTER A	5	6	4	7	8
CRANEMAN	6	5	6	1	4
PLATER	7	11	5	8	2
DRILL-PRESS OPERATOR	8	9	10	9	12
ASSEMBLY, BENCH	10	7	13	14	13
INSPECTOR-TESTER	9	8	14	13	14
TRUCKER, ELECTRIC	12	10	11	6	10
HELPER, TRADES	11	12	2	10	9
JANITOR	13	13	3	11	5
LABORER	14	14	1	12	1

COMMITTEE CHAIRMAN: *[signature]*
DATE: July 15, 1948

Fig. 2-6.—Record of final average job rankings in terms of whole numbers.   Used in factor comparison method.

MONEY APPORTIONMENT TABLE

KEY JOB TITLE	RATE	SKILL		MENTAL EFFORT		PHYSICAL EFFORT		RESPONSIBILITY		WORKING CONDITIONS	
		$	R	$	R	$	R	$	R	$	R
TOOL AND DIE MAKER	1.68	1.041	1	0.178	1	0.136	9	0.172	2	0.153	11
ELECTRICIAN A	1.45	0.782	3	0.160	4	0.152	7	0.164	3	0.192	3
MACHINIST A	1.48	0.854	2	0.168	2	0.124	11	0.156	5	0.178	7
AUTOMATIC SCREW MACHINE SETUP MAN	1.40	0.742	5	0.166	3	0.146	8	0.162	4	0.184	6
CARPENTER A	1.40	0.764	4	0.146	6	0.172	4	0.144	7	0.172	8
CRANEMAN	1.33	0.642	6	0.152	5	0.162	6	0.186	1	0.188	4
PLATER	1.25	0.634	7	0.118	11	0.164	5	0.138	8	0.196	1
DRILL-PRESS OPERATOR	1.10	0.566	8	0.126	9	0.132	10	0.134	9	0.142	12
ASSEMBLER, BENCH	1.00	0.498	10	0.141	8	0.112	13	0.118	13	0.131	13
INSPECTOR-TESTER	1.02	0.552	9	0.142	7	0.098	14	0.116	14	0.112	14
TRUCKER, ELECTRIC	1.04	0.488	11	0.122	10	0.120	12	0.148	6	0.162	10
HELPER, TRADES	0.95	0.344	12	0.108	12	0.204	2	0.126	10	0.168	9
JANITOR	0.93	0.388	13	0.092	14	0.192	3	0.122	12	0.186	5
LABORER	0.95	0.326	14	0.094	13	0.212	1	0.124	11	0.194	2

$ = MONEY APPORTIONMENT
R = MONEY RANKING

COMMITTEE CHAIRMAN: _____
DATE: July 21, 1948

Fig. 2-7.—Table showing record of composite opinion of committee members as to apportionment of money between factors for each key job. Used in the factor comparison method.

MONEY RANKING-JOB RANKING COMPARISON SCHEDULE

KEY JOB TITLE	SKILL		MENTAL DEMAND		PHYSICAL DEMAND		RESPONSIBILITY		WORKING CONDITIONS	
	JR	MR	JR	MR	JR	MR	JR	MR	JR	MR
TOOL AND DIE MAKER	1	1	1	1	9	9	2	2	11	11
ELECTRICIAN A	3	3	4	4	7	7	3	3	3	3
MACHINIST A	2	2	3*	2*	12*	11*	4*	5*	7	7
AUTOMATIC SCREW MACHINE SETUP MAN	4*	5*	2*	3*	8	8	5*	4*	6	6
CARPENTER A	5*	4*	6	6	4	4	7	7	8	8
CRANEMAN	6	6	5	5	4	4	1	1	4	4
PLATER	7	7	11	11	5	5	8	8	2*	1*
DRILL-PRESS OPERATOR	8	8	9	9	10	10	9	9	12	12
ASSEMBLER, BENCH	10	10	7*	8*	13	13	14*	13*	13	13
INSPECTOR-TESTER	9	9	.8*	7*	14	14	13*	14*	14	14
TRUCKER, ELECTRIC	12*	11*	10	10	11*	12*	6	6	10	10
HELPER, TRADES	11*	12*	12	12	2	2	10	10	9	9
JANITOR	13	13	13*	14*	3	3	11*	12*	5	5
LABORER	14	14	14*	13*	1	1	12*	11*	1*	2*

MR = MONEY RANKING
JR = JOB RANKING

* MONEY RANKINGS AND JOB RANKINGS NOT IN COINCIDENCE. ADJUSTMENT OR ELIMINATION FROM GROUP NECESSARY.

COMMITTEE CHAIRMAN: *[signature]*
DATE July 31, 1948

Fig. 2-8.—Form used in the factor comparison method for comparing composite money rankings and job rankings as determined by the ranking committee.

into line with the job rankings, the job is eliminated from the key job group.

Establishing Evaluation Scales.—In the event that the committee is unable to agree on the money apportionments for machinist A, automatic screw machine setup man, trucker, electrician, and laborer, for example, these jobs are dropped from the group of key jobs to be used in establishing job evaluation scales. When these five jobs are dropped and other discrepancies corrected, the committee chairman fills in a form similar to Figure 2–9. This completes the establishment of factor comparison rating scales and makes possible the evaluation of all remaining jobs under the factor comparison method.

Evaluation of Jobs.—As a result of the job rankings, five separate factor rating scales have been established for the purpose of evaluating jobs. It will be noted, however, that the spread between money apportionments is not consistent. As a further check on the accuracy of scales and as a means of filling in or narrowing some of the spreads, additional jobs may be ranked in the same manner as before and added to the scales. Additions to scales and any changes resulting therefrom should be made only with the consent of the committee.

The balance of the jobs to be evaluated can then be placed in their proper positions within each of the scales, taking into consideration job content, factor definitions, and rankings of jobs previously evaluated. For example, assume that the job of punch-press setup man is to be evaluated and that the committee has decided that under the skill factor it belongs somewhere between carpenter A and craneman. Punch-press setup man would then appear on the skill scale as shown in Figure 2–10, and the committee would negotiate the punch-press setup rate somewhere between sixty-five and seventy-five cents per hour. In a similar manner rates for the other factors would be determined, the five rates totaled, and a total rate for the occupation established.

Advantages and Disadvantages of the Factor Comparison Method.—Because the factor comparison method utilizes the breaking-down of jobs into characteristics rather than the consideration

KEY JOB FINAL RANKING SCHEDULE

KEY JOB TITLE	SKILL			MENTAL DEMAND			PHYSICAL DEMAND			RESPONSIBILITY			WORKING CONDITIONS		
	JR	MR	MV	JR	MR	MV	JR	MR	MV	JR	MR	MV	JR	MR	MV
TOOL AND DIE MAKER	1	1	1.05	1	1	0.18	7	7	0.13	2	2	0.18	7	7	0.14
ELECTRICIAN A	2	2	0.78	2	2	0.17	6	6	0.14	3	3	0.17	2	2	0.19
CARPENTER A	3	3	0.76	4	4	0.15	3	3	0.17	4	4	0.16	5	5	0.16
CRANEMAN	4	4	0.65	3	3	0.16	5	5	0.15	1	1	0.19	3	3	0.18
PLATER	5	5	0.63	8	8	0.11	4	4	0.16	5	5	0.15	1	1	0.20
DRILL-PRESS OPERATOR	6	6	0.59	7	7	0.12	8	8	0.12	6	6	0.14	8	8	0.13
ASSEMBLER, BENCH	8	8	0.53	5	5	0.14	9	9	0.11	10	10	0.10	9	9	0.12
INSPECTOR-TESTER	7	7	0.56	6	6	0.13	10	10	0.10	9	9	0.11	10	10	0.11
HELPER, TRADES	9	9	0.37	9	9	0.10	1	1	0.20	7	7	0.13	6	6	0.15
JANITOR	10	10	0.36	10	10	0.09	2	2	0.19	8	8	0.12	4	4	0.17

COMMITTEE CHAIRMAN: *[signature]*

DATE: *Aug 18, 1948*

JR = JOB RANKING
MR = MONEY RANKING
MV = MONEY VALUE

FIG. 2-9.—Form used in the factor comparison method for recording final job rankings agreed to by the committee.

JOB TITLE	MV	JOB TITLE	MV
MONEY SCALE — SKILL FACTOR			
TOOL AND DIE MAKER	1.05		
ELECTRICIAN A	0.78		
		ASSEMBLER, BENCH	0.56
CARPENTER A	0.76		
		INSPECTOR-TESTER	0.53
PUNCH-PRESS SETUP MAN	?		
CRANEMAN	0.65		
PLATER	0.63		
DRILL-PRESS OPERATOR	0.59	HELPER TRADES	0.37
		JANITOR	0.36
MV = MONEY VALUE		COMMITTEE CHAIRMAN: *W. R. Prada*	
		DATE: *Aug. 18, 1948*	

Fig. 2–10.—A money scale used for evaluating jobs in the factor comparison method.

of jobs in their entirety, it can claim the advantage of arriving at more accurate results. Further accuracy is attained by comparing jobs, factor against factor. Accuracy, therefore, affords this method its primary advantage over the job ranking method (which it is a substantial refinement of) and the predetermined grading method. Another advantage lies in the flexibility of the method, for there are neither top nor bottom limits confining the relative positions into which jobs may be placed—an advantage not claimed by the predetermined grading method or by poorly devised point rating plans.

On the other hand, the factor comparison method is encumbered with a disadvantage that may easily lead to its failure, namely: it is difficult to explain to employees—therefore, difficult to sell before it is put into operation. Also, dealing with a monetary scale as it does, a continuation of inequities is likely to result because of the influence of present rates on the judgment of the committee. This disadvantage can be overcome by the application of conversion factors, but this further complicates the method and magnifies one of its disadvantages. Another disadvantage is that union and management will be faced with increasing collective bargaining difficulties, for this method does not divorce job evaluation from monetary considerations. Further criticism of the method emanates from those who believe that the use of relatively few job characteristics does not permit as accurate an appraisal of a job as is possible and that to increase the number of factors to a practical ten to fifteen would render the method exceptionally cumbersome.

QUESTIONS

1. The job evaluation plan of the National Electrical Manufacturers' Association has been applied by a very large number of companies. Does this fact indicate that it is adaptable to any type of manufacturing company?
2. What are the first steps to be taken in selecting a job evaluation plan?
3. Describe briefly the predetermined grading method. What are its advantages? Its disadvantages?

4. Explain the job ranking method. What are its advantages over the predetermined grading and factor comparison methods?

5. Assume that a plant has 2,000 employees who occupy 300 jobs. Would you use the job ranking method to evaluate these jobs? Why?

6. Both the job ranking and factor comparison methods require the selection of key jobs. What factors govern the type of jobs selected and the number of jobs in the group?

7. What are the six basic steps involved in the factor comparison method?

8. How many factors are generally employed by the factor comparison method? Do you believe that this number permits accurate differentiation between jobs? What disadvantages are there in increasing the number of factors?

9. What are the advantages of the factor comparison method over the predetermined grading and job ranking methods? What are the comparative disadvantages?

10. If you were called upon to sell a program of job evaluation to a group of employees and to their union representatives, what method—predetermined grading, job ranking, or factor comparison—would be easiest for you to sell? To explain? Why?

CHAPTER 3

POINT RATING

FUNDAMENTALLY, the point rating method compares the characteristics of a job with a set of standards or definitions, awarding points to a particular occupation in proportion to the degree of presence of the requirements and conditions measuring the worth of the job. How many different point rating plans are in use at this time is a matter of conjecture. Polls have been taken, but there appears to be little available and reliable information on the extent of their use. There are, however, sufficient number of plans in use to afford a wide choice and the benefit of considerable experience to those interested in learning how these plans work.

Rarely, however, will a plan meet the requirements and fit the circumstances of two or more companies equally well, even though the concerns may be engaged in similar operations. Variances in policy, working conditions, and operating methods may preclude the application of a single plan by more than one company. It is well to consider such variations before endeavoring to apply a plan used with success by another company. Such matters as the comparative quantity and quality of supervision required by policy in one plant may not be the same in another, thereby causing differences in the general level of required skill. One company may purchase castings and forgings while another may operate a foundry and forge, a situation which obviously will mean differences in working conditions between the two plants.

While there may be some value in using identical plans as a means of securing comparative locality and industry wage rate information, it should be realized that the comparison will be less useful if weights are distorted, definitions misapplied,

47

or unnecessary factors included. If a plan which is designed to emphasize responsibility characteristics and to de-emphasize skill characteristics is applied in a plant where there is a preponderance of skilled employees who have relatively little responsibility, the requirements of the occupations evaluated will not be properly recognized. Under such circumstances, the plan, if applied at all, should be altered to reflect the higher level of skill and the lower responsibility requirements.

Some plans considered may be basically satisfactory except for a few alterations necessary to meet unusual situations or conditions. However, it has been the experience of those who have tried to alter a plan to suit their needs that the effort usually results in an almost entirely new plan; for it is unusual to find a company whose policies, operating methods, and working conditions are so similar as to make possible identical treatment in the measuring of job worth.

Originating a Point Rating, Job Evaluation Plan

Where time and capable personnel are available, it is recommended that companies installing job evaluation projects design their own plans. However, building a new plan is a tedious process, replete with problems—many of which are entirely new to persons called upon to solve them—and burdened with details which require much time of valuable personnel. Thus, prepared plans have been used much more extensively than those specifically designed by companies for their own use.

For the most part, only large companies, such as General Electric, Western Electric, Montgomery Ward, General Foods, and United States Steel, have developed their own point rating plans. All companies, however, regardless of size, can enjoy a large measure of success with original point rating plans. An original plan will better meet the requirements and fit the circumstances of the company involved than will a borrowed plan. The original plan is developed by those closely associated with the problems, by those best qualified to formulate the plan to the satisfaction of those most concerned with accurate results. Also, when the persons developing the original plan begin the rating of jobs, they have a greater mutual understanding of definitions. In fact, the entire plan has more meaning to a company when it is originated by that company. Point rating plans can be patterned after those of other concerns, but they must be properly modified to meet individual needs. Definitions, for example, must be reworded and not copied exactly from the definitions of the original, borrowed plan.

Those responsible for designing the plan, will gather a considerable amount of information, through consultation and study, which will serve to educate them in sound job evaluation fundamentals. This, in turn, will induce a greater degree of consistency in ratings and a close co-ordination of effort. Originating a plan enables use of experiences of others and thereby reduces the number of pitfalls encountered when applying plans whose features are not custom made. Although more time, effort, and expense may be involved in the early stages of developing a new plan, the ultimate benefit to be gained will result in economies that will far exceed the increase in original cost.

Five Basic Steps.—Devising a point rating plan embodies the following steps:

1. Studying the jobs to be evaluated so as to determine the characteristics to be used in measuring job worth.

2. Studying the maximum and minimum possible degree of presence of each characteristic so that all jobs to be evaluated will fall within the degrees provided and so that no unnecessary degree will be provided.

3. Preparing suitable definitions for the characteristics or factors provided and for the degrees determined to be necessary.

4. Agreeing on the weights to be accorded each factor and degree and assigning the points to each degree of each factor.

5. Selecting the key jobs and evaluating them according to the plan developed.

This chapter, in addition to amplifying the five steps listed above, will include a discussion of the advantages, disadvantages, and wide acceptance of the point rating method.

Selecting Factors

The factors to be used in appraising the relative worth of jobs will depend upon the general type of occupations to be evaluated. Generally, attempts to devise plans which are suitable for evaluation of both shop and clerical occupations have met with little success; for the characteristics of the two types of jobs are, in too many instances, not comparable or common to one another.

For instance, most plans used in the evaluation of plant jobs include the factors of hazard and working conditions, which rarely, if ever, apply to clerical positions. By the same token, some plans for evaluation of clerical and executive positions include the factor of responsibility for confidential data, which rarely applies to plant occupations. Executive positions should not be evaluated under the same plan as clerical and manual occupations, primarily because there is danger of misaligning supervisory with manual and clerical jobs.

The occupations to be evaluated must be studied before any plan is considered in order to determine the scope of general job characteristics. Frequent discussions with workers and foremen will aid in determining what jobs are characterized by maximum and minimum degrees of such factors as hazard, experience, working conditions, and physical effort. The committee or individual should record his findings in a manner permissible for incorporation into a report for presentation to management and to the union. Those requirements common to all occupations in identical degrees should be closely watched for so that they may be eliminated from consideration at a later date. It might prove advantageous to select ten or twelve commonly used factors and to note the jobs requiring their maximum and minimum degrees.

The important point to be remembered is to include the factors sufficient for appraisal of all jobs to be evaluated and to include no unnecessary factors. A factor, to be legitimate, must be one that is present in varying degrees; for unless the degree of presence varies, the factor is incapable of differentiation. Factors should not overlap. To give credit because a task requires operation of a machine and to give the same job additional credit because it involves training on the machine would mean duplication of data. Each factor must be such that it and its varying degrees of presence are readily definable.

Number of Factors to Use.—Job characteristics are generally grouped under four general headings, namely: skill, effort, responsibility, and working conditions. Basically, these four characteristics are present in all jobs, although in different degrees. Thorough analysis, however, requires that these characteristics be broken down into component parts. The number of factors used should exceed the number required for maximum simplicity (four or five) but should be less than the number required for maximum theoretical accuracy (twenty to thirty). Ten to fifteen factors strike a balance between simplicity and theoretical accuracy—ten and eleven being the most widely used figures.

Figure 3–1 lists twenty-one point rating plans, the total factors each employs, and the number of components into which each general factor is broken down. The figure indicates the extent of disagreement over the number of factors to be incorporated into a plan and the degree of refinement which each general factor requires. Of the twenty-one plans listed, four have a tendency toward extreme simplicity, using three to seven factors; two have a tendency toward extreme accuracy, using twenty-four and thirty-five factors; while the others appear to have maintained a balance between simplicity and accuracy.

Considerations in Selecting Factors.—Persons doing the rating should not be required to distinguish between more job characteristics than can be visualized. Characteristics should have, by nature, a significant bearing on the recognition of wage differentials. Factors should be reducible to simple terms and easily related to the experiences of those rating or observing the jobs. Although simplicity should be an objective in selecting or designing a point rating plan, job evaluation technicians

COMPANY	SKILL	EFFORT	RESPONSIBILITY	WORKING CONDITIONS	TOTAL FACTORS
GENERAL FOODS CORPORATION	7	1	2	0	10
GENERAL ELECTRIC COMPANY	2	2	1	1	6
REVERE COPPER AND BRASS, INC.	2	2	3	2	9
WESTINGHOUSE ELECTRIC CORPORATION	3	3	4	0	10
AMERICAN OPTICAL COMPANY	1	1	1	1	4
CHENEY BROS. COMPANY	1	0	1	1	3
R.G. LE TOURNEAU, INC.	8	2	4	2	16
INLAND STEEL COMPANY	3	2	5	3	13
CARNEGIE-ILLINOIS STEEL CORPORATION	4	2	4	2	12
BALDWIN LOCOMOTIVE	4	2	3	3	12
WESTERN TABLET AND STATIONERY CO.	4	2	3	2	11
CESSNA AIRCRAFT COMPANY	3	2	4	2	11
LOCKHEED AIRCRAFT CORPORATION	2	2	1	2	7
GREENFIELD TAP AND DIE CORP.	4	2	2	2	10
AN UNDERWEAR MANUFACTURER	6	2	4	3	15
A TEXTILE MILL	2	2	2	2	8
NATIONAL ELECTRICAL MFRS. ASSN.	3	2	4	2	11
INDUSTRIAL MANAGEMENT SOCIETY	5	1	3	2	11
STIGERS AND REED *	14	5	1	15	35
GEORGE S. MAY CO. †	6	4	3	4	17
MC CLURE, HADDEN, AND ORTMAN †	7	6	6	5	24

*"THE THEORY AND PRACTICE OF JOB RATING"
† MANAGEMENT CONSULTANTS

FIG. 3-1.—A comparison of twenty-one point rating plans showing the number of factors used and the number of components into which each general factor is broken down.

have, in too many instances, been biased toward ultrafine distinctions and mechanical frills presumed to increase the accuracy of ratings. Actually, a relatively large number of simple factors is preferable to a combination of simple factors into complex groups which require involved and arbitrary weighting and estimates in the evaluation process.

The following list will give some insight into the large variation of factors used. The list was compiled from plans in use, and no factor is included which has not been included in at least two plans. It will be noted that many factors are synonymous, while some border on general characteristic headings. The list can be of value in selecting factors where a new plan is to be devised or where an existing plan is to be refined, supplemented, or otherwise altered.

SKILL

Accuracy
Accuracy of calculations
Accuracy of measurement
Accuracy of selection
Accuracy of reading
Accuracy of record
Adaptability
Adjustability
Analysis
Analytical ability
Aptitude
Artistic ability
Attention to orders
Complexity
Co-ordination
Co-operation
Decisions
Details
Education
Foresight
Ingenuity
Initiative
Inventiveness
Job knowledge

Job skill
Judgment
Know other operations
Knowledge of equipment and tools
Knowledge of materials
Knowledge of methods
Leadership
Length of schooling
Management ability
Manual dexterity
Manual skill
Mechanical ability
Mental capability
Mentality
Motor accuracy
Originality
Personal requirements
Physical skill
Precision
Previous training
Resourcefulness
Tact and diplomacy
Training time
Versatility

EFFORT

Alertness	Mental stability
Application	Monotony
Endurance	Muscular co-ordination
Exertion	Physical effort
Fatigue	Physical pace or energy
Honesty of effort	Quickness of comprehension
Memory	Strength
Mental effort	Visual effort

RESPONSIBILITY

Avoidance of shutdowns	Material
Company policy	Money
Confidential data	Product
Cost of errors	Quality
Effect on subsequent operations	Safety of others
Equipment	Reports and records
Good will	Work of others
Maintenance of pace	

WORKING CONDITIONS

Accident hazard	Environmental deterrents
Clothing spoilage	Eyestrain
Contact of body	Health hazard
Current expense	Nervous strain
Discomfort	Surroundings

The above factors were taken from plans designed for evaluating plant jobs; however, many of them are applicable to clerical, technical, and supervisory occupations.

Balancing Factors.—There are students of job evaluation who strongly hint at, if not openly advocate, the inclusion of what are sometimes referred to as "balancing" factors to be used to compensate for outside influences on wage scales. A few such influences are: supply and demand for certain skills, seasonal or other irregularity of employment, tradition, organized group pressures, and opportunities for advancement. While it may be argued that such factors have no place in consideration of the job content upon which jobs are evaluated, it is an irrefutable fact that they play an important part in determining the relative positions of jobs within wage structures. Considerable thought and research may afford an answer to this controversial problem.

Defining Factors

Having selected the factors most suitable for measuring the relative worth of the jobs to be evaluated, the next step is to clarify the meaning of the factors through the preparation of definitions.

Those who have been members of evaluation committees faced with the problem of trying to rate jobs on the basis of poorly defined factors and degrees will agree that too much stress cannot be placed on the accuracy with which definitions are written. Endless discussion results from definitions that are not clear, concise, objective, and positive, and in which simple language and correct nomenclature are not used. Definitions should consist of easily understood phrases which mean what they say; dictionary accuracy is not so important as are semantic precision and usefulness as guiding criteria for evaluators. A group doing the rating should, through properly expressed definitions, have the same concept as to what each degree means with regard to job content. Such an identity of concept obviously averts much discussion and thereby accelerates the rating of jobs. Clearly understood definitions also ease the work of handling grievances, for arguments over the relations of degrees to job content are lessened. Further, where there is mutual understanding of meanings, greater consistency in ratings will result.

Plan of the National Electrical Manufacturers' Association.—An insight into the need for clarity in definitions can be gained by studying some of the definitions actually in use. The following are the factor and degree definitions for "Visual and/or Mental Demand" employed in the point rating plan of the National Electrical Manufacturers' Association.[1]

---

[1]Industrial Relations Department, National Electrical Manufacturers' Association, Job Rating Manual, *Definitions of the Factors Used in Evaluating Hourly Rated Jobs* (New York, 1946), p. 7.

MENTAL AND/OR VISUAL DEMAND.—This factor measures the job requirements which induce mental fatigue and/or visual strain in terms of duration of time that mental and/or visual application is required, and the required intensity of such application. It does not relate to the degree of intelligence or mental development but to the quantity and concentration of mental application.

First Degree.—Little mental and only intermittent visual attention since either the operation is practically automatic or the duties require attention only at long intervals.

Second Degree.—Frequent mental and/or visual attention where the flow of work is intermittent or the operation involves waiting for a machine or process to complete a cycle with little attention or checking.

Third Degree.—Continuous mental and/or visual attention where the flow or work is repetitive or the operation requires constant alertness.

Fourth Degree.—Must concentrate mental and visual attention closely, planning and laying out complex work; or co-ordinating a high degree of manual dexterity with close visual attention for sustained periods.

Fifth Degree.—Concentrated and exacting mental and visual attention, usually visualizing, planning, and laying out very involved and complex jobs.

Clarity versus Brevity.—The foregoing definitions include terms that can hardly avoid controversy. The words "little," "intermittent," and "long" mean one thing to one person and something else to another person. The word "frequent" may mean once every hour or once every fifteen minutes; but to refine a definition to specify the exact time intervals fitting the word may lead to some inconsistency, for "frequent" in one operation may mean something entirely different in another operation. How is frequency of mental and visual attention measured? By using one's best judgment is probably the answer; but even here differences will undoubtedly occur as to what constitutes mental and visual attention, particularly if varied levels of mentality are represented on the evaluation committee. Some will argue that so long as the work is being performed, regardless of whether it is almost wholly mechanical or not, mental application must exist and that, therefore, any work requires continuous mental application. Such adjectives as "involved" and "complex" may be interpreted by a graduate engineer as applying to very few jobs, but a floor sweeper may apply them to a great many jobs. From these examples, it can thus be seen how brevity achieved at the cost of clarity greatly impairs the necessary, accurate interpretation of terms.

In contrast, the second degree of the factor "mental effort" is incorporated and defined in the plan used by the Carnegie-Illinois Steel Corporation as follows: "Light mental or visual application required for performing work where there is some variety, but actions to be taken and decisions made are limited to few possibilities. Work requiring some coordination with others or process. Set up, regulate, adjust simple machines and processes; weigh and count product, record data; ordinary crane hooking. Do simple trades work, such as concrete finishing, connecting pipe, simple torch cutting, etc. Routine lubrication."[2] This definition leaves far less to the imagination, but it may still cause some disagreement among committee members owing to the use of such terms as "some variety" and "simple machines."

The same problem of clarity exists with regard to the factor and degree definitions incorporated in the plans used for evaluating technical, clerical, and supervisory positions. Examples of such definitions are given in Figure 3–2.

Use of Bench Marks.—As a means of reducing the probability of misunderstood definitions, bench marks may be used. The Industrial Management Society point rating plan makes extensive use of "bench mark" jobs, which are key occupations whose job content properly falls into one of the several degrees of a factor.[3] For example, under this plan, the first degree of the factor "schooling" is defined briefly as "unable to speak, read, or write English," and opposite the definitions are listed the bench mark jobs of ditch digger and section hand, thus indicating to what type of occupation the first degree of the fac-

---

[2] *Intraplant Wage Rate Inequities Agreement between Carnegie-Illinois Steel Corporation and the United Steel Workers of America (C.I.O.), October 23, 1945*, p. 44.

[3] Industrial Management Society, *Occupational Rating Plan.* (Chicago: Modern Franklin-Company Press, 1943), p. 76.

RESPONSIBILITY FOR CONFIDENTIAL DATA

This factor appraises the degree to which integrity must be exercised in the keeping of the company's confidential matters.

	1st Degree	2nd Degree	3rd Degree	4th Degree	5th Degree
Degree of Responsibility	None—or a negligible amount of confidential data involved.	May work with confidential material or data but disclosure would not have an appreciable effect on company.	Works regularly with confidential data, and disclosure might have an appreciable effect on company.	Works continuously with confidential data of considerable importance which, if disclosed, may be detrimental to the company's interest.	Complete access to all confidential material such as plans, procedures, etc., which are necessary to safeguard company's progress and future.

EXECUTIVE RESPONSIBILITY

This factor appraises the degree and scope of supervisory responsibility.

	1st Degree	2nd Degree	3rd Degree	4th Degree	5th Degree
Degree of Responsibility	None or very little supervision.	Supervision over several employees in the same occupation, performing the same work most of the time.	Supervision over a group of employees. Most of time is spent assigning, reviewing, eliminating ordinary difficulties, when procedure is somewhat standardized.	Supervision of a section, a large group of workers. Organizes and coordinates with the next level of responsibility.	Supervision of a department, involving accountability for results in terms of costs, methods and personnel.

EDUCATION OR ITS EQUIVALENT—MENTALITY

While actual formal education is not essential, it will here be expressed in terms of schooling equivalent to the required MENTAL AND GENERAL INTELLIGENCE, AND ABILITY TO ABSORB, CORRELATE AND UTILIZE KNOWLEDGE.

	1st Degree	2nd Degree	3rd Degree	4th Degree	5th Degree	6th Degree
Requirement	Read, write, add and subtract.	Knowledge of simple arithmetic, English, checking, posting. Adaptability to simple office or plant routine.	Knowledge of ordinary clerical and typing. Interpret simple drawings or instructions.	Knowledge of higher type clerical work, bookkeeping, secretarial essentials.	Knowledge of specific field such as accounting, drafting, time study, also involves a background of practicable knowledge to interpret complicated drawings and manufacturing methods.	Requires equivalent education of technical nature to understand complicated technical or electrical subjects, or any of the professional fields, such as accounting, engineering, chemistry, etc.
Mental and General Intelligence Equivalent to	Grammar School (8 grades)	1 - 2 years High School	3 - 4 years High School	High School and Business College	Partial College 1 - 2 years	College Graduate

RESPONSIBILITY FOR MONEY AND MATERIAL

This factor appraises the degree of monetary worth of the responsibility or the probable effect, in monetary loss, of errors on the job.

	1st Degree	2nd Degree	3rd Degree	4th Degree	5th Degree
Degree of Responsibility	Small or negligible monetary loss resulting from errors or mishandling.	Some definite loss ($25.00 to $100.00 monthly) resulting from errors or mishandling. Work requires a fair degree of accuracy, infractions usually confined to one department.	Considerable loss ($100.00 to $500.00 monthly) may result from errors or infractions. The effect is usually confined within company.	Infractions difficult to detect and may involve relations outside the plant. Work seldom checked or audited. Monetary loss may amount to $500.00 to $1,000.00 monthly.	Infractions may involve a major monetary loss (over $1,000.00).

FIG. 3-2.—Examples of definitions that might be found in job evaluation plans covering technical, clerical, and supervisory positions.

tor applies. The use of bench marks for each degree of each factor obviously clarifies the problem of understanding the meaning of the definitions. (Fig. 3–3.)

Weighting Factors

Relative Importance of Characteristics.—It is generally recognized that certain characteristics are more important than others in measuring the difficulty and responsibility of occupations. For example, in a tool and die making shop the greatest weight would be placed on skill factors, while in a foundry the greatest weight might be applied to working conditions. Criticism of factor weighting in point rating evaluation plans has arisen primarily out of the differences in weights assigned to the factors employed. Although the criticism may not be fully justified, it should not be overlooked; for it it becomes widespread, confidence will be lost in the effectiveness of point rating evaluation plans.

There is no proven system or mathematical formula for establishing factor weightings. Reliance must be placed on pooled human judgment, past experience, and trial and error in order to arrive at equitable weightings; and under such circumstances opportunity for error will be present. Checking the results of judgment against successfully applied plans can reduce somewhat the margin of error in weightings. In many instances the estimates of committee members are averaged to arrive at the figure to be used, but the procedure is advocated only where discussion cannot bring the estimates into line; for averaging a few figures often results in inaccuracies, averages being a means of errors.

Weightings are often expressed as percentages of the total maximum or minimum points allowed by a plan. It makes little difference what point totals are used—whether they are 300 or 1,000—just so long as there will be no indication of what the resulting rate will be when the totals are computed. When the first degree of each factor calls for no points, as in the plan used by the Carnegie-Illinois Steel Corporation, weighting of the minimum points will not be possible and weights must be

PRE-EMPLOYMENT TRAINING—1

Consider the mentality required to absorb training and exercise judgment for the satisfactory performance of the job. This mentality may be tne result of native intelligence, and schooling or self study.

Code	The Job Requires the Mentality to Learn To:	Benchmark Jobs	Numerical Classifi- cation
A	Carry out simple verbal or simple written instructions necessary to the performance of a repetitive manual task, or a closely super- vised nonrepetitive task. Make out simple reports such as crane reports and production cards. Operate simple machines and make simple adjustments where ad- justments are limited. Use measuring devices such as scales, rules, gauges, and charts in the performance of work where action to be taken is obvious. Operate powered mobile equipment performing simple tasks where little judgment is required.	Stocker O. H. Laborer Loader—Shipplng Thread, Mach. Oper. Barb Wire Mach. Oper. Pipefitter Helper Ingot Buggy Operator	Base
B	Perform work of a nonrepetitive or semirepetitive nature where judgment is required to obtain results. Lead or direct three or more helpers in a variety of simple tasks. Exercise judgment in the operation of powered mobile equipment servicing a number of units or performing a variety of tasks. Set up and operate machines or processes requiring a variety of adjustments. Post detailed data to standard forms or write reports based on observation and judgment.	Pickler Stocker Keeper—B. Fce. Truck Driver Guide Setter—Bil. Slitter Operator	0.3
C	Make general repairs to equipment involving the knowledge of mechanical or electrical principles. Interpret detailed assembly and complex part drawings such as involved in performing trades- man's duties. Direct the operation of a complex production unit which deter- mines size, shape, analysis, or physical property of the product. Plan complex work details and procedures to obtain desired results.	Millwright B. M. Machinist "A" Heater—Hot Strip Tandem Mill Roller Moulder "A"	1.0

SURROUNDINGS—11

Consider the general conditions under which the work is performed, other than hazard, and the extent to which these conditions make the job disagreeable.

Select the description from the table which best describes the average working conditions for the job.

Code	Work Requires Exposure To:	Benchmark Jobs	Numerical Classifi- cation
A	Inside machine shop or average factory type of building. Slightly dirty, noisy and not uniformly heated.	Machinist "A" Sheet Bundler Slitter Operator	Base
B	Heat in summer due to proximity to furnace or hot materials. Inside and outside conditions but not required to remain out in extreme weather. Outside weather conditions but protected part of time by roofs, pulpits or cabs. Continually dirty or greasy work, or exposure to wetness and some fumes and smoke.	Coil Oper. Rod Mill Pipefitter "A" Ore Bridge Oper. Dryerman—B. P.	0.4
C	All weather conditions where weather is severe. Exposed to considerable wetness, acids, fumes, dust, or glare necessitating the wearing of protective clothing or devices. Extreme conditions of dirt where man becomes covered with ob- noxious dirt such as tar, paint, etc. Extreme heat for intervals but not for extended periods. Exposed to intense noise for extended periods.	Welder "A" Keeper—Blast Fce. Nail Mach. Oper.	0.8
D	Exposed to extreme heat of intense degree and for considerable time.	Craneman—Soak. Pit.	1.6
E	Exposed to extreme heat approaching the point of endurance where relief from surroundings at regular intervals is a necessity.	Bottom Maker—S. P.	3.0

FIG. 3–3.—Use of bench mark jobs to clarify factor degree definitions under Carnegie-Illinois Steel Corporation plan. From *Intraplant Wage Rate Inequities Agreement between Carnegie-Illinois Steel Corporation and the United Steel Workers of America (C.I.O.), October 23, 1945*, pp. 24 and 48.

geared to maximums. Some plans, however, use scales which
have no top limit. Such scales allow a specified number of
points for each month or year of experience, for each dollar of
materials worked on, etc. Additional flexibility is provided, but
the problem of weighting may become somewhat difficult.

Application of Points to Factors.—Once weightings have been
agreed upon, point values can be applied to factors and degrees.
This may be done by dividing the number of points allocated
to a factor by the number of degrees in that factor. For example, if the plan has a total of 720 points and a factor a weight

TABLE 3-1

DEGREE OF FACTOR	POINTS ALLOTTED		
	Constant Progression	Geometric Series	Arbitrary Progression
1.....................	16	5	10
2.....................	32	10	20
3.....................	48	20	40
4.....................	64	40	60
5.....................	80	80	80

of 10 per cent, the factor would be allotted 72 points; if there
are six degrees in that factor, then each degree would be worth
an additional 12 points, provided a constant progression between degrees is desired.

There are, however, differences of opinion among students
of job evaluation as to whether the points between degrees
should be constant or whether they should increase progressively
as the higher degrees of the factor are approached. Table 3-1
illustrates the difference in point allotments under three methods
of allotting points to degrees, i.e., under constant progression,
geometric series, and arbitrary progression.

The constant progression eliminates some of the judgment
ordinarily required and, therefore, leaves less room for accusa-

tions of arbitrariness and simplifies the matter of explaining and selling the plan. On the other hand, a geometric series or arbitrary point progression may provide a more accurate reflection of relative job worth. To some students of the problem it hardly seems logical to assume that the difference between the first and second degree of a factor should carry the same weight as the difference between the fourth and the fifth degree. Using the factor "education" as an example, it is argued that the difference between an elementary and a two-year high school education should not be valued as highly as the difference between the two-year college and four-year college education. These arguments merit consideration. This matter of point progression is discussed further in the chapter devoted to wage scales and conversion lines.

Number of Degrees Necessary.—The number of degrees should depend upon the desired degree of differentiation and clarity of definitition. Because one factor can be broken down into five clearly definable degrees does not mean that five degrees will always serve with maximum effectiveness. Uniformity in the number of factor degrees often results in misunderstood definitions.

Figure 3–4 exemplifies arithmetic point progression and uniformity in the number of degree factors, and, therefore, identical weightings for maximum and minimum point totals. The weights shown in this plan closely approach the averages of weights applied in the majority of point rating plans.

In contrast, the plan illustrated in Figure 3–5 exemplifies a nonarithmetic point progression and a nonuniformity of degrees within factors. It is the plan used by the Carnegie-Illinois Steel Corporation and was developed to meet unusual circumstances and peculiar requirements.[4] It will be noted that the weights applied to factors vary from 2.3 per cent to 23.2 per cent, while the degrees per factor range from three to nine.

---

[4]For broader treatment read Robert Tilove, "The Wage Rationalization Program in United States Steel; *Monthly Labor Review*, June, 1947.

Factors	1st Degree	2nd Degree	3rd Degree	4th Degree	5th Degree	Weight Per Cent
SKILL:						
Education........................	14	28	42	56	70	14
Experience.......................	22	44	66	88	110	22
Initiative and ingenuity..........	14	28	42	56	70	14
EFFORT:						
Physical demand.................	10	20	30	40	50	10
Mental and—or visual demand.....	5	10	15	20	25	5
RESPONSIBILITY:						
Responsibility for equipment or process....	5	10	15	20	25	5
Responsibility for material or product.....	5	10	15	20	25	5
Responsibility for safety of others.......	5	10	15	20	25	5
Responsibility for work of others........	5	10	15	20	25	5
JOB CONDITIONS:						
Working conditions...............	10	20	30	40	50	10
Hazards.........................	5	10	15	20	25	5

Fig. 3–4.—Factors, point allocations, and weights—National Electrical Manufacturers' Association plan.

Factors	A	B	C	D	E	F	G	H	J	Weight Per Cent
SKILL:										
Pre-employment training	0	0.3	1.0		1.6	2.0	2.4	3.2	4.0	2.3
Employment training and experience	0	0.4	0.8	1.2	2.8	3.5				9.3
Mental skill	0	1.0	1.6	2.2	2.0					8.1
Manual skill	0	0.5	1.0	1.5	2.0					4.7
EFFORT:										
Mental	0	0.5	1.0	1.5	2.5					5.8
Physical	0	0.3	0.8	1.5	2.5					5.8
RESPONSIBILITY:										
For materials*	0	2.3	3.7	8.5	10.0					23.2
For tools and equipment*	0	0.5	1.0	2.0	3.0	4.0		6.5		9.3
For operations	0	0.5	1.0	2.0	3.0	4.0	5.0			15.1
For safety of others	0	0.4	0.8	1.2	2.0					4.7
JOB CONDITIONS:										
Surroundings	0	0.4	0.8	1.6	3.0					7.0
Hazards	0	0.4	0.8	1.2	2.0					4.7
Total										100.0

*There is a point range within each degree of these factors. The figure shown is the top of the range.

FIG. 3–5.—Factors, point allocations, and weights—Carnegie-Illinois Steel Corporation plan.

Advantages of Point Rating

Any method of job evaluation will be at a disadvantage if improperly applied, either through lack of knowledge of the subject or failure to adhere to generally accepted principles of soundness. Because of its relative simplicity, the point rating method appears to be well entrenched, not only as a method but as a teacher of sound principles.

The human judgment element so prevalent in all job evaluation systems is at a minimum in point rating because of the gauges or standards provided by definitions. The factor comparison method calls on human judgment to determine whether job A requires more or less skill than job B, and later it calls on the same human judgment to say how much of the going rate for job A and for job B is compensation for that skill. Point rating merely asks that the skill required of the two jobs be compared with the definitions or standards established. Another advantage is that a more definite gauging is provided through expansion in the number of factors used in appraisal. The larger number of factors forces the analysis of jobs, thus precluding over-all blanket judgment and the possibilities of bias. By the proper use of points as a measure of worth, judgment is not warped through a consideration of existing rates and possibilities of perpetuating inequities are reduced. Of utmost importance is the fact that point rating plans require the maintenance of permanent records which are useful as substantiating evidence of how jobs were appraised and of the resulting appraisal.

While not as simple as the job ranking and predetermined grading methods, either in application or in salability, point rating does have the advantage over factor comparison in this respect: it is complex enough to arouse curiosity and, at the same time, it is easily explained to those who are not acquainted with the generalities of job evaluation.

Disadvantages of Point Rating

The most frequently heard criticism of point rating concerns its nonflexibility. This weakness of the system stems from the application of ceilings to factors and weights placed on factors prior to using the plan. The weakness, however, does not warrant the concern over the soundness of the method so often evinced by advocates of factor comparison.[5] Although the ceiling placed on a factor does not allow the assigning of points to a particular job in excess of those called for by the highest degree of the factor, the indisputable fact is that in those plans where such a situation exists there has been failure to select the proper plan or there has been lack of thought in devising one. No plan should be used where the jobs to be evaluated do not fall within the degrees provided. Many point rating plans place no limit on many factors; some place no ceiling on the number of points that might be assigned. A certain number of points may be allowed for each year or month of experience required, for each dollar of responsibility for equipment and materials, for each dollar of payroll of those supervised, or for each year of schooling required, etc.

The problem of weighting applies to either the factor comparison or the point rating method. Under the former, weighting is accomplished by assigning a portion of the going rate to the factor, thus automatically establishing the weight of the job characteristic. In the latter method, group judgment establishes the weight when the plan is chosen or devised.

However, there is considerable flexibility in that each degree calls for different point values, which results in a wide range of points assigned to the degree of a factor in relation to the total points assigned. For example, under the National Electrical Manufacturers' Association plan, total possible points range between 100 and 500; and factors carry values of 5 to 22 points for the lowest degree and 25 to 110 points for the highest degree. It is altogether possible, then, to have a situation wherein 5 out of a possible 480 points or a percentage of 1.04, might measure the presence of a job characteristic. It is also possible to assign 25 out of 120 points, or a percentage of 20.8, to measure the presence of the same characteristic in another job. Under the same plan, skill factors may account for 20 to 75 per cent of

[5]For a severe criticism of the point rating method, read E. J. Benge, *Job Evaluation and Merit Rating*, (National Foremen's Institute, Inc., 1941).

the total points assigned. In some instances, plans will provide degrees unnecessary to the measurement of jobs, in which case they are never applied; this obviously distorts weightings, but that is a failure of the plan and not of the point rating method.

Wide Acceptance of the Point Rating Method

Of the four generally recognized methods of job evaluation, point rating enjoys the widest acceptance. As with other systems, it has certain deficiencies but appears to best fit the requirements of the majority of concerns. It is employed successfully not only by the larger companies, such as Westinghouse Electric Corporation, United States Steel Corporation, and General Electric Company, but by countless smaller enterprises as well. Point rating is recommended by such bodies as the National Electrical Manufacturers' Association, an association which estimates their plan to be employed by 1,200 to 1,500 plants, and the National Metal Trades Association which estimates 500 users of their plan.[6]

Further indications of the favored position of point rating are evidenced in its widespread use by management consultants and in the fact that the Industrial Management Society plan embodies the point rating technique. However, because the point rating method is the most widely accepted does not conclusively prove that it is the best; but this does indicate that it evidently gives satisfactory results. There has been considerable criticism of point rating, particularly by those who strongly advocate the factor comparison method, but such criticism is actually the result of disagreement over the manner in which the plans have been set up or applied, rather than of the general point rating idea. Job evaluation is still in its infancy, and for this reason, no one method of evaluation has proved itself to the extent of justifying claims of perfection.

This chapter has been devoted in general to the consideration of point rating as a method of job evaluation. Specifi-

[6]Smyth and Murphy, *Job Evaluation and Employee Rating* (New York: McGraw-Hill Book Co., Inc., 1946), p. 29.

KEY JOB TITLE	EDUCATION		EXPERIENCE		INITIATIVE AND INGENUITY		PHYSICAL DEMAND		MENTAL AND VISUAL		EQUIPMENT OR PROCESS		MATERIAL OR PRODUCT		SAFETY OF OTHERS		WORK OF OTHERS		WORKING CONDITIONS		HAZARDS		TOTAL
	D	P	D	P	D	P	D	P	D	P	D	P	D	P	D	P	D	P	D	P	D	P	
TOOL AND DIE MAKER	4	56	5	110	5	70	2	20	4	20	3	15	5	25	3	15	3	15	2	20	3	15	381
ELECTRICIAN A	4	56	4	88	4	56	2	20	3	15	3	15	4	20	3	15	3	15	3	30	5	25	355
MACHINIST A	4	56	4	88	4	56	2	20	4	20	2	10	4	20	3	15	2	10	3	30	3	15	340
AUTOMATIC SCREW MACHINE SETUP MAN	3	42	4	88	4	56	2	20	4	20	3	15	2	10	3	15	3	15	3	30	3	15	326
CARPENTER A	3	42	4	88	4	56	3	30	3	15	2	10	2	10	3	15	3	15	3	30	3	15	326
CRANEMAN	1	14	2	44	3	42	3	30	4	20	4	20	4	20	5	25	1	5	3	30	4	20	270
PLATER	1	14	3	66	3	42	3	30	2	10	4	20	2	10	2	10	2	10	4	40	3	15	257
DRILL-PRESS OPERATOR	2	28	2	44	2	28	2	20	3	15	2	10	2	10	2	10	1	5	2	20	2	10	200
ASSEMBLER, BENCH	2	28	2	44	2	28	2	20	3	15	2	10	2	10	1	5	1	5	2	20	2	10	195
INSPECTOR-TESTER	2	28	2	44	2	28	2	20	3	15	2	10	2	10	1	5	1	5	2	20	2	10	195
TRUCKER, ELECTRIC	1	14	1	22	2	28	3	30	3	15	3	15	2	10	4	20	1	5	2	20	3	15	194
HELPER, TRADES	1	14	1	22	2	28	4	40	2	10	2	10	1	5	3	15	1	5	3	30	3	15	194
JANITOR	1	14	1	22	2	28	3	30	2	10	2	10	1	5	3	15	1	5	4	40	3	15	194
LABORER	1	14	1	22	1	14	4	40	2	10	1	5	2	10	3	15	1	5	4	40	3	15	190

D=DEGREE
P=POINTS

FIG 3-6.—Application of point rating under the N.E.M.A. plan.

cally, it has treated the problems of selecting or devising a point rating plan through a discussion of the selecting, defining, and weighting of factors to be used in the measurement of relative job worth. The process of evaluating jobs under the point rating system is given detailed treatment in Chapter 5. However, for purposes of comparing this system with other systems, the key jobs used for illustrating the principles of job ranking and factor comparison methods have been evaluated under the National Electrical Manufacturers' Association plan. The results of this point rating application are illustrated in Figure 3–6.

QUESTIONS

1. Why is it more desirable for a company to design its own point rating plan? Why is this not done more often?

2. What are the basic steps involved in originating a point rating plan?

3. What bearing do the occupations to be evaluated have on the selection of factors? Explain.

4. What is meant by a "legitimate" factor? Give an example of a factor that is not legitimate.

5. Do you believe five, fifteen, or twenty-five to be the most desirable number of factors to use with the point rating method? Why? Would you use the same number with the factor comparison method? Why?

6. Visit a factory in your general area; and after seeing it in operation, select from the list of factors those you would use if you were to devise a point rating plan. Select only as many factors as you would employ in your plan. Give reasons for your selections.

7. What is your opinion as to the use of balancing factors? Why do you feel as you do?

8. What are the characteristics of a good factor definition?

9. Take one of the factors you selected in question No. 6 above and compose your own definition of it. Assume there are five degrees to the factor and compose definitions for each of the degrees.

10. What is meant by a "bench mark"? Name a bench mark job for each of the degree definitions you have written for question No. 9.

11. Why is it necessary to weight factors? How would you apply weights to factors? Would you change your weights if the total number of maximum or minimum points allowed by the plan was doubled? Why?

12. Upon what does the number of degrees within a factor depend?

13. If you were to select a method of job evaluation, which would be your choice—factor comparison or point rating?

CHAPTER 4

JOB DESCRIPTIONS

THE two preceding chapters were devoted to the subject of selecting and originating evaluation plans, and the chapter to follow will be concerned with the process of evaluating jobs. Regardless of the plan selected or originated, the evaluation process requires that information, setting forth just what constitutes each job to be evaluated, be made available to those charged with rating jobs. Unless jobs are clearly defined and delimited, those doing the evaluating may have differences in concept which will result in failure to agree on the relative worth of a job. Fundamentally, then, job descriptions are necessary to enable the raters to differentiate and to standardize the concepts of job content. Job descriptions are the subject matter of this chapter, and discussion will be based on the following topics:

1. Uses of job descriptions.
2. Considerations preliminary to preparing descriptions.
3. How data are secured.
4. What information to include.
5. Forms of job descriptions.
6. Maintenance of files.

Terminology

Throughout this chapter and later in this text confusion may arise over the meaning of the terms "job," "occupation," "grade," "job description," and "job specification." Therefore, in the interest of clarity, these terms are defined as follows:

JOB.—A work assignment having a specific set of duties, responsibilities, and conditions different from those of other work assignments.

OCCUPATION.—A group of closely related jobs having common characteristics. For example, the operator of an external grinder in a machine shop might be engaged in the "occupation" of "grinder hand." His "job," however, might be termed "piston grinder."

POSITION.—Work performed without stating whether or not such work differs from the work assignments of other individuals. In other words, a group of piston grinders may occupy similar jobs but different positions.

GRADE.—A definite bracket or cell distinguishing the levels of work. For example, one grade of grinder hand may do intricate shoulder, contour, and taper grinding, while a grinder hand of a lower grade may do only simple repetitive work on straight shafts.

JOB CLASSIFICATION.—The arrangement of jobs having similar characteristics into logical groups and subgroups.

JOB ANALYSIS.—The process of studying the duties, operations, and organizational aspects of a work assignment.

JOB DESCRIPTION.—A written report delineating the duties, responsibilities, and conditions attendant to the job.

JOB SPECIFICATION.—A job description to which has been added the skill, effort, responsibility, and working condition requirements necessary to the fulfillment of the work assignment.

JOB TITLE.—A distinctive, designative term for a particular job.

Uses of Job Descriptions

The primary concern of the analyst in writing job descriptions is to furnish information necessary to the evaluation of jobs. If, however, through the addition of a little time and effort, the descriptions can be made to serve multiple purposes, their value to management may be considerably enhanced.

Personnel departments often use job descriptions and specifications as guides in the hiring and transferring of personnel or in the preparation of schedules of promotions. With the increase in the use of more scientific methods of selection, i.e., the application of psychological test batteries, information included in the description can be a guide as to what batteries to use. Furthermore, study of descriptions to ascertain what jobs are most hazardous and injurious to health may assist the Industrial Relations Department in directing safety campaigns and in efforts to reduce occupational disease. Further uses of job descriptions include: aid in establishing training programs, estimating of costs, methods improvements, budgetary control, timekeeping and payroll simplification, and installing of wage incentives. Prior to writing job descriptions, the analyst should be informed as to how other than for job evaluation the descriptions will be used and if any additional data must be incorporated to render them useful to other functions. The use to which job descriptions are put must be known so that proper distribution of copies can be made.

Considerations Preliminary to Preparing Descriptions

Analyst and Employee Should Be Informed.—No effort should be made to prepare job descriptions until certain preliminary steps have been taken. Analysts should not enter the shops for purposes of gathering data until management and the union have announced the program of job evaluation and have prepared the employees for co-operating with those seeking information. If the worker is acquainted with the reasons why information is being sought, it saves the time of worker and of analyst and more intelligent and complete answers will be forthcoming. The analyst must know the plan to be used, for the information desired should include all the facts necessary to consideration of all factors used in the plan.

Review of Titles.—Of utmost importance is the review of titles, for in many cases similar titles do not denote similar jobs, and like jobs are often referred to by different titles. For example, a machine operator and a machinist may do the same work in one plant, but in another plant there may be substantial differences between the two jobs. In many plants it is difficult to differentiate between the job content of trades helpers and common labor. In offices considerable title confusion exists between such positions as cost accountant and cost clerk, bookkeeper and accountant, stenographer and typist.

The possibilities of combining jobs should receive thorough consideration, for many opportunities for reducing the number of jobs to be evaluated may present themselves. A common failure of analysts is the excessive refinement of and the consequent expansion in the number of titles. One company went so far as to prepare a description for each machine in the plant; this resulted in approximately 1,300 descriptions when a total of about 400 would have been sufficient. The number of job titles required will frequently depend on the type of business and its operating policies and methods, for the greater the degree of specialization among workers the more job descriptions will be required.

Union Attitudes.—Because many unions fear the effect on seniority of too many titles, they have exerted considerable pressure in order to reduce the number of titles to a minimum. On the other hand, however, some unions have required management to set up an excessive number of titles, with the result that very slight changes in job content have led to many grievances and discontent with the principles of job evaluation.

It should be remembered that there is no measure of the proper number of jobs within a given plant. Very often the range of skills will be the determinant as to the number of titles involved.

Base Descriptions on Normal Operations.—Where a plant or department is operating substantially above or below normal capacity so that job content is distorted, it may be well to postpone the analysis of jobs until such time as the operations are on a normal basis. During World War II, many plants were forced to adopt production methods that would allow for expansion in volume; and job content was changed substantially as a result. After the war, however, jobs reverted to their normal content, and it was necessary to rewrite the descriptions that had been formulated on the basis of wartime operations.

There must be assurance that jobs are reasonably definite or standardized, for the time of the analyst will be wasted if the jobs are subjected to constant change. Analysts should be watchful for proposed changes in methods, operations, working conditions, and policies that may have future effects on job content.

Job descriptions, therefore, should only be made after the analyst has been informed of the plan to be used and the use to which the descriptions will be put, after the employees have been prepared for the program, and after the job titles have been reviewed and the operations are on a normal basis. When these points have been considered, then the process of accumulating data can begin.

How Data Are Secured

The job analyst is charged with the task of securing accurate data, sufficient for intelligent appraisal of job content. Observation, discussion, and questionnaire are the most commonly used techniques, although they are not always employed under similar circumstances.

Techniques Used in Shops.—Observation is the method used extensively in shops, but it should be supplemented with discussions with the operator. Rarely will an observer be able to gather all data necessary by merely watching an operator at work, for the range of duties will be spread over a day's or perhaps a week's time. For example, a lathe operator may be required to perform six different operations, such as turn, face, form, chamfer, counterbore, and ream; but he may perform only the turning operation during the period his job is observed. Discussion with the operator would be necessary in order to learn the additional operations required. Also, consultation with the foreman or supervisor usually brings to light additional facts. Many operators are reticent about talking too freely, feeling that their statements will have adverse effects on their earnings or will be misconstrued; in such instances, the foreman or steward will be able to furnish most of the information.

Too much stress cannot be placed, however, on the advisability of consulting with the operator. Not only is this a means of securing information, but it also makes the operator feel that he is an important part of the program and is receiving equal treatment. It is important, too, that the foreman be asked his opinion of jobs, for he also must be made to feel that he is a vital part of the project. A study of layouts, blueprints, and written instructions is another additional source of information for the analyst as are organization charts and policy manuals.

The use of employee questionnaires in the shop is not advisable. Shop personnel rarely have the ability or aptitude for expressing themselves well in writing. The questionnaire, if filled out by the analyst for the operator, may be an improvement; but this is a little different from the preferred practice of the analyst of taking notes during his observation and of discussing the job with the operator.

Techniques Used in Offices.—In analyzing clerical and technical occupations, the questionnaire has been used with considerable success. It should not, however, be used without also discussing the information provided in it with the supervisor and, in some cases, with the employee. When the questionnaire is filled out by the employee, there is the possibility of exaggeration of the importance of the job; but there is the advantage of having the employee's own statements when the evaluations must be substantiated.

Figure 4–1 is a questionnaire which has been used successfully in securing data for clerical job descriptions. The form was designed to bring out the facts necessary to evaluating the jobs under a specific plan. Employees, therefore, in filling in the form not only analyzed their positions but took a large part in evaluating them. Contrary to expectations, most employees had a tendency to underrate their jobs.

Observation of clerical jobs is a long and tedious process which usually involves studies of clerical systems and procedures. Discussion with employees is usually confined to those cases where questionnaire answers are lacking in clarity or where the supervisor is not sufficiently acquainted with the details of the position.

Briefly, observation augmented by frequent discussions with the operator and supervisor is the most satisfactory method of securing data in the shop; while in offices the questionnaire, coupled with conferences with the supervisor, generally secures the best results with the least expenditure of time and effort.

What Information to Include

Clarity and Accuracy.—The purpose of the job description is to convey a set of facts to job evaluators; descriptions serve their purpose only to the extent to which they accomplish this end. Clarity and accuracy are essential, and a prerequisite of a satisfactory job description is that the writer have a clear understanding of the material presented.

Certain writing methods are helpful in expressing desired information clearly and concisely. Sentences should begin with active, functional verbs, such as "tests," "performs," "uses," etc. Quantitative words should be used. It is inadequate to say "pushes loaded truck"; instead "pushes truck loaded with 100 to 500 pounds of material" gives more exactitude to the description. The use of specific, rather than of vague words, gives a more accurate picture of what the worker is required to do. For example, rather than say that a patternmaker "makes" patterns, it is more informative to say that he "saws stock to length on circular saw and roughly to width on ripsaw; shapes with woodworking machines and hand tools." Too detailed a statement, however, may result in a motion or operation analysis. It is easier to visualize the job if the various tasks are stated in proper order, such as setup, feed, remove, maintain.

The material should be complete, carefully selected, and organized thoroughly in advance of writing. Complete standardization of the writing of descriptions is not desirable, for there is the danger of inflexibility that may hinder the expansion of statements concerning salient features of the job described. There should, however, be a measure of uniformity so that those who are to benefit from the descriptions will know where to look for specific facts.

As with any type of report, there should be a definite distinction between fact and opinion. Here consensus is severely divided as to whether the analyst has or has not the right to insert his personal estimate into a description. If the analyst states his personal opinion on job requirements, there may, if his opinion is regarded, be little left for the evaluators to do

QUESTIONNAIRE—TECHNICAL and CLERICAL POSITIONS

Please read this entire questionnaire over carefully before answering any of the questions. Do not leave any questions blank. Answer each question as specifically and as completely as possible. If a particular question does not apply to your job, do not leave that question blank—fill in the words "none", "no", or "does not apply". Remember that this information is for a person not familiar with the duties of your position or your department. Make your information sufficiently clear to be understood by such a person. If you do not understand any question, contact your supervisor.

The company has found it advisable to determine the full content of all of its office and clerical jobs as a basis for organization of office functions. In order to do so, we are requesting all of the employees themselves to describe just what they are doing, of what their respective jobs consist, and the amount of knowledge, skill, experience and responsibility required therefor. Your careful preparation of the information asked in this questionnaire will be of great help to your Company and will allow us accurately to classify and describe the various positions.

This questionnaire is **not** intended to obtain any information about the particular person holding a particular job. We desire only information **about the job itself.** Your answers, regardless of the information given, will not cause any reduction in your pay or job status.

Your wholehearted expression is earnestly requested.

Department_____ Date_____

Name of
EMPLOYEE_____ Title of Position_____

—Immediate Superior—

Name_____ Title of Position_____

A. DESCRIPTION OF THE DUTIES OF YOUR POSITION:

1. Daily duties (in answering this question be sure to include all those duties in your daily routine).

Approx. hours
per day

_____

_____

2. Regular, periodic duties (weekly, monthly, etc.)

3. Occasional duties at irregular intervals.

4. What is the general purpose of your work?

Fig. 4-1.

B. EDUCATIONAL REQUIREMENTS OF YOUR POSITION: (indicate by check ✓).

State what **you think** is required, not your own education.

Formal Schooling	Equivalent
1. ☐ Grammar School (8 grades)	Read, write, add, subtract.
2. ☐ 1 - 2 yrs. High School	Simple arithmetic, checking, posting, etc.
3. ☐ 3 - 4 yrs. High School	Ordinary clerical, typing, interpret simple drawings.
4. ☐ High School and Business College	Higher type clerical, bookkeeping, secretarial.
5. ☐ Partial College 1 - 2 yrs.	Knowledge of specific field—Accounting, Engineering, etc., or practical knowledge required to interpret complicated drawings and manufacturing methods.
6. ☐ College Graduate	Technical background (advanced knowledge of Accounting, Engineering, Chemistry, etc.) required to understand complicated subjects.

C. EXPERIENCE AND TRAINING REQUIRED FOR YOUR POSITION:

(Consider and state what you think should be the combined amount of previous experience and training required to fulfill your position.)

	Months			Years					
From	0	3	7	1	3	5	7	9	11
To	2	6	12	2	4	6	8	10	12
Check									

D. EQUIPMENT USED:

Does the work of your position require the use of any machines or equipment?   Yes ☐   No ☐

If so, indicate the name and type, and extent of use.

_____ (Name)   _____ (Type)

☐ OCCASIONAL

☐ FREQUENT

☐ REGULAR

E. CONFIDENTIAL DATA: (Does your position require working with confidential data? If so, indicate by ☑)

INDICATE EXTENT BY SYMBOL OF
THE FOLLOWING:

(A) Limited

(B) Moderate

(C) Considerable

1. ☐ None

2. ☐ Wages, salaries _____ (Extent)

3. ☐ Costs _____ (Extent)

4. ☐ Financial statements _____ (Extent)

5. ☐ Corporate structures _____ (Extent)

6. ☐ Confidential and secret
       contract data _____ (Extent)

7. ☐ OTHER _____ (Specify) _____ (Extent)

Indicate by ☑ the access which your position gives to information or data requiring a high degree of integrity, to safeguard the company's
confidential or competitive position.

1. ☐ NONE   2. ☐ REPORTS   3. ☐ PLANS   4. ☐ PROGRAMS

5. ☐ Other _____ (Specify)

Fig. 4-1.—*Continued.*

F. CONTACT WITH OTHERS

1. ☐ Little or no contact except with immediate associates or superiors.

2. ☐ Contacts within department only.

3. ☐ Contacts with other departments, furnishing and obtaining information.

4. ☐ Contacts with other departments, requiring tact and judgment to avoid friction.

5. ☐ Frequent contacts with major executives on matters requiring explanations and discussions.

6. ☐ Outside contacts with customers or others, presenting data that may influence important decisions.

7. ☐ Frequent contacts involving the carrying out of programs and schedules requiring the influencing of others to obtain the desired result.

8. ☐ Regular and frequent outside contacts with persons of high rank, requiring tact and judgment to deal with and influence people. Requires well developed sense of strategy and timing.

G. EXTENT TO WHICH WORK IS SUPERVISED: (indicate by check ☑)

1. ☐ Immediate or frequent supervision.

2. ☐ Short assignments—supervised.

3. ☐ Follow standardized procedures with little immediate supervision in normal routine or work.

4. ☐ Follow established procedures generally, refer only unusual cases to superior.

5. ☐   Broad assignments, procedure not standardized; usually with little guidance or checking. Rarely refer to superiors except as to matters of policy.

6. ☐   Organize own work, assign and check work, rarely refer specific problems to supervisors.

7. ☐   Under administrative direction, set up own standards of performance; Virtual self-supervision.

H. EXERCISE OF DISCRETION AND INDEPENDENT JUDGMENT:

Does the work of your position require the exercise of discretion and independent judgment?   Yes ☐   No ☐

If yes, give a typical example of a situation in which discretion and independent judgment must be used, and the extent to which damage or loss could result from an error by you.

I. REMARKS:

State here any additional information which you believe would help in describing or understanding the duties of your position.

FIG. 4–1.—*Continued.*

THE FOLLOWING IS TO BE ANSWERED ONLY BY EMPLOYEES WHO SUPERVISE OTHERS

J. SUPERVISION OF OTHERS:

I Character of Supervision:

Consider here the nature of the supervision; responsibility for disciplining, hiring, transferring, etc., or is it merely assigning and checking work, or acting as understudy to a supervisor? If totally responsible for any of the following, please check items; if partially responsible, insert "P" in the block preceding item.

1. ☐ ASSIGNS WORK	8. ☐ PERSONNEL
2. ☐ CHECKS WORK	9. ☐ GRIEVANCES
2. ☐ HIRING	10. ☐ PLANNING
4. ☐ TRANSFERRING	11. ☐ ROUTING
5. ☐ DISCIPLINING	12. ☐ SCHEDULING
6. ☐ COSTS	13. ☐ QUALITY STANDARDS
7. ☐ METHODS	14. ☐ QUANTITY STANDARDS

II Type of Employee Supervised:

State the job titles of employees and the number in each classification.

a.

FIG. 4-1.—*Continued.*

but to record points. A description stating what the responsibility and skill requirements of an occupation are ceases to be a description and becomes a specification. If unbiased group judgment is to evaluate the jobs, it appears advisable for the analysts to include nothing but factual data in job descriptions.

Figure 4–2 illustrates a description in which the analyst has done a considerable part of the actual evaluation of the job. The education, experience, and mental effort requirements and the amount of responsibility for money and materials has been included, as well as statements concerning the amount of independent judgment necessary. If the evaluating committee accepts the word of the analyst, there will be little for them to do but to award the required number of points allowed by the plan for the degree of education, experience, mental effort, and responsibility for money and materials.

Composition of the Description.—The heading of the description should include the job title, date of analysis, job number or code, and exact location of the operation, including machine and department numbers. The date is highly important in determining the elapsed time between the observation and the evaluation of the job and the possibilities of a change in job content having occurred during the interim. Careful noting of the location of the job will save time if it is necessary to visit the job to verify the content of the description. Many forms include provisions for entering the names of the workers engaged in the job described. Such a practice may defeat the cardinal principle of the plan which is to evaluate the job, not the operator. If the proper location of the job is shown, along with the machine number and other identifying data, the name of the operator should not be required and will best be excluded. Including any rate information on the form before a rate has been established through evaluation of the job is not advisable, for such practice may have a distorting effect on judgment.

The body of the description should be composed in such a manner as to facilitate the finding of such facts as are necessary to intelligent evaluation. In general, the body of the descrip-

JOB DESCRIPTION

JOB TITLE: Chief Stenographer   DATE: June 7, 1948

JOB CODE No.: 800   Dept.: 310   LOCATION: Bldg. 6, 2nd Fl.

JOB SUMMARY:

To supervise and to co-ordinate the activities of the stenographic department.

JOB DUTIES:

Check work into department, classify into one of three classes recognized by department, and assign work to department employees. Proofread and mail out completed work. Sort and mail out service department order forms to branch houses. Check department equipment for accuracy and operating condition. Make out weekly report of employees daily typewriter key stroke count. Make weekly check of department stationery and supplies and requisition necessary items. Make out monthly dictaphone report of number of letters typed and cylinders used. Instruct employees in their duties and in how to do unfamiliar work. Take and type dictation of a confidential nature.

REQUIREMENTS:

This employee should possess stenographic and supervisory ability, a clerical aptitude for verbal clerical reasoning, and a vocational interest in the clerical field. Independent judgment and discretion must be exercised in planning and assigning the work. Duties are reasonably varied, and a wide scope of stenographic material is encountered. Continuous mental application is required.

The employee makes frequent contacts with major executives on matters requiring explanation and discussion but has little responsibility for money and materials. The position gives regular access to confidential data, such as wages, costs, financial statements, contracts, reports, and programs. Employee must be well versed in the operation of stenographic equipment, such as typewriters, dictaphones, and duplicating devices.

EDUCATION AND EXPERIENCE:

A high school and business college education, or its equivalent, is required, for the employee must have a knowledge of higher type clerical and secretarial routines and procedures. Three to four years' experience in stenographic work is required for the purpose of learning the various types of work and equipment that may be encountered.

SUPERVISION:

This employee supervises the activities of ten to fifteen typists, dictaphone operators, and duplicating machine operators and is responsible to the general office manager to whom she reports.

Fig. 4–2.—Example of a job description that pre-evaluates job

tion usually includes a summarizing paragraph stating, in abbreviated terms, the content of the job. This is followed by a paragraph stating in detail the specific duties of the employee and the variety and types of operations performed.

Since job descriptions are prepared as a means of facilitating the evaluation of jobs, the items included will be governed to a large extent by the plan used and particularly by the factors employed in the plan. In other words, the description should state what information the plan calls for. The most common fault in preparing job descriptions is failure to strike a balance between saying too much and omitting needed factual data. It is almost a universal practice to include statements concerning tools, equipment, and materials used in the performance of the job, since such information is indicative of the nature and complexity of the work, hazards, and working conditions.

One suggested form of description calls for, in addition to a job summary and description of detailed duties, four paragraphs each devoted to descriptive data concerning one of the four general job characteristics: skill, effort, responsibilities, and working conditions. Such a method of presentation not only aids the evaluation committee in locating information necessary to the appraisal of each characteristic but also acts as a reminder to the analyst that each paragraph provides information vital to the process of evaluating the job.

Where more than one analyst prepares the job descriptions, it may be well to compose a list of standard terms or phrases to be used in order that consistency in description of content will be followed. Analysts will differ in their ability to express themselves in writing, and a drab literary style may tend to give an evaluation different from one described in more colorful terms.

Forms of Job Descriptions

The form of the description is secondary to the accomplishment of its purpose. The method of gathering and assembling

JOB DESCRIPTION

JOB CODE: 123   DATE: Dec. 23, 1948

JOB TITLE: Cutter   DEPT.: 120

PURPOSE:

To operate a semiautomatic machine that shears such materials as paper, press board, and cardboard to required sizes.

JOB DUTIES:

Picks up a stack of material and loads on table of machine, positioning the material against the back gauges. Actuates two hand levers which lower the shearing knife and cuts the material stock to the desired size. May depress foot pedal to clamp stock into position while cutting. Operator disposes of scrap ends and repeats the positioning and cutting operations until the desired dimensions are obtained. Removes the finished stock from machine table and lays on skid or rack for transportation to the next operation. Operator occasionally rubs wax on edge of knife blade. Stock is delivered to the operator. Operator adjusts his machine gauges and replaces knives, which requires removal of dull knife with a wrench. Transports knife to sharpening station, exchanges for a sharp knife, returns, and sets up in machine. Cuts such materials as paper, press board and cardboard.

RESPONSIBILITIES:

Operator must acquire the ability to correctly measure his cuts in order to avoid scrap. Co-ordination of hand, foot, and eye is required in operation of machine.

Operator has little opportunity to damage equipment if average care is used in operating and setting up the machine.

Continuous mental and visual attention is required but not to an exacting degree.

Fingers, hands, and arms are in continuous motion within a small area in normal course of work and frequent lifting or stretching may be required in procuring materials or in the disposal of finished work. Work is normally performed in a standing position with walking involved only in the procurement of materials or the disposal of finished material.

TOOLS AND EQUIPMENT:

Seybold paper cutting machine, Oswego cutting machine, wrench, and various types of paper, pressboard, and cardboard.

WORKING CONDITIONS:

The work area is warm and well ventilated, though somewhat noisy from operation of machines in the vicinity of the operator. Loss of fingers may be sustained from edge of knife during operation of machine if care is not taken.

SUPERVISION:

Operation is highly repetitive and little supervisory attention is required except in the case of machine trouble. Work assignments are received from the foreman.

EDUCATION AND EXPERIENCE:

Since only the ability to read, write, add, and subtract is required of the worker, an equivalent elementary school education is required. Up to four months' training on the job and two to three years of previous experience is sufficient to provide the average worker with the ability to operate the machine and to perform setups.

FIG. 4–3.—Example of prose type job description.

JOB DESCRIPTION

CODE: 519-1   DATE: Sept. 20, 1946
TITLE: Locker Room Attendant   LOCATION: Lawson

PURPOSE:

To control the admission of members and guests to the physical section and to render service to members using the facilities of the physical section by checking their personal belongings and complying with their requests for supplies and equipment.

GENERAL DUTIES:

The worker may perform all or any of the following tasks as directed by his superior:

(a) Checks membership cards, for the purpose of determining if members are paid up and entitled to use the facilities of the physical section.

(b) Issues gym baskets, soap, and towels and receives members' personal belongings for safekeeping.

(c) Issues small equipment, such as volley balls, basketballs, handballs, and other items provided for general use of members. May receive deposits on some items until they are returned.

(e) Allows persons to use the locker room and other gym facilities and equipment on presenting guest passes or upon paying entrance fee at the locker room cage.

(f) May maintain a card file of members having baskets.

(g) May keep a daily record on all activities showing frequency of use of the various facilities and equipment in the physical section.

(h) Checks out cash or cash register and submits report of cash taken in and services or items sold.

(i) May procure own supplies of pop, candy, and other food or beverage items.

(j) May take periodic inventories of equipment, towels, and merchandise connected with the locker room operation and may requisition supplies for sale, designating required sizes of gym equipment.

(k) Sees that guests comply with house rules.

(l) Gathers, counts, records, and sends out soiled linen.

(m) Receives incoming linen for the locker room, counts and stores.

(n) May clean locker room area and keep all fixtures in the cage in neat and orderly manner.

(o) May guard the swimming pool for short periods in absence of regular personnel.

REQUIREMENTS:

No specific skill required on this job. The worker must have some knowledge of the simple clerical procedures required in keeping activity reports, recording inventories, maintaining file cards of baskets, and handling of guest passes and membership cards. The worker has considerable responsibility for maintaining efficient operation of the locker room and for extending prompt and courteous service to members and guests.

Some physical effort is necessary since the majority of time is spent in servicing requests or storing baskets and involves considerable walking back and forth. A small amount of time is spent in cleaning and sweeping tasks plus some handling of soiled linens. A minimum of visual and mental effort is required in making change, keeping records, and handling the personal belongings of others.

FIG. 4-4.—Example of prose type job description.

TOOLS AND EQUIPMENT:
  A cash register and sales receipt machine may be used.

WORKING CONDITIONS:
  Surroundings are pleasant and clean. Humidity at various times can be annoying to a small degree. Probability of an accident in this work is very remote.

SUPERVISION:
  Follows established procedures generally; refers only unusual cases to superior.

EDUCATION AND EXPERIENCE:
  A one- or two-year high school education or equivalent clerical training and experience is necessary to the worker since the ability to maintain cash and other simple clerical records is required. Some previous experience in serving the public is desired but not required. One to two weeks of experience on the job will provide a knowledge of procedures and routines.

LINE OF ORGANIZATION:
  The locker room clerk receives directions from and reports to the physical education director.

Fig. 4–4.—*Continued.*

data, however, must be conductive to future reference and usefulness in case substantiation of evaluations becomes necessary. For this reason the analyst should follow a definite procedure in gathering, recording, interpreting, and filing data used in the composition of job descriptions.

The Prose Type.—There are two general types of description: prose and check list, but very often combinations of the two types are used. Figures 4–3, 4–4, 4–5, and 4–6 exemplify the prose type. It affords the writer unlimited expression of thought and an opportunity to include everything deemed necessary in presenting the facts. Its primary advantage lies in its flexibility. On the other hand, it opens the way to pre-evaluation of jobs by allowing the analyst a free choice of statements and the inclusion of opinion as well as of fact. There may also be a tendency on the part of the analyst to be "wordy" in his style of expression, thus increasing the time required to read and to interpret the description.

When the prose form of description is used, the analyst will probably take rough notes during his observation of the job

MEMORIAL HOSPITAL
of
DuPAGE COUNTY

Standard Job Description

DEPARTMENT: Nursing
JOB NO.:   N-8-S
DATE: Dec. 27, 1948

JOB TITLE:

Head Nurse: Medical-Surgical Patient Care. (First floor west; second floor center; second floor west).

PURPOSE:

To have charge of and be responsible for sectional nursing service on the medical-surgical floors and to supervise and direct nursing activities within the section assigned.

GENERAL DUTIES:

(a) Collaborate with medical staff and directors of nursing and carry out their orders in the care and treatment of patients residing in their respective sections.
(b) Oversee the general administration of the section and the nursing care and treatment of patients.
(c) Train and supervise nurses and nurses aides under her direction.
(d) Be responsible for the carrying-out of established administrative policies and procedures.
(e) Attend to transfers and discharges.
(f) Requisition needed supplies.
(g) Supervise the administration of medicines and treatments as prescribed by the medical staff.
(h) Originate ideas and make recommendations for general improvement of nursing, nursing service, and related activities.
(i) See that administration detail, reports, and records are properly prepared and processed or assist in same.
(j) Visit patients and confer with relatives and visitors as necessary.
(k) Assist in care of critically ill or injured patients.
(l) Make rounds of inspection.
(m) Assign nurses to cases; schedule nurses' work schedules; and see that section is adequately staffed.
(n) Clear doctors' orders through various clinical departments.
(o) Orient and instruct new personnel.
(p) Perform other related duties as required.

REQUIREMENTS:

A broad knowledge of general nursing care and treatment and the ability to supervise and direct others is required. Must have skill in dealing with patients. Considerable judgment and analytical ability is essential in order to effectively operate the section. Considerable tact and diplomacy is necessary on occasions. Must have ability to teach, train, and lead others. Must be able to follow exacting procedure and see that subordinates do the same. Must be able to organize a group and to manage the administrative affairs of the position. Must be alert and keenly observant. Physical effort is generally moderate, but considerable nervous tension is associated with the position.

FIG. 4-5.—Example of prose type job description.

WORKING CONDITIONS:
   Conditions generally good. Exposure to contagious diseases, infections, and injury from violent patients are present in the work and constitute some hazard.

SUPERVISION:
   Supervises all nurses and nurses aides within the section. Receives general supervision from the director of nursing or her assistants.

EDUCATION AND EXPERIENCE:
   High school graduate and a graduate of an accredited school of nursing. One or two years of graduate experience.

LINE OF ORGANIZATION:
   The head nurse of medical-surgical patient care receives orders from and reports to the director of nursing.

FIG. 4–5.—*Continued.*

and his discussions with the operator and foreman. Such notes should be recorded neatly and in sequence, preferably on a form prepared for that purpose. After the interview, the analyst should read to the operator and foreman the general content of his notes and make the necessary corrections on the spot. From such notes the description can then be written or dictated. The first draft of the description should be approved by the operator, foreman, and, in many instances, the union steward before it is finally submitted for evaluation.

The Check List Type.—The check list or data sheet method of description has the advantage of speed and brevity, not only for the analyst but for the evaluation committee as well. There is the danger, however, of having too detailed a form which may lead to overstatement of opinion on the part of the analyst, leaving little use for the judgment of evaluators. Check or data sheets should be so composed that only questions of fact are checked or noted thereon, while those questions requiring judgment are left for the rating committee to answer. There is always a possibility, too, of having too sketchy a form which will not include all the data needed by the evaluators, thus necessitating numerous trips to the scene of the operation to gather the missing information. The check list, therefore, must

---

DESCRIPTION OF JOB

JOB TITLE: Voluntary Ad Taker   DEPT.: Classified Advertising

JOB PURPOSE:

To receive, transcribe, and transmit classified ads from customers and to perform numerous other clerical duties for the department where contact with the public is a factor.

DUTIES AND RESPONSIBILITIES:

Receives voluntary classified ad insertions by telephone. Transcribes copy to ad form and forwards to copy desk.

Occasionally substitutes at information counter in building lobby receiving want ad insertions, selling back copies of paper, and answering information queries. Independent judgment restricted to answers given.

Performs other incidental duties as requested by immediate superior.

Exercises no supervision of others.

Reports to office manager.

EXPERIENCE AND EDUCATIONAL REQUIREMENTS:

No previous experience required. Follows well-established lines of procedure under normal supervision.

Knowledge of job and department routine may be acquired by three months' training if person makes a good appearance and has ability to talk to the public.

A three-to four-year high school education would suffice to qualify person for position.

FIG. 4–6.—Example of prose type job description.

be carefully designed to strike a balance between simplicity and complexity and to fit the requirements of the evaluation plan being employed.

Figure 4–7 is a job rating data sheet that might be used under the National Metal Trades or National Electrical Manufacturers' Associations' plans. Properly filled in, the form should provide ample data for satisfactory accomplishment of its purpose with relatively little possibility of the analyst recording too many of his own opinions.

Job Rating Data Sheet

Job Name: _____

Job Description:

Typical Examples:

Occ. No. _____

Dept. _____

Class _____

Points _____

Grade _____

FACTOR	D	POINTS
EDUCATION		
EXPERIENCE		
INITIATIVE		
PHYSICAL		
MENTAL		
EQUIP		
MATERIAL		
SAFETY		
W OF O		
WORK CON		
HAZARDS		

1. EDUCATION OR TRADE KNOWLEDGE

	Simple	Ordinary	Complex
Able to read, write			
Decimals, fractions			
Shop arithmetic			
Handbook formulas			
Geometry, trigonometry			

Explain use:

Measuring Instruments

Rule, scale, calipers, square			
Micrometers			
Fixed gauges—plug, ring, snap			
Dial indicator			
Vernier—height			
Vernier—calipers			
Bevel protractor			
Sine bars			
Jo-blocks			
Pyrometer			
Weigh scales			
Shrink rule			

Drawings

	Simple	Ordinary	Complex
Sketches			
Drawings			
Number of dimensions			
Wiring diagrams			
Specifications			

Extent used:

Trade Knowledge

_____ Feeds, speeds, tools, work holding methods on specialized machine operation

_____ Fundamentals of construction and operation of_____

_____ Broad knowledge of_____
requiring_____ years apprenticeship or trades training covering_____

2. EXPERIENCE

Analyze job to determine the length of time usually required to learn to do the job duties satisfactorily, over and above any trades training where required.

_____ Up to and including 1 month
_____ Over 1 month up to 3 months
_____ Over 3 months up to 6 months
_____ Over 6 months up to 12 months
_____ Over 1 year up to 3 years
_____ Over 3 years up to 5 years
_____ Over 5 years

Do not include apprenticeship or trades training in experience. Consider it under Education.

FIG. 4–7. (*See next page.*)

3. INITIATIVE AND INGENUITY

Analyze the job as to complexity, variety of work assigned, standardization of duties, length of cycle per unit, amount and kind of planning required, kinds of decisions made, diagnosing and remedying trouble.

Work Assignment:

Who directly assigns work?   How often?

Who checks work?   How often?

Describe inspection, if any:

Variety of Work: Quantity of Lots   Approximate Time per Unit   Tolerances

Highly repetitive   _____   _____   _____

Repetitive   _____   _____   _____

Short runs   _____   _____   _____

Jobbing   _____   _____   _____

Repair and maintenance _____   _____   _____

                        (jobs per day)

Planning Work: State typical examples of planning that job requires.

Decisions Required:

        Examples   Effect of Error in Judgment

Trouble Shooting: State below typical examples of diagnosing and remedying trouble

4. PHYSICAL DEMAND

Analyze job requirements as to work position, elements of work which produce physical strain or fatigue, lifting, bending, etc.

Work Position	Per Cent of Time
___ Sit	_____
___ Stand	_____
___ Walk	_____
___ Bend—stoop	_____
___ Lift—handle	_____
___ Hold	_____
___ Shovel sand	_____
___ Ride	_____
___ Push or pull	_____
___ Carry _____ lbs	_____
___ Arms in unsupported position	_____

Material Handling

Weight of Material.	N	O	F	C
Up to 1#				
1 to 5#				
Over 5 to 25#				
Over 25 to 60#				
Over 60#				

N = Up to 5% of time
O = 5% to 20% of time
F = 20% to 50% of time
C = 50% or more of time

Explain use of any material handling equipment, such as hoists or cranes. Describe any difficult work positions which may produce physical strain or fatigue.

Fig. 4–7. (See next page.)

5. MENTAL OR VISUAL DEMAND

Analyze job as to mental or visual attention and alertness required.

Degree:

___ Little—up to 20% of time
___ Frequent—20% to 50%
___ Continuous—over 50%

Reasons:

___ Intermittent duties
___ Length of cycle
___ Handle small parts
___ Check work
___ Speed of manipulation

Operating points requiring attention:

___ Close attention on complex work
___ High manual dexterity—close visual attention
___ Concentrated and exacting attention on very complex jobs as

___ Parts or equipment difficult to manipulate
___ Tolerances difficult to maintain
___ Machine adjustments necessary
___ Co-ordinate hand and eye—highly repetitive

6. RESPONSIBILITY FOR EQUIPMENT

Equipment Involved	How Can It Be Damaged through Carelessness	Estimated Cost to Repair
_____	_____	_____
_____	_____	_____
_____	_____	_____

7. RESPONSIBILITY FOR MATERIAL

Analyze job for causes of scrap or rework caused by carelessness on the job. Consider amount of spoilage that may occur before detection, the value of labor and material up to this point, the salvage value if any and cost to repair.

Causes	Where Discovered and by Whom	Scrap or Rework	Probable Loss
_____	_____	_____	_____
_____	_____	_____	_____
_____	_____	_____	_____

8. RESPONSIBILITY FOR SAFETY OF OTHERS

Analyze job to see how some employee may be hurt through carelessness on this job. What care must be used to prevent injury to others?

Hazard Causing Injury	Who Can Be Injured	How Can They Be Injured
Air Hose		
Dropped Tools		
Dropped Work		
Electric Shock		
Flying Part or Chips		
Flying Work		
Hot Material		
Molten Metal		
Wheel Breakage		

9. RESPONSIBILITY FOR WORK OF OTHERS

Is employee responsible for directing other employees? _____ How Many? _____

If so, describe nature of duties:

10. WORKING CONDITIONS

Analyze job to see what disagreeable elements there are in working conditions.

N = Up to 5%;   O = 5-20%;   F = 20-50%;   C = Over 50%

Element	Cause or Source	Degree	Per Cent of Time Exposed	Remarks
Acid				
Cold				
Dust				
Fumes				
Grease				
Heat				
Noise				
Oil				
Steam				
Vibration				
Water				
Weather				
Respirator				

FIG. 4-7. (See next page.)

11. UNAVOIDABLE HAZARDS

Analyze job for possible hazards, either accident or health, even though safety devices are in use.

Hazard	Cause	How Can Employee Be Injured

- Abrasions
- Burns—minor
- Burns—major
- Crushed fingers
- Crushed toes
- Cuts
- Eye injury
- Falls—ladder, etc.
- Fractures
- Hernia
- Loss fingers, toes
- Loss arm, leg
- Shock

Employees Who Regularly Do This Job:

Remarks:

Man No.	Rate			Man No.	Rate		
	Day	Base	Earn.		Day	Base	Earn.

Approvals:

I approve the facts and ratings unless otherwise noted above.

	Date	Man
Written Up		
Rated		
Checked		
Typed		
Revised		

FIG. 4—7—*Concluded.*

Figures 4–8, 4–9, and 4–10 are examples of job description forms most commonly used. Figure 4–8 has the information usually included in the heading; and the body of the description includes a general outline of job content, a listing of detail duties, and special qualification and information on work surroundings. It leaves information regarding tools, equipment, and materials worked with, supervision given or received, and other necessary data to the judgment of the analyst. The reverse side of the form, however, is devoted to statements of why the specific job was evaluated as it was, thus substantiating the points allotted to each factor. Such a method improves the consistency of ratings and affords a permanent record for use in settling grievances.

Figure 4–9 was drawn up with greater care and provides more extensive data. It will be noted, however, that the heading, contrary to good practice, calls for the operator's name and information on rates. The reverse side of the form is a check and data sheet and is used for assigning point values to each of the twenty-three factors employed as measurements. The lower right-hand corner of the front of the form is used for computations necessary to the constructing of a least squares conversion line, which will be discussed later.

Figure 4–10 is a form providing a maximum of brevity and a minimum of analyst's opinion. The work of the analyst is confined to writing, in brief terms, the actual content of the job, while the filling in of the evaluation check sheet is left to those evaluating the jobs. The form was designed to fit a particular clerical occupation evaluation plan. Its advantage lies in its compactness and in the fact that it requires a minimum of time and effort in preparation.

Regardless of the form used, no description should be turned over to the evaluators until it has been read and approved by the operator, his supervisor, and a representative of the union in its final form. One copy should be signed, or at least initialed, by those approving the description and filed in case of future need.

JOB DESCRIPTION

DATE:_____

JOB NAME: _____ DEPT.: _____ JOB CODE: _____

MACHINE: _____ NO.: _____

CLASSIFICATION: _____

GENERAL JOB DESCRIPTION:

DETAIL DUTIES:

SPECIAL QUALIFICATIONS:

WORKING CONDITIONS AND HAZARDS:

PREPARED BY:_____ PERSON INTERVIEWED:_____ APPROVED:_____

FIG. 4–8. (*Front*)

Maintenance of Files

All data used in preparing job descriptions should be filed for future reference in case of grievances, changes in job content, or other matters requiring verification. The original notes, rough draft, and check and data sheets should be clipped or stapled to one copy of the final description; and each time a revision is made a revised copy, with explanatory notations, should be attached. This affords a file of material for each job, and, properly maintained, it will result in savings of time and **effort.**

| JOB FACTORS | | EVALUATION | | ANALYSIS OF FACTORS |
		DEG.	PTS.	
SKILL	EDUCATION			
	EXPERIENCE			
	INITIATIVE AND INGENUITY			
EFFORT	PHYSICAL DEMAND			
	MENTAL OR VISUAL DEMAND			
RESPONSIBILITY	EQUIPMENT OR PROCESS			
	MATERIAL OR PRODUCT			
	SAFETY OF OTHERS			
	WORK OF OTHERS			
JOB CONDITIONS	WORKING CONDITIONS			
	HAZARDS			
TOTAL POINTS				

Fig. 4–8. (*Back*)

Files may be arranged alphabetically or numerically by job code, departments, or other locations, depending on the number of jobs involved whose supervision the files are under, and the cross reference methods employed.

QUESTIONS

1. What must be added to a job description to transform it into a job specification?
2. Differentiate between the terms "job," "occupation," "position," and "grade."

		CURRENT BASE RATE	
JOB EVALUATION		POINT VALUE	
		PROPOSED BASE RATE	
		OCCUPATIONAL RATE	

DIVISION

MACHINE NAME	DAY WORK
MACHINE NUMBER	PIECE WORK
JOB TITLE	DATE

OPERATOR   CLOCK NUMBER

REPORT TO   SUPERVISES   EMPLOYEES

1. OPERATES:

2. DUTIES CONSIST OF:

3. MATERIALS CONSIST OF:

4. INFORMATION IS FURNISHED.

TOOLS OR EQUIPMENT USED:

PERSONNEL REQUIREMENTS: Male_____ Female_____ Either_____   EXP: Yes_____ No_____

FIG. 4–9.

RESPONSIBILITY	Money and Property	Not more than $						
	Equipment	Not more than $						
	Materials	Not more than $						
	Service and Good Will	None		Little			Some	
	Safety of Others	None	Little		Some		Considerable	
	Executive	Self Supervised Supervises None			1 to 4		4 to 8	8 to 16
JOB CONDITIONS	Discomfort	Average		Some			Considerable	
	Accident Hazard	Minor—Seldom Severe—Seldom		Occasional Occasional		Frequent Frequent		
	Clothing Spoilage	Slight		Some			Considerable	
	Health Hazard	None	Minor		Some		Considerable	
	Adaptation Period	to weeks						
EDUCATION AND SKILL	Education	Equivalent to grade				years High School		
	Experience	months						
	Dexterity	Little	Fair Degree		Slightly Below Ave.	Average		Slightly Above Ave.
	Precision	Several factors involved Tolerances to plus minus						
	Versatility	Repetitive	Little		Medium	Large		Extreme
	Initiative and Ingenuity	Minimum of one		Both		Moderate amount		
MENTAL AND PHYSICAL EFFORT	Perseverance	Little		Some			Considerable	
	Concentration	Little	Some	Slightly Below Ave.		Average		Somewhat Above Ave.
	Judgment	Minor decisions				By Precedents & Standards		
	Acuteness of Senses	Normal use		Slightly Above		Somewhat Above	Acute	
	Strength	Up to pounds						
	Endurance	Little		Ordinary Exertion		Sustained	Not Sustained	

COMMENTS				TOTAL POINTS (X)
				Y
				XY
				X^2
PREPARED BY	CHECKED BY	APPROVED BY	DATE	

Fig. 4–9.—*Continued*.

SALARY ANALYSIS SHEET

DEPARTMENT: ------------------------------**JOB TITLE:** ------------

JOB DESCRIPTION:

EDUCATION

1. Read, write, add, subtract
2. One or 2 yrs. High school
3. Three or 4 yrs. High school
4. High School and Business College
5. Partial College
6. College Graduate

RESPONSIBILITY FOR COMPANY POLICY

1. Superior only
2. Associates within department
3. Contacts other departments
4. Contacts individuals outside Company
5. High degree of tact and diplomacy

JOB KNOWLEDGE
1. Prev. Exp. Wks. Mo. Yrs.
2. Training Wks. Mo. Yrs.

JUDGMENT
A. Complexity of duties
1. Simple
2. Varied routine
3. Reasonably varied
4. Semi-difficult
5. New or difficult
6. Diversified
B. Analytical ability
1. Minimum
2. Limited
3. Wide range of material
4. Wide scope—2 or more departments
5. High degree

MENTAL APPLICATION
1. Minimum
2. Occasional
3. Close
4. Continuous
5. High degree

ANALYSIS CHECKED BY ....

RESPONSIBILITY FOR MONEY AND MATERIALS
1. Little or none
2. Some
3. Considerable
4. Great
5. Major

RESPONSIBILITY FOR CONFIDENTIAL DATA
1. None
2. Little
3. Regularly
4. Continuously
5. Complete access

EXECUTIVE RESPONSIBILITY
1. Very little or none
2. Few employees
3. Group
4. Section under superior
5. Department—cost, method, etc.

TOTAL POINTS

ANALYSIS MADE BY ....

FIG. 4–10.

3. What is the fundamental reason for writing the job description? What other uses may it be made to serve?

4. What steps must be taken prior to analyzing jobs and accumulating data?

5. Is observation alone sufficient for gathering data in the shop? What must supplement the observation? Why?

6. What technique do you advise using when data on office jobs is being gathered? Why?

7. Do you believe that job specifications should be used as a source of data by committee members when they are evaluating jobs? Why?

8. What information must be included in a job description? Name two items of information that should not be included. Why should they be omitted?

9. Do you prefer the prose, check list, or combination prose and check list type of description? Why?

10. Write a description of a job you have held, using any type of description you choose. If you have never held a job, describe some other occupation, such as housewife or student.

Chapter 5

THE EVALUATION PROCESS

A T THIS point, it is assumed that the necessary steps pre-liminary to the actual evaluation of jobs have been taken. As described in previous chapters, the policies have been decided upon, the plan selected, the bench marks established, and the job descriptions written. In later chapters, it will be discussed how employees and supervisors will be sold on the idea of job evaluation and the necessary personnel selected and trained to carry out the program. The evaluation process, which is the subject matter of this chapter, will be treated through a discussion of the following topics:

1. Activities prior to rating of jobs.
2. Evaluation procedure under point rating.
3. Consistency.
4. Forms for recording evaluations.
5. Checking evaluations.
6. Combining and grouping jobs.
7. Employee classification.

Activities Prior to Rating of Jobs

At the first meeting held for the purpose of evaluating jobs, the group that is to evaluate the jobs will review the plan to be used and the procedure to be followed during the evaluation process. The meaning of factor and degree definitions should be recited and any misunderstandings clarified. Any forms to be used should be explained. When there is a satisfactory meeting of the minds among all present, the evaluators should visit the department where the first jobs to be evaluated are located. Here the department supervisor and, when appropriate, the union steward escort the group on a tour of inspection so that they can become acquainted with the department's operations, methods, flow of work, work surroundings, and record systems. Section heads should be available to answer questions and to explain operational details if necessary. When the tour of the department has been completed, the group can start evaluating the jobs.

On some installations a practice has been followed of requesting the foreman to rank the jobs in the order of what he believes to be their relative worth. This provides a guide for the evaluators during the rating process. Another method is to have the analyst rank the jobs of a department by each factor, similar to the manner employed in establishing the measuring scales under the factor comparison method. Divulging these rankings prior to the evaluation of the jobs, however, may sway the judgment of the evaluators and, where the foreman's blanket ranking is concerned, perpetuate inequalities. Such opinions of the foreman or analyst, if he is not a member of the evaluation group, will better be reserved for use as a check against the evaluations made by the committee.

Evaluation Procedure under Point Rating

The first step in the process of evaluating a job is to read the job description. Any disagreement as to job content should be reconciled at that time, or the description changed to reflect the actual facts. When agreement as to the content of the job has been reached, the group should determine what degree of each factor best describes the job being evaluated. If disagreement arises, the problem should be discussed until agreement is reached. When the degrees for each factor of one job have been chosen, the members or one member of the group should record, on an appropriate form, the degrees, degree point values, and total points for that job. The reasons for awarding the degree should also be recorded. This process should be repeated for each job that is evaluated. The records of degrees and point values assigned, etc., should be permanently retained for all jobs.

Consistency

Inconsistencies are one of the outstanding job evaluation headaches, suffered by union grievance committeemen and wage administrators, which often spell the difference between success and failure of a project.

Many inconsistencies arise as a result of appraising the capabilities of a person and of reading such data into the recorded job content. During the evaluation process, evaluators should constantly bear in mind that they are evaluating the job only on the basis of the job content as reflected in the description, not on what the operator is capable of doing or has done in the past. Factor and degree definitions, if ambiguous, will also result in improper differentiation between occupations. Such ambiguity should be eliminated before, not after, the evaluation of the job starts; for once a pattern is set, there can be no change in the concept of a meaning unless all jobs are reviewed and re-evaluated to reflect the change. Once definitions are definitely established, they should be closely followed. Deviating from bench marks or factor degrees assigned to key jobs and failing to make comparison with jobs previously evaluated are additional sources of inconsistency in evaluation.

The personalities involved in evaluating jobs will be an important determinant as to whether or not proper differentiations between jobs are established. An evaluation committee is no place for management to put an old work horse out to pasture, nor should membership be made a reward for exceptional loyalty to the union. Above-average mentality and a flexible mind are essential. Under conditions where group judgment must be consolidated in order to attain satisfactory results, an adamant attitude will result in continuous bogging-down of effort.

The statement has often been made, after the evaluation of jobs was completed, that the jobs were rated consistently high or consistently low, whichever the case may have been. The consistency may be commendable, but very often it defeats itself by causing a bunching of jobs at the top or bottom of the wage scale, thus narrowing the spread between them and,

HOURLY ANALYSIS SHEET

Job Title and Description

Date............

I. Education
1. Read ....
2. Write ....
3. Add and Subtract ....
4. Decimal and Fractions ....
5. Com. Calculating ....
6. Simple Drawings ....
7. Aver. Mach. Drawings ....
8. Elementary Tech. Probs. ....
9. Aver. Tech. Problems ....
10. Complicated Tech. Probs. ....

II. Job Knowledge
1. Previous Experience
   Wk........ Mos........ Yrs. ....
2. Required Training on Job
   Wk........ Mos........ Yrs. ....

III. Judgment
1. Type of Operation
   A. Standard ....

V. Mental Effort
1. Degree of Concentration
   A. Little or none ....
   B. Some ....
   C. Frequent ....
   D. Continuous ....
   E. High degree ....
2. Type of Operation
   A. Standard ....
   B. Semi-Standard ....
   C. Reasonably Varied ....
   D. Diversified ....

VI. Physical Effort
1. Observation ....
2. Operating Levers ....
3. Bending, Stooping ....
4. Muscular Effort ....

X. Hazard
1. Probability of Accident
   A. Little or none ....
   B. Potential ....
   C. Definite ....
   D. High Susceptibility ....
2. Extent of Injury
   A. None ....
   B. Cut ....
   C. Burn ....
   D. Bruise ....
   E. Broken Limb ....
   F. Permanent ....
   G. Fatal ....

XI. Work Surroundings
1. Good ....

B. Semi-Standard
C. Reasonably Varied
D. Diversified

2. Accuracy
A. Rough or Inexact
B. Approximate
C. Close
D. Exact

IV. Resourcefulness

1. Initiative (Ability to introduce new procedure)
A. Little or none
B. Some
C. Considerable

2. Ingenuity (Ability to plan new procedure)
A. Little or none
B. Some
C. Average
D. Considerable
E. High

3. Set Ups
A. Simple
B. Average
C. Difficult

5. Strenuous
6. Strain

VII. Resp. for Equipment and Material

1. Negligible
2. Little
3. Some
4. Considerable
5. Exceptional

VIII. Resp. for safety of others

1. Probability of Accident
A. Very Little or None
B. Potential
C. Care Necessary
D. High Degree of Car
E. Dangerous

IX. Resp. for Work of Others

1. None
2. Helper or Helpers
3. Group

2. Dirty
3. Very Dirty
4. Greasy
5. Very Greasy
6. Noisy
7. Very Noisy
8. Hot
9. Very Hot
10. Fumes

XII. Miscellaneous

ANALYSIS MADE BY ....

ANALYSIS CHECKED BY ....

Fig. 5–1.

therefore, distorting differentials. In addition, consistencies o this kind throw weightings out of balance. For if ratings are high, there is a possibility, if not a probability, that the lowest degrees will never be applied; and if ratings are low, the highest degrees may be disregarded.

There have been cases where agreement could not be reached on the degree to be applied to a factor, with the result that a point value midway between two degrees was used. Such a procedure is a deviation from the plan and will lead to inconsistent ratings. There is a tendency to follow such practice where not enough degrees have been provided or where degrees of factors have not been clearly defined.

Forms for Recording Evaluations

Check Sheet.—Throughout the committee evaluation sessions, members should record the job evaluations not only to provide permanent records but to have sources of reference against which prior and future evaluations may be checked. One such permanent record is the analysis or evaluation check sheet (Fig. 5–1). At the top of the sheet the group member enters the title, a brief description of the job being evaluated, and the date the evaluation took place. As each job is evaluated, the member enters in the appropriate space the points assigned to each factor of the job and places check marks in the spaces opposite those descriptive elements which substantiate the points assigned. Such a record has the advantage of reflecting not only the points assigned to the job but the reason why such points were assigned. When employed, the form should be adapted to fit the plan to be used.

Summary Rating Sheet.—Another form used for recording point ratings is the summary rating sheet (Fig. 5–2). The job title is entered in the space provided; and as the evaluation group reaches a decision as to what degree is applicable to each factor, the degree and/or the corresponding points are entered in the appropriate columns. When all factors have been considered, the points are cross-totaled and entered. Entries

DEPARTMENTAL SUMMARY SHEET — JOB RATING

202 _____ DEPARTMENT

6-29-48

| OCCUPATION | SKILL | | | | | | EFFORT | | | | RESPONSIBILITY | | | | | | | | JOB CONDITIONS | | | | TOTAL X | AVG. HOURLY RATE Y | XY | X² |
| | EDUCATION | | EXPERIENCE | | INITIATIVE AND INGENUITY | | PHYSICAL DEMAND | | MENTAL AND VISUAL | | EQUIPMENT OR PROCESS | | MATERIAL OR PRODUCT | | SAFETY OF OTHERS | | WORK OF OTHERS | | WORKING CONDITIONS | | HAZARDS | | | | | |
	D	P	D	P	D	P	D	P	D	P	D	P	D	P	D	P	D	P	D	P	D	P				
ASSEMBLY BENCH	2	28	2	44	2	28	2	20	3	15	2	10	2	10	1	5	1	5	2	20	2	10	195			
AUTOMATIC SCREW MACHINE SETUP MAN	3	42	4	88	4	56	2	20	4	20	3	15	2	10	3	15	3	15	3	30	3	15	326			
CARPENTER A	3	42	4	88	4	56	3	30	3	15	2	10	2	10	3	15	3	15	3	30	3	15	326			
CRANEMAN	1	14	2	44	3	42	3	30	4	20	4	20	4	20	5	25	1	5	3	30	4	20	270			
DRILL-PRESS OPERATOR	2	28	2	44	2	28	2	20	3	15	2	10	2	10	2	10	1	5	2	20	2	10	200			
ELECTRICIAN	4	56	4	88	4	56	2	20	3	15	3	15	4	20	3	15	3	15	3	30	5	25	355			
HELPER, TRADES	1	14	1	22	2	28	4	40	3	15	2	10	1	5	3	15	1	5	3	30	3	15	194			
INSPECTOR-TESTER	2	28	2	44	2	28	2	20	3	15	2	10	2	10	1	5	1	5	2	20	2	10	195			
JANITOR	1	14	1	22	2	28	3	30	2	10	2	10	1	5	3	15	1	5	4	40	3	15	194			
LABORER	1	14	1	22	1	14	4	40	2	10	1	5	2	10	3	15	1	5	4	40	3	15	190			
MACHINIST A	4	56	4	88	4	56	2	20	4	20	4	20	4	20	3	15	2	10	3	30	3	15	340			
PLATER	1	14	3	66	3	42	3	30	2	10	2	10	2	10	2	10	2	10	4	40	3	15	257			
TOOL AND DIE MAKER	4	56	5	110	5	70	2	20	4	20	3	15	5	25	3	15	3	15	2	20	3	15	381			
TRUCKER, ELECTRIC	1	14	1	22	2	28	3	30	3	15	3	15	2	10	4	20	1	5	2	20	3	15	194			

D = DEGREE
P = POINTS

Fig. 5-2

SHEET 1 — JOB RATING SUMMARY SHEET — TECHNICAL AND CLERICAL POSITIONS — 1-20-48

Code	POSITION	EDUCATION	JOB KNOWLEDGE	JUDGMENT	MENTAL APPLICATION	COMPANY POLICY	RESPONSIBILITY			TOTAL X	HOURLY RATE Y	XY	X²
							MONEY AND MATERIALS	CONFIDENTIAL DATA	EXECUTIVE				
57-1	KEY-PUNCH OPERATOR	90	200	200	80	60	150	60	120	960			
57-2	KEY-PUNCH OPERATOR	90	160	160	70	60	120	60	120	840			
113-1	TYPIST	90	240	200	80	60	120	60	120	970			
113-2	TYPIST	90	200	200	70	60	120	60	120	920			
201-1	ACCOUNTANT CLERK	120	360	280	80	70	180	80	120	1,290			
210-1	BLUEPRINT-MACHINE OPERATOR	90	240	240	80	60	150	80	120	1,060			
210-2	BLACK AND WHITE PRINT-MACHINE OPERATOR	90	200	200	70	60	150	80	120	970			
210-3	BLUEPRINT TRIMMER	90	200	160	70	60	120	80	120	900			
220-1	CALCULATING-MACHINE OPERATOR	90	320	200	80	70	150	60	150	1,120			
220-2	CALCULATING-MACHINE OPERATOR	90	280	200	80	70	150	60	120	1,050			
220-3	CALCULATING-MACHINE OPERATOR	90	240	160	70	60	150	60	120	950			
220-4	CALCULATING-MACHINE OPERATOR	90	160	160	60	60	150	60	120	860			
228-1	COST WRITER	120	400	320	80	70	210	70	120	1,390			
228-2	COST WRITER	105	360	280	80	70	180	70	120	1,265			
232-1	SHIPPING CLERK—LEADER	105	360	280	70	70	180	50	150	1,265			
232-1	CLERK GENERAL—LEADER	105	360	280	80	80	150	80	150	1,275			
232-1A	ORDER-SCHEDULING CLERK—LEADER	105	360	320	80	80	180	70	120	1,395			
232-1C	STORES-CONTROL CLERK—LEADER	105	360	360	80	80	210	50	150	1,355			
232-1D	REPAIR-ORDER SPECIFICATION CLERK—LEADER	105	320	320	80	80	210	60	180	1,355			
232-1E	TOOL-MACHINERY CLERK—LEADER	105	360	280	70	70	180	80	150	1,295			
232-1F	RECEIVING CLERK—LEADER	105	320	320	80	80	210	50	150	1,315			
232-1G	EQUIPMENT AND MAINTENANCE CLERK	90	200	240	70	70	150	60	120	1,030			
232-1H	BILLING CLERK—LEADER	105	360	320	80	70	210	70	120	1,335			

Fig. 5-3

recorded on the figure are for the key jobs used in describing the job ranking method of job evaluation; the form was designed for use with the National Electrical Manufacturers' Association plan. Columns have been provided for entering the hourly rate for the job and for the computations necessary to calculations by the least squares method explained in a later chapter. The summary rating sheet has the advantages of compactness, in that numerous jobs are recorded on one sheet, and of affording a factor-by-factor comparison of jobs previously evaluated, particularly if similar occupations are recorded on one sheet. Use of this type of form, therefore, is an aid to rating consistency. Figure 5–3 is a summary rating sheet for recording points only.

Substantiating Data Sheet.—It is sometimes the practice of the evaluation group to record the points assigned to each job and also to state why the points were assigned. This can be done as the jobs are evaluated by entering the substantiating data on a form similar to Figure 5–4. The descriptive material may be entered prior to when the evaluators meet; it may be entered when the job is evaluated; or, if the form is reproduced on the reverse side of the job description, it may be eliminated entirely. (See Figure 5–4.) The substantiating data provide an excellent reference in cases of grievances and where changes in ratings that reflect changes in job content are contemplated. A disadvantage lies in the fact that the speed with which jobs are evaluated may be retarded in order to record the data.

Punch-Card Accounting.—Where punch-card accounting equipment is available, excellent records can be compiled for reference purposes and for checking evaluations factor by factor. Key punch operators can punch cards directly from summary rating sheets or other forms, punching in either points or degrees and total points. The hourly rate and the labor grade may also be included. After the cards have been punched, sortings may be made by labor grade, rates, and factor degrees; or a tabulation of all jobs may be made in the order of the point totals. Once the cards have been punched, any desired comparison may be made with a minimum of time, effort, and expense.

JOB GRADE SUBSTANTIATING DATA

(HOURLY RATED JOBS)

Job Title: AUTOMATIC SCREW MACHINE OPERATOR

JOB DESCRIPTION:

Operate only multiple spindle automatic screw machines, involving complex tooling, and tolerances or finish requirements difficult to maintain. Work from drawings, layouts, specifications, etc. use gages; re-sharpen and readjust tools; assist and instruct helper.

Job Factors	Evaluation		Substantiation of Factor Rating
	Deg.	Pts.	
EDUCATION	3	42	Requires a general knowledge of machines and specialized knowledge in the principle of screw machine operation acquired by vocational training specializing on screw machines. Works from fairly complicated drawings, layouts and specifications.
EXPERIENCE	3	66	Requires from 2½ to 3 years generalized automatic screw machine or related experience to sharpen and reset tools and effect adjustments necessary to maintain satisfactory production and quality requirements on multiple spindle machines.
INITIATIVE AND INGENUITY	3	42	Makes general decisions in resetting of tools and in making machine adjustments to maintain difficult requirements. Works with minimum supervision.
PHYSICAL DEMAND	2	20	Involves continuous standing and circulating among machines. Requires restocking of machines, handling rod stock and containers of parts. Effort is equivalent to occasionally

Mental and/or Visual Demand	3	15	Continuous mental and visual attention is required in observing operation of machines, frequently checking products to insure satisfactory quality, and to replenish stock.
Responsibility for Equip. or Process	3	15	Improper tool adjustments such as tools not tightened, or tool interference when indexing, may cause jamming and breakage. Cost of repair could exceed $25.00, but would seldom exceed $150.00.
Responsibility for Material or Prod.	2	10	Failure to check products or observe faulty machine operation could result in loss of product which could exceed $10.00 but would seldom exceed $100 at any one time.
Responsibility for Safety of Others	2	10	Carelessness in handling rod stock and pans of parts could result in minor bruises to other employees in area.
Responsibility for Work of Others	2	10	Responsible for assisting and instructing helper.
Working Conditions	3	30	Continuously exposed to oily conditions from cutting lubricants used in machines and from noise of machines in operation.
Hazards	3	15	Exposed to lost time accidents such as crushed hands or fingers or eye injuries from flying particles.
TOTAL POINTS		275	SCORE RANGE 272-293

Fig. 5-4

Checking Evaluations

Assurance against Inconsistency.—When all jobs have been evaluated, the ratings should be thoroughly checked against each other as an assurance against inconsistencies. The first review should be made by the group to determine whether all members are in agreement with the relative positions of the jobs. When the chairman is assured that the group is satisfied, the ratings should be presented to the shop foremen or office supervisors; and, if desired by the union, the stewards should also review the ratings and make suggestions to the group in case certain jobs appear to be out of line.

Factor Comparison Check.—Probably the most commonly used rating check is the factor-by-factor comparison. Those jobs assigned the same degree of a factor are listed, and comparisons are made to determine whether all the jobs so listed should receive that degree of the factor. Any jobs which appear to be improperly included in the group should be moved to the group to which they appear to belong. Where there are numerous jobs, the work of listing them in factor degree groups is tedious. A great deal of time can be saved if punch-card accounting equipment is used for listing purposes. If a company has none of this equipment, other concerns in the general area may have it and be willing to provide the necessary assistance.

Combining and Grouping Jobs

Objections to a large number of job titles are frequently overcome by combining and grouping the jobs to be evaluated. A substantial part of the combining of jobs will be done by the job analyst at the time his observations are made and descriptions written. This is a natural function of the analyst, for he is the one best qualified to recognize jobs which have identical content. In cases where more than one analyst is used—all analysts working in different departments—it is entirely possible that the similarity of jobs will not be realized until such jobs are evaluated. Such a possibility can be reduced by having all the descriptions reviewed by a chief job analyst, but even then some possible combinations and groupings will not be noticed.

If the combining and grouping of jobs is a function delegated to the group evaluating such jobs, it will be found generally, that the opinion of the analyst will be relied upon to a very considerable extent. The evaluators frequently are not equipped with the knowledge necessary to determine whether or not a grouping or combination of jobs is feasible. This is one reason why the analyst should be an active member of the evaluation group. Although the analyst will do most of the combining and grouping, a check on additional possibilities should be made by the group after the evaluation has been completed.

The simplest method of combining jobs is to list them in the order of their total assigned points. Jobs having identical point values are then compared by title and job content and also factor by factor. Where two jobs receive identical point values on all factors and where job content is the same, there should be little question as to whether combining is advisable. In some instances jobs may have similar content and identical total points, but because of minor inconsistencies the distribution of points between factors may not be the same. In such cases a reconsideration of the evaluations may enable a combination of the jobs without a change in point values. All jobs of identical title which fall within a reasonable point range should be considered for combination. It is not advisable, however, to make adjustments in total points for purposes of facilitating the combination of jobs until such time as the wage scale is constructed and the point ranges and rates are known. Altering of total point values may cause a change in the rate that would properly go with the job and lead to future grievances and perhaps to a lack of faith in the entire evaluation.

Employee Classification

There can be no expectancy of a reduction in grievances if, after the jobs are evaluated, the employees are improperly classified. Employee classification is the process of assigning to employees the titles of the jobs which they perform as well as an appropriate grade and wage rate. Once assigned, the title should be retained by the employee until a transfer, promotion, or demotion takes place; and even under these circumstances, union agreement provisions may require that the worker retain his classification or title. In order for an evaluation project to reap maximum benefits, there must be a drastic lessening in the tendency of some supervisors to sanction improper classification of workers either through carelessness or giving in to constant pressure on the part of employees or their representatives.

Problems of Classification.—The problem of how to classify employees is not difficult when a worker is performing one job all of the time. It is in those situations where an operator works on more than one job, each being separately described and evaluated, that the classification will require careful thought. If the operator continually performs two tasks, such as machining and layout, and the job is described as requiring both operations, then the job will be evaluated to include these operations and no problem will arise. If, however, machining constitutes one job and layout another and both jobs carry different rates, then a policy will have to be established to handle the problem. Very often the problem can be solved through collective bargaining, and many union agreements include provisions covering such possibilities.

There are a number of ways of treating this problem, one of which is to record a change of classification each time the employee switches from one job to another. Obviously, where numerous changes are made, an excessive amount of clerical work will be involved. Classifications may not need to be changed if cost accounting records do not require it. However, if there is a difference in rates for the jobs worked on, then a close timekeeping control will be required.

Another method is to classify the employee on the basis of the highest rated job which he performs. While this may appear, at first, to be expensive, a large part of the expense will be absorbed through the elimination of clerical and timekeeping effort. It must also be considered that, if the jobs worked on by an employee were combined under one description, the content of the job would require the rate of the highest classified job, and perhaps a higher one. This manner of classification is the one most acceptable to unions and to employees.

It is possible, however, to classify employees on the basis of the job worked on the majority of the time. The disadvantage of this type of classification lies in the fact that employees dislike to work on a higher rated job at a lower rate of pay. There is also the difficulty of determining how much time the employee has spent on various jobs.

Changes in Classification.—At times employees will be transferred from their regular jobs to other jobs thus necessitating a change in classification. Often such changes are covered in union agreements. Where transfers are made at the option of the company and are not the result of the employee's shortcomings, the employee should retain his old rate and, if seniority is involved, his old classification, provided such transfer is to a lower classification. If the employee is transferred to a higher classification, he should receive the new title and new rate.

Transfers made at the worker's request usually carry the new rate and title, whether the transfer is to a higher or to a lower classification. In those cases where an employee is transferred to a lower classification in order to avoid layoff, the transfer is usually accompanied by a lowering in classification and rate. There are numerous other situations that may arise, all of which should be foreseen, if possible, and provided for by policy. Fairness to the employee in framing such policies will help to avert future grievances.

Classification Procedure.—The responsibility for correct classification rests with supervision. Where there is a union, however, classifications may be subject to the approval of union representatives. The most expeditious procedure for classifying employees is to send to each supervisor and, if appropriate, to

each union steward a list of employees of their respective departments (see Fig. 5–5) with the request that proper classifications
be assigned and the list returned. When the lists are returned,
the classifications assigned by supervision and by the union are
compared, and any disagreements are settled through discussions between management and the union.

Periodic Reviews.—Classifications should be checked periodically. The check can be accomplished by sending the listings
of employees' names and the classifications to the department
for correction and return. Five- or six-month intervals between
checks are usually correct under average circumstances, although such factors as stability of production schedules, rate
of labor turnover, and frequency of change in product lines
may determine the interval.

In place of periodic reviews, frequent test checks may be
made. Frequency should determine the extent of the check to
be made; but where an entire department is suspected of having
faulty classifications, all the jobs in that department should be
checked. The process of keeping classifications in line cannot
be accomplished from a desk. Those who are assigned the
responsibility for such checking should actually observe the jobs
prior to making any decisions as to whether reclassification is
necessary. Supervisors and stewards, job analysts, and time-
study personnel usually are the most active in maintaining
correct job classifications.

Results of Faulty Classification.—Improper classification results
in underpayment or overpayment of workers, and either condition can mean an increased volume of grievances. The
underpaid worker will feel that he has been unjustly treated,
while the worker who is fairly paid may compare his earnings
with those of the overpaid worker and feel that he too is being
slighted. Errors in computing manufacturing costs will also
result if job classifications do not truly reflect the work being
done by the employee. Overpaid employees may be concerned
over the fact that they are receiving more than their just wage
and may live in fear that the error will be found and corrected.
The best preventive against improper classification is to classify
employees on the basis of the job actually being performed.

JOB CLASSIFICATION RECORD

JOB TITLE: _____ JOB CODE: _____ LABOR GRADE: _____ EVAL. POINTS: _____ RATE RANGE: _____ PAGE _____

CLOCK NO.	NAME	DATE ASSIGNED	TIME ON JOB		MERIT RATING CODE	BASE RATE	AVG. HOURLY EARNINGS	TRANSFERRED TO		
			YRS.	MOS.				DATE	RATE	JOB CODE

Fig. 5-5.—One type of form used as a record of employees classified under the same occupation.

QUESTIONS

1. Assume that you are in charge of a group assigned the task of evaluating jobs. What action would you take before evaluating any jobs?

2. What is meant by "inconsistency in rating"? What are a few reasons for such inconsistency? How can it be avoided?

3. Why should a record of evaluations be maintained as the work of the evaluation group progresses? Describe a form used for that purpose.

4. Checking evaluations is an assurance against inconsistencies. How may this be accomplished?

5. Who do you believe should group and combine jobs? Why?

6. Describe a method of grouping and combining jobs.

7. What are the results of improper employee classification?

8. What classification problems arise when an employee works on two jobs, each carrying a different rate? How would you solve them? Why?

9. How often do you believe employee classifications should be reviewed in a fruit-packing company? Why?

CHAPTER 6

THE WAGE SURVEY

WAGE surveys have an important bearing on the final form of the wage scale, for before wage scales can be determined, a general survey of wages must be made. The discussion of wage surveys in this chapter is based on the following topics:

1. Purpose of the survey.
2. Data desired.
3. Form of the survey.
4. Jobs to include.
5. Number of jobs to include.
6. Firms to be surveyed.
7. Number of firms to be surveyed.
8. Gathering the information.
9. Summarizing the data.
10. Analyzing the data.
11. Time interval between surveys.

Purpose of the Survey

After the evaluation of jobs and the classification of employees has been completed, management, with union consent, frequently uses the existing rate scale in applying money values to job worth. While the use of the present scale may turn out to be a harmless procedure, it is usually done on a dangerous assumption, i.e., that the present scale is adequate. For purposes of illustrating the fallacy of such an assumption, a simple but somewhat extreme set of circumstances may be used. If a company has 100 jobs having maximum and minimum evaluated point values of 380 and 150, respectively, and the rate scale has a $1.40 maximum and a $1.20 minimum, it can be seen that the relative point worth of the high and low jobs could hardly be reflected in the money assigned to the labor grades. A 230-point evaluation range would have to be sandwiched into a 20-cent money range. This would result in extremely wide worth ranges if reasonable money increments between labor grades are to be used. If reasonable worth ranges are employed, the money increments would be so small that difficulties in substantiating them might arise. In any event, there must be an acceptable rate spread between, for example, the laborer and the diemaker. In the given example, 20 cents per hour hardly reflects the difference in worth of the two jobs.

Within a given area companies compete for labor, and within a given industry they compete for profits. Because the labor cost has a substantial effect on profits, it can be concluded that area and industry wage rates must be given due consideration in somewhat the same manner as competitive selling prices. When a wage scale—no matter how free it is of inequities—is below the competitive level, it will eventually become misaligned through the necessity for reaching upward to secure the desired working force. Therefore, the use of a wage scale which is not geared to industry and area rates may easily render an evaluation ineffective. One purpose of job evaluation is to maintain the correct wage levels. For this reason, no negotiations of the scale should take place until the company is assured that its rates are competitive with those of the area and industry labor market. Unions should have no objections to a company seeking such assurance.

Data Desired

The basic reason for conducting a wage survey is to determine the labor cost to a company of securing and of maintaining an adequate force of efficient workers. In order to know the cost of attracting and keeping such a force, information must be secured from competing companies to provide an insight into what wage structure must be constructed to meet this competition.

The employee is primarily interested in his take-home pay and not in whether the amount he takes home results from the base rate, incentive, overtime, or other factors which effect his earnings. The wage survey, on the other hand, is interested in segregating all the elements going into the wage structure so that a comparative picture may be secured. One company may have unusually low base rates, but owing to rather loose incentive rates the employees may enjoy hourly earnings considerably above the industry and area average. In such an instance a comparison of base rates only may be misleading and cause considerable harm to the company conducting the survey by leading them to believe that their wage scale is inadequate. It is essential, therefore, that all elements entering into the compensation of the employee be considered in the survey.

Four Comparisons between Company and Survey Data.—In general, four comparisons between company and survey data are desirable; therefore, the survey information secured must include facts which will permit these four comparisons to be made. Survey information should be broken down to segregate those facts pertaining to (1) hiring rates, (2) base rates, (3) average earned rates, and (4) additions to income.

Where hiring rates are the same as base rates, no particular problem is posed; but where there is a differential, some explanation of policy is desirable. How long the employee receives the hiring rate and what qualifications are necessary to raise the employee from the hiring rate to the regular base rate are two facts which have an important bearing on the comparisons that may be made. Caution must also be exercised in securing information on average hourly rates and salaries. If incentive earnings are included, the kind of incentive should be known. Comparisons of earnings on straight piecework with those on a standard hour, or similar plan with a guaranteed minimum, may be misleading. Overtime, shift differentials, and conditions under which past average hourly earnings are paid must be clearly set forth and understood. It is of particular interest to know how the base rates and salaries were established and what job evaluation plan, if any, was used in eliminating and preventing inequities. Full details concerning additions to income, such as group life and hospital insurance, pension and profit-sharing plans, and vacations with pay, are necessary to a satisfactory comparison of wages.

Who Conducts Survey?—The task of conducting the survey should be assigned to individuals who are familiar with the content of the jobs to be included in the survey, for it is imperative that jobs which have identical content be compared. In addition, those who conduct the survey should have a knowledge of wage payment methods, incentive systems, and other practices and principles of wage administration; for it is necessary when comparing wage rates and earnings to know what elements comprise the wage rates and earnings and whether a justifiable comparison is possible. If the company conducting the survey has personnel who can meet these requirements, then there will be no problem of what individuals will be assigned the task. In most instances the wage administrator or job analyst will have the qualifications. However, if the surveying concern is not so fortunate, it is advisable to secure the services of an outside firm qualified to conduct a wage survey.

Form of the Survey

Necessity for Complete Facts.—It is essential that those conducting the survey understand the necessity for gathering a complete set of facts. It is better to conduct no survey at all than to get misleading results through superficial efforts or short cuts. Telephone conversations, brief visits to personnel offices, and the use of poorly composed, brief forms and letters usually provide information which may be more damaging than constructive. Such brevity in conducting a survey does not assure that the same jobs are being compared and that all facts reflecting the true earning potentialities of the employees are being secured.

Considerable thought must be given to the method of survey to be employed and to the conditions under which the survey is to be made. If association, industry, or Department of Labor surveys are used, it should be remembered that, while as a rule they are very well organized and tabulated, they are too general to be of much use to a particular company unless used as a check against broad trends. It is usually possible to obtain a complete set of facts, however, for most companies are willing to exchange information and are only too glad to be of assistance, particularly if they are informed of the results of the survey. Unions, too are frequently a source of material. Many of them maintain very complete and up-to-date files covering wage and salary information secured from their numerous locals.

Survey data should be gathered in such a manner that it assumes a useful form, but the compilation should not require excessive time and effort by either the company conducting the survey or the company being surveyed. Too cumbersome an assemblage of facts is a waste of time and reduces the extent to which other companies are willing to co-operate. Data should be limited to just what is required to do the job; when properly summarized, this data should show at a glance the picture of the wage rates of the industry and area that were surveyed.

Information obtained should not include figures which require excessive computation on the part of the companies furnishing the information. Requesting that such computations be made is an unwise encroachment upon those co-operating in the survey; further, such an accumulation of previously assembled and consolidated figures may prevent getting the actual figures required. The more satisfactory approach is to secure the individual rates of the companies surveyed and to make the necessary accumulations and analyses without recourse to the help of those furnishing the information. In this way the calculations will be standardized, the results will be more consistent, and the company will be able to make its own computations of ranges and going rates for jobs. When surveyed companies furnish their own computations, there is the danger that estimates rather than calculations will be presented, owing to the pressure of time or to a disinterested attitude. In brief, the company making the survey should seek a simple but complete set of facts and do its own summarizing.

Use of Survey Forms.—Form design plays an important part in conducting wage surveys, not only from the standpoint of completeness of data secured but from the standpoint of summarizing and analyzing results. The forms should be simple to understand and easy to fill in. Wherever possible, use should be made of check marks; essay answers should be held to a minimum. It will be an aid to all parties concerned if ample instructions and, where necessary, definitions of terms are provided. Ordinarily, three forms are used in requesting the desired information (1) a general form for securing information about the wage structure; (2) a form for recording information about specific jobs; and (3) an instruction sheet explaining the use of the forms. Enough forms should be provided to permit copies to be retained by the surveyed companies.

Jobs to Include

In selecting jobs for which comparative wage data will be gathered, the following five points should be considered:

1. The jobs must be likely to exist in the area or industry being surveyed. Obviously, if there are no jobs in the area or industry surveyed comparable to the ones of the company making the survey, no comparative data will be provided. For example, while it is conceivable that a garment manufacturer might have a lathe operator in its maintenance department, the probability of other companies in the industry being so equipped would be somewhat remote. Therefore, using a lathe operator classification for survey purposes would result in little, if any, satisfactory information.

2. The group of jobs selected should pretty well cover the range of the jobs evaluated. In the case of point rating plans, jobs carrying maximum and minimum points as well as jobs well scattered between the two extremes should be included.

Under the ranking method, jobs well scattered among relative rankings should be chosen.

3. The jobs selected should be characterized by a stability of content over a period of years. These are the occupations upon which all other jobs are founded; and, therefore, they are the backbone of the wage structure. For this reason the surveys made of new industries or in areas where new industries predominate are not as reliable as those conducted in areas or industries where the jobs have experienced little change in content over the years.

4. The jobs selected should be filled by a large group of employees. Use of such jobs in the compilation of comparative data is conducive to greater statistical accuracy and to a better indication of the financial impact on the company which may occur from future adjustments resulting from the survey.

5. The fifth point to consider in choosing jobs for the wage survey is the effect that a present abundance or shortage of persons available to occupy the jobs will have on present rates. If rates are being driven out of line by an abnormal supply of or demand for certain jobs, such jobs should not be considered for comparison. It may be advantageous in some instances to survey some jobs where the supply of occupants is short, for this may afford an insight into the adjustments necessary to meet competition.

Number of Jobs to Include

A relatively few well-chosen jobs may provide better results than a large number of jobs selected with less care. In actual practice the number of occupations used ranges from ten up into the hundreds. In most cases, however, it is difficult to find a large group of jobs meeting the five requirements stated above; therefore, if care is exercised in selecting the jobs, the number will seldom be excessively large. Some companies have used a large number of jobs in their surveys in the hope that enough information would be secured to provide reliable, statistical data. Such a technique, however, gives no more reliable results, requires the handling of an excessively large number of figures, and demands that the other companies co-operating in the survey expend an unnecessary amount of effort.

The relative reliability between using a large number of jobs chosen with little care and using a few select jobs chosen with considerable thought can be seen by computing the line-of-best-fit for both groups of jobs and by comparing the two curves. The difference in the curves will be negligible, despite the fact that one survey was the result of an amount of effort far in excess of the effort required by the other survey. The excellent results obtained by the various consumer and public opinion polls and surveys tend to substantiate the small sampling theory, which indicates that a wage survey covering approximately twenty-five jobs should provide satisfactory results.

Firms to Be Surveyed

As stated previously, the companies included in the survey should have occupations similar to those of the company conducting the survey. For that reason the firms to be surveyed should be carefully chosen on the basis of the type of business or industry of which the surveying company is a part and on the basis of the intensity with which the company conducting the survey competes for labor with the other firms in the area. Where the labor is of a very specialized nature, it tends to shift within the same industry. This means that a competitive demand for labor exists. Therefore, the company conducting the survey should include other concerns in the same industry, particularly if there is a loss of skilled workers to these other firms.

Companies surveyed that are located reasonably near by should also be included, for the company conducting the survey competes for labor with those industries in the general geographic area. If the companies to be surveyed are selected purely on the basis of location in the same geographic area, they should be chosen from those located within an hour's commuting time from the area. Workers rarely are willing to spend more than an hour traveling to or from work; therefore, this usually limits the area to a radius of approximately fifty miles.

The companies should be generally considered by employees in the community as being good places to work, and they should be large enough to make it worth while, from a statistical standpoint, to include them in the survey.

Number of Firms to Be Surveyed

The number of companies to include in the survey may range from one upward, depending on a number of factors. If the community is dominated by one large company, then it may be satisfactory to include only the dominating company in the survey. The nature of the industry may also be such that only a few firms similar to the surveying company exist in the area, with the result that the few companies surveyed will give the only available comparative data for the industry. In general, the survey should embrace those companies most likely to have occupations comparable to those of the surveying concern. The fact that a company is considered the industry or area leader and, therefore, to establish the rate level, should not preclude the conducting of a survey; for little harm will result from learning the extent of its leadership status and the possibilities for raising or lowering the wage scale.

In some instances there may be no industry competition within the immediate area because of peculiarities of product, patents, or other circumstances. If, under such circumstances, a survey is still deemed necessary, it will have to embrace companies of other industries which have comparable occupations.

For the reasons already stated, a few carefully selected companies will provide data as reliable as that gathered from a large number of concerns. Under average circumstances, approximately twenty-five companies should provide satisfactory data, but it is not uncommon to find five to twenty companies surveyed with excellent results. Such a small number, unless slipshod methods are used, will frequently furnish much more than a mere sample of wage rate conditions. There is a substantial probability that the small number include the entire competition, and, therefore, the results should be quite accurate and reliable.

In larger cities it is possible to conduct wage surveys by contacting the large, reliable employment agencies. These firms have access to much wage data of companies in the area, particularly for salaried office jobs. If after a test check indicates that the data is reliable, this source can be used with a substantial saving of time and effort.

Gathering the Information

Once the firms who are to participate and the jobs that are to be included in the survey have been selected, the problem resolves itself into one of securing the desired information. A greater measure of co-operation from other companies can be expected if a member of general management writes to one of the top ranking officials of the other firms, informing them of the project and requesting that company's participation in it. Figure 6–1 is an example of such a letter.

When appointments have been secured with the proper parties in the companies to be surveyed, the interviewer should proceed to secure the information. The wage administrator, job analyst, or whoever is assigned the task should first secure information concerning the wage administration policies and practices. This data should be entered on the form shown in Figure 6–2 during the course of the interview.

Obtaining information about specific jobs, however, is a more time consuming procedure, for time must be taken to assure that the jobs are being properly matched for comparative purposes. In many instances the person being interviewed will request that the forms be left with him in order that he may devote the necessary time to properly matching the jobs. This is not a satisfactory procedure, however, for the analyst may want to see the jobs himself so that he can compare them with the jobs described.

$\mathcal{T}he$ **ALGIN** $\mathcal{C}ompany$

2442 WEST ROSEMONT AVENUE   ::   CHICAGO 45, ILLINOIS

June 1, 1948

Mr. John J. O'Brien
231 South LaSalle Street
Chicago, Illinois

Dear Mr. O'Brien:

Our company is in the process of installing a program of job
evaluation, and our Director of Industrial Relations has asked
that I request your cooperation in making a survey of the
salaries and hourly rates paid in this locality.

It will be sincerely appreciated if you would arrange for our
job analyst, Mr. Oliver P. Johnson, to meet the proper personnel of your company to discuss the information desired. Such
information will be held in strictest confidence.

Each company participating in the survey will receive copies of
the attached summary completely filled in with the results of
the survey. If in the future your company should undertake a
similar program, we will be only too glad to reciprocate.

Very truly yours,

General Manager

EPA:hoc

Enc. 1

Fig. 6–1.—Letter requesting co-operation of firm participating in survey.

Jobs should be compared on the basis of job content only
to make sure that information on comparable jobs is being
secured. For this reason, the job title may not appear on the

WAGE SURVEY GENERAL INFORMATION SHEET

PARTICIPATING COMPANY:_____ASSIGNED CODE:_____ __
ADDRESS_____TYPE OF BUSINESS_____
PERSON CONTACTED:_____TITLE:_____DATE:_____

	Hourly		Salary	
1. Number of employees in company?				
Male	—— ——		—— ——	
Female	—— ——		—— ——	
2. Minimum Hiring Rate:	Hourly		Salary	
Male	—— ——		—— ——	
Female	—— ——		—— ——	

	Hourly		Salary	
	Yes	No	Yes	No
3. Do you employ some form of wage incentive?	——	——	——	——

	Hourly	Salary
4. What is average percentage of base rate earned on incentive?	%	%

	Hourly		Salary	
5. Are bonuses, other than incentive, paid in addition to regular earnings?	Yes	No	Yes	No
Profit sharing	——	——	——	——
Christmas	——	——	——	——
Other	——	——	——	——

Please explain:_____

	Hourly		Salary	
	Yes	No	Yes	No
6. Does each job carry a:				
Single rate?	——	——	——	——
Rate range?	——	——	——	——

	Hourly		Salary	
7. What method of progression through a rate range is used:	Yes	No	Yes	No
Merit increase only?	——	——	——	——
Automatic increase only?	——	——	——	——
Part merit and part automatic?	——	——	——	——

	Hourly		Salary	
	Yes	No	Yes	No
8. Are employees guaranteed an annual income?	——	——	——	——

Please explain if "yes"_____

FIG. 6–2.—Wage survey form for recording general data.

9. Number of hours worked per year, on an average, by your average shop employee (estimate if necessary)_____

10. What is the basis of your overtime payments?_____
_____
_____

	Hourly	Salary
11. How many holidays per year do you observe?	_____	_____

	Hourly		Salary	
	Yes	No	Yes	No
12. What are employees paid for working on holidays?				
Time and one-half	____	____	____	____
Double time	____	____	____	____
Other	____	____	____	____
13. Are employees paid if they do not work on holidays?	____	____	____	____
14. Do you have night shifts?	____	____	____	____
15. Do you pay shift differentials?	____	____	____	____

If "yes" what amounts apply to each shift?
_____
_____
_____

	Hourly		Salary	
	Yes	No	Yes	No
16. Is employee's lunch time paid for?	____	____	____	____
17. How much lunch time is allowed?	____	____	____	____
18. Is clean-up time allowed at end of shift?	____	____	____	____
19. Is employee paid for clean-up time?	____	____	____	____
20. Are rest periods granted?	____	____	____	____
21. Is employee paid for rest periods?	____	____	____	____
22. How much time is allowed for rest periods?	____	____	____	____

23. What plans for employee benefits do you have excluding those required by law?	Yes	No	Contributed By Company %	Contributed By Employee %
Death	____	____	_____	_____
Accident	____	____	_____	_____
Sickness	____	____	_____	_____
Hospitalization	____	____	_____	_____
Pension	____	____	_____	_____
Savings	____	____	_____	_____
Other	____	____	_____	_____
_____	____	____	_____	_____
_____	____	____	_____	_____

FIG. 6–2.—*Continued.* (*See next page also.*)

	Hourly		Salary	
24. Are employees paid for:	Yes	No	Yes	No
A. Vacations granted?	——	——	——	——
B. Sick leave?	——	——	——	——
C. Other leaves of absence?	——	——	——	——
D. Layoff due to lack of work?	——	——	——	——

Where answer is "yes," please explain policy concerning

A. _____

_____

_____

_____

B. _____

_____

_____

_____

C. _____

_____

_____

_____

D. _____

_____

_____

_____

25. If an employee is called in on an emergency, what pay policy do you pursue?_____

_____

26. What work clothing is furnished employee and how often?_____

_____

27. What tools are employees expected to furnish?_____

_____

_____

28. Do you pay a separation allowance when service terminates? Yes__No__
If "yes," explain basis of allowance_____

_____

_____

29. Do you have a suggestion system?   Yes__No__
If "yes," are employees rewarded by: % of Savings?_____
Flat cash award?_____
Maximum award payable, if any_____
Minimum award payable, if any_____

FIG. 6–2.—*Concluded.*

job comparison sheet (Fig. 6–3). Wherever there is doubt as to the similarity of job content, the job should be personally observed; and if observation is not possible, the data should be eliminated, so far as the company interviewed is concerned. Figure 6–4 illustrates a form on which job titles are shown. This form is taken from the job evaluation manual of the National Electrical Manufacturers' Association.

In making a comparison of jobs, it may be of some benefit to evaluate them according to the plan used by the surveying company. In this manner the jobs will be compared on the basis of factors and their differences more clearly set forth. When the similarity of jobs has been determined, the rates may be entered; or the forms may be left at the company being surveyed to be filled in and mailed to the interviewer.

This procedure may appear to be overly painstaking at first. However, experience will prove that carelessness and superficial methods will not only produce inaccurate results but may require a repetition of interviews and unnecessary inconvenience to the representatives of the participating companies.

Summarizing the Data

When all forms have been completely filled in and checked for accuracy and completeness, the data should be summarized so that it is presentable in easily understood terms to those responsible for conducting the survey and to those participating in it. The data should also be tabulated to determine the adequacy of the company's present rate structure through statistical analysis.

Figure 6–5 is a form that might be used for treating statistically the general information collected. Where answers to questions are in essay form, a narrative summary or tabulation will be necessary. The forms used, however, will in all probability be designed to fit the general form of the original questionnaire.

In addition to a general information summary, a tabulation of hourly rates and weekly salaries should be compiled, using

YOUR JOB TITLE		BASE RATE	NO.	AVG. EARNED HOURLY RATE	NO.	BASE RATE	NO.	AVG. EARNED HOURLY RATE	NO.	BASE RATE	NO.	AVG. EARNED HOURLY RATE	NO.
OUR JOB DESCRIPTION													
1	YES ☐	NO ☐			YES ☐	NO ☐			YES ☐	NO ☐			
2													
3													

1. ENTER HERE AVERAGE HOURS SCHEDULED PER WEEK, ESTIMATED IF NECESSARY.
2. ENTER HERE HOURS WORKED LAST WEEK BY AVERAGE EMPLOYEE.
3. IS JOB COVERED BY INCENTIVE PLAN?

FIG. 6-3.—Wage or salary survey information sheet.

IN HORIZONTAL COLUMN MARKED "ACTUAL RATES" SHOW DISTRIBUTION OF EMPLOYEES BY HOURLY RATES, EXCLUDING INCENTIVE AND PREMIUM SUCH AS OVERTIME, ETC. LIST TRAINEES SEPARATELY AND MARK WITH "T". IN HORIZONTAL COLUMN MARKED "STRUCTURE" ENTER THE MINIMUM AND MAXIMUM RATES WHICH HAVE BEEN ADOPTED AS THE RATE RANGE, WHERE AUTOMATIC INCREASES ARE GIVEN, SHOW ON THE MACHINE RATE THE SUCCESSIVE RATES AND ON THE HORIZONTAL LINE MARKED "INT.", THE TIME INTERVAL AT WHICH THEY ARE GIVEN. ALSO POST YOUR GRADE NUMBER UNDER "GRADE."

JOB DESCRIPTION			AVG. RATE AND TOTAL EMPL.
HELPER (TRADES) GRADE 9 ASSIST TRADESMEN AND PERFORM MINOR ASSIGNMENTS IN CONNECTION WITH TRADES WORK WHICH GENERALLY INCLUDE TASKS OF A MANUAL LABOR NATURE AND SPECIFIC TRADES ASSIGNMENT UNDER CLOSE DIRECTION.	ACTUAL RATES	RATE / EMPL.	
	STRU. RATES	RATE / EMPL. / INT.	GRADE
INSPECTOR AND/OR TESTER GRADE 9 VISUAL, MECHANICAL, OR ELECTRICAL INSPECTION AND CHECK, USING STANDARD METHODS, ON SOMEWHAT DIVERSIFIED WORK UNDER FREQUENT SUPERVISION INVOLVING HANDLING OF AVERAGE WEIGHTS. WORK FROM SIMPLE TO AVERAGE DRAWINGS AND SPECIFICATIONS. USE SIMPLE GAGES AND DC OR SIMPLE AC TEST SETS.	ACTUAL RATES	RATE / EMPL.	
	STRU. RATES	RATE / EMPL. / INT.	GRADE
INSPECTOR AND/OR TESTER GRADE 10 VISUAL, MECHANICAL, OR ELECTRICAL INSPECTION AND CHECK OF SMALL PARTS OR ASSEMBLIES. WORK FROM SIMPLE TO AVERAGE DRAWINGS AND SPECIFICATIONS. INSPECT FOR GENERAL CONSTRUCTION AND USE TEST EQUIPMENT SUCH AS INDUCTANCE BRIDGE.	ACTUAL RATES	RATE / EMPL.	
	STRU. RATES	RATE / EMPL. / INT.	GRADE
INSPECTOR AND/OR TESTER GRADE 12 INSPECT OR CHECK SMALL PARTS OR ASSEMBLIES, WORKING FROM SIMPLE INSTRUCTIONS, DRAWINGS, OR FINISH STAMPINGS. USE FEELER, PLUG AND INDICATOR GAGES AND SIMPLE ELECTRICAL TESTING EQUIPMENT SUCH AS WHEATSTONE BRIDGE. WORK REQUIRES SOME JUDGMENT.	ACTUAL RATES	RATE / EMPL.	
	STRU. RATES	RATE / EMPL. / INT.	GRADE
JANITOR GRADE 9 SWEEP AND CLEAN SHOP AREAS, INVOLVING REMOVING OILY AND DIRTY SCRAP METALS AND OTHER MATERIALS FROM MACHINE AREAS. DISAGREEABLE WORKING CONDITIONS AND MODERATELY HEAVY PHYSICAL EFFORT.	ACTUAL RATES	RATE / EMPL.	
	STRU. RATES	RATE / EMPL. / INT.	GRADE

Fig. 6-4.

QUESTION 6

Does each job carry A:	Hourly		Salary	
	Yes	No	Yes	No
Single rate?	14	10	20	4
Rate range?	10	14	4	20

QUESTION 7

What method of progression through a range is used:	Hourly		Salary	
	Yes	No	Yes	No
Merit increase only?	6	4	1	3
Automatic increase only?	3	7	3	1
Part merit and part automatic?	1	9	0	4

QUESTION 8

	Hourly		Salary	
	Yes	No	Yes	No
Are employees guaranteed an annual wage?	1	23	0	24

Please explain if "yes." *All hourly paid employees having 10 or more years service are guaranteed a minimum of 1600 hours work annually.*

QUESTION 9

Number of hours worked per year, on an average, by your average shop employee?

1,400–1,500	1	1,500–1,600	3	1,600–1,700	4
1,700–1,800	5	1,800–1,900	8	1,900–2,000	1

QUESTION 10

How many holidays per year do you observe? Four: _1_ Five: _2_ Six: _21_

QUESTION 11

What are employees paid for working on holidays?	Hourly		Salary	
	Yes	No	Yes	No
Time and one-half		24		24
Double time	24		24	
Other		24		24

FIG. 6–5.—Page from wage survey general information summary.

separate forms for hourly paid and salaried occupations. Similar jobs paid on an hourly basis by some companies and on a weekly basis by others should be entered on both forms—the hourly wages being converted to weekly rates and the salaries converted to hourly rates, for comparative purposes.

The amount of detailed information compiled and entered for each job will be limited only by the scope of information required. Figure 6–6 is a suggested form to be used in tabulating rate information concerning specific jobs. While additional information may be added by expanding the form, experience has shown it to be satisfactory in the large majority of cases, not only from the viewpoint of those conducting the survey but also from that of the participants.

Once data has been assembled and recapitulated, copies of all the forms are sent, with an appropriate letter of transmittal, to those who originally authorized participation in the survey. Code numbers of all the companies, excepting the one conducting the survey and the one to whom the particular copies are sent, are kept confidential; but the names of all companies participating in the survey are usually mentioned.

Analyzing the Data

Four Basic Comparisons.—In order to draw reasonably accurate conclusions from the data obtained from the wage survey, four basic comparisons of company and survey data should be made. Some comparisons utilize single statistical methods, while others require considerable judgment. The four comparisons are of base rates, average earned rates, minimum hiring rates, and additions to income.

Base Rate Comparison.—The comparison of company base rates with those reflected in the survey requires, as a first step, an analysis of the company's payroll. This is done by listing all the jobs by labor grade. Thus, if there are ten labor grades, there will be ten lists of jobs, each list made up of the jobs belonging to one particular labor grade. The second step is the tabulation of each employee's base rate under the labor grade.

JOB TITLE																	
JOB DESCRIPTION																	
COMPANY CODE	AVG. EARNED HOURLY RATE	BASE RATE			AVG. EARNED HOURLY RATE	BASE RATE			AVG. EARNED HOURLY RATE	BASE RATE		
		MIN.	MAX.	AVG.		MIN.	MAX.	AVG.		MIN.	MAX.	AVG.
MINIMUM												
MAXIMUM												
AVERAGE												
COMPANY MEDIAN												

Fig. 6–6.—Wage survey summary of hourly rates.

The tabulation within each labor grade should be in rank order from highest to lowest. The rates that fall in the middle of each tabulated group constitute the median base rates for the respective labor grades. The median, rather than the arithmetic average, is used because it is not subject to distortion by a small number of extremely high or low rates. However, where there are no extremely high or low rates, an average can be considered reliable; likewise, where the number of rates is small,

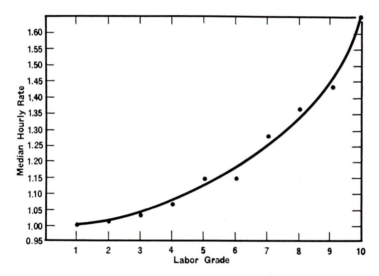

Fig. 6–7.—Median rate curve: company rates—base.

the median may not be as accurate as the average. After tabulating the company's jobs in the described manner, the same process is repeated, using the base rate data gathered during the survey. This data should be simplified by proper design of survey forms. Upon completion of the survey data tabulation, the median rate for each labor grade is selected.

The median rates are then plotted; a separate graph for each set of rates, the labor grade along the abscissa, and the money rates up the ordinate. Curves are then constructed. The comparison will be facilitated if the curves are then replotted on a single sheet of graph paper (see Figs. 6–7, 6–8 and, 6–9). In this manner, the base rate structure of the com-

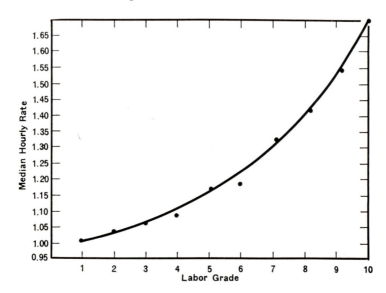

Fig. 6-8.—Median rate curve: survey rates—base.

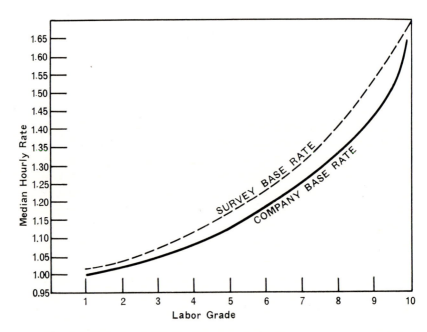

Fig. 6-9.—Median rate curves: comparison between company base rates and survey base rates.

pany and the composite base rate structure of the surveyed companies may be directly compared.

Two items are considered in the comparison, namely: monetary differences and slopes of curves. If the company curve falls above the other curve at all points, then its basic wage structure is generally higher than the composite structures of other companies; but if the company curve falls below the other curve, then the opposite would be true. The amount of difference for each labor grade may be measured directly from the graph. The relative slope of the two curves must also be considered. When the curves run parallel and close together, they indicate that the basic rate structure is close to being identical with that of the companies surveyed; such a comparison very seldom exists, however. Such being the case, an element of judgment must be injected; but no final decision should be made until average earned rates, minimum hiring rates, and income additions have been compared. When such comparisons have been made, then judgment can be applied to bring the curves into a relationship compatible with the labor market policy of the company.

Average Earned Rate Comparison.—Comparison of the average earned rates of the company with those of the companies surveyed is accomplished in the same manner as described for the base rate comparison, using, of course, the average earned rates instead of the base rates.

Minimum Hiring Rate Comparison.—The procedure used when comparing minimum hiring rates is very simple. Rates reported in the survey are arranged in rank order, and the median minimum hiring rate for the lowest evaluated jobs of the companies surveyed is determined. This rate is then compared with the rate paid the lowest evaluated job of the company, exclusive of apprentice, trainee, or learner rates. This comparison will then indicate any changes in minimum hiring rates which the company may deem advisable in the light of established policy.

Addition to Income Comparison.—It can be readily understood, when comparisons are made with what various companies do for their employees in addition to paying salaries or wages, why some companies which have below average base, earned average, and minimum hiring rates find little difficulty in maintaining a better-than-average labor force. These additions to income include such employee benefits as pensions, various types of insurance, profit-sharing, paid leaves, vacations, and periods of one kind or another, shift differentials, and other types of premiums for compensating employees for inconveniences.

Making comparisons of such items cannot be reduced to simple formulas or procedures. However, reasonable care and the application of some system to the tabulation of survey results will enable the company to determine with a reasonable degree of accuracy where it stands in relation to prevailing practice. For example, if one firm out of fifty surveyed has a pension plan but forty-five firms grant night shift differentials, then it may be logically concluded that the company not granting premiums for work performed during the night shift should modify its policy and that the pension plan, seriously considered as a means of stabilizing the present working force, could be forgotten without fear of adverse results.

Because a change in the base rate structure will necessarily result in a change in the average earned and minimum hiring rate, the results of the comparisons resolve into two problems of judgment, namely, "Shall the base rate structure be changed?" and, "Shall policies as to income additions be altered?" Only in instances where income additions are so liberal as to compensate for unduly low base rates will policies dictating such a liberal attitude have an effect on the base rate curve. Because such instances are indeed rare, it is the base rate curve, therefore, which must receive the most consideration in the final analysis. If the base rate curve is to be changed, the rates to be adjusted and the magnitude of the adjustment must be determined. What rates and to what extent these rates should be changed will be determined only after a study of each particular case. It is possible, however, for the base rate structure to remain unchanged if the management adopts a program of wage incentives or of increased working hours as a means of increasing the earned average rate.

Time Interval between Surveys

The frequency with which labor market surveys will be made will depend largely upon the attitude of management toward their usefulness. In many cases a survey has been made in conjunction with a job evaluation project, after which all thought of continuing a wage comparison has ceased.

For an evaluation to remain effective, the adequacy of the wage scale should be checked periodically, particularly if the companies within the industry or locality are subject to general and frequent revisions of their wage structures and policies as a result of union bargaining. As much as a stable wage structure is desired, it is a condition difficult to attain because of constant day-to-day pressure to change the existing rates or policies.

Periods of labor unrest or rapid change in economic conditions call for more frequent surveys than periods when the reverse is true. It is advisable, when conducting a survey, to find out from each company surveyed when their union agreement expires and when a new agreement will be negotiated. In larger industrial areas, where there is a large number of companies to choose from, the company conducting the survey might select companies having similar union contract termination dates. In this way the participating companies can be resurveyed immediately after the new contracts have been negotiated, with the resulting assurance to the company conducting the survey that the rates will remain fairly stable for the following year. Such a procedure, however, is not always possible.

Under ordinary circumstances, surveys are conducted at least twice a year, unless unusually stable labor and economic conditions exist. The quality of the survey, particularly with regard to the care exercised in the selection of the occupations and companies surveyed, will have an effect on the frequency with which the effort must be repeated.

During the negotiation of a new union contract, the question of the general wage level will undoubtedly arise and management and union alike will want to know the position of the concern's wage scale relative to that of the industry and locality. The survey, therefore, should be started in time to provide an opportunity for satisfactorily completing the survey and for analyzing the data prior to negotiations.

QUESTIONS

1. What is the danger of using an existing wage scale when applying money values to job worth?
2. What do you believe a wage survey tells management?
3. What basic sets of facts should survey information furnish?
4. What points should be considered in selecting jobs from which wage data will be gathered?
5. Do you believe that by using a large number of jobs when conducting a wage survey the resulting statistical data will be more accurate than if a smaller number of jobs, selected with greater care, were used? Why?
6. How would you determine what companies to select for making your wage survey? How many companies would you survey?
7. How would you proceed to gather the data you desire? What forms would you need?
8. After you had collected the necessary data, explain how you would compare it with your own company's base rate structure.
9. After comparing the base rates of your company with the composite base rates of the companies surveyed, you find that your company's rates are 15 per cent higher. What would you do?
10. How often do you believe wage surveys should be conducted? Why?

CHAPTER 7

THE WAGE CURVE

CONVERSION, as applied to job evaluation, is the translation of relative job values, determined through job evaluation, into money. The conversion takes place after jobs have been evaluated and employees properly classified, and it is a problem to be solved regardless of the evaluation method employed. Before taking the step, however, decisions must be reached on certain fundamentals, such as: what will form the basis of the rate structure—negotiation, wage survey, present scale, or a combination of them? And what differentials will be incorporated into the wage structure? These and other matters affecting the wage curve are discussed in this chapter under the following topics:

1. Job ranking and predetermined grading conversion.
2. Factor comparison and point rating conversion lines.
3. Rates for individual jobs.
4. Labor grades.
5. Single rates versus rate ranges for labor grades.
6. Number and limits of rate ranges.
7. Preliminary considerations in applying money to labor grades.
8. Assignment of money to labor grades.

Job Ranking and Predetermined Grading Conversion

Job Ranking.—Under the job ranking method of evaluation, relative job worth will be converted to money, either through negotiation or the sole judgment of management. Where a union is involved, the problem will most likely be solved through negotiation.

Referring to the table of key job rankings used for explanation of the job ranking method (Fig. 2–3), it will be noted that certain rates, denoted by asterisks, are not in the proper order and must be adjusted. First, however, it may be necessary to negotiate the top and bottom rates, for the union may feel, for example, that the rates for the tool and die maker and janitor are low and should be increased. However, if the increase is negotiated, it might be necessary to adjust the rates of all jobs ranked by the same amount to maintain the proper relative relationship. Even with the top and bottom rates negotiated, some jobs may still be out of line and rates reflecting proper relative job value must be attached to them. In the example, because of the relative positions assigned to the jobs during the ranking process, the electric trucker should receive less than the inspector–tester, bench assembler, and trades helper; and the janitor should receive more than the laborer. One way of bringing the jobs into line would be to decrease the rate of the electric trucker and to increase the rates of the trades helper and janitor. Another way would be to increase the rates of the inspector–tester, bench assembler, trades helper, and janitor without decreasing the rate of the electric trucker. The second method would be the one used if collective bargaining pressure was sufficiently strong.

Predetermined Grading.—Under the predetermined grading method, when broad classifications have been established and jobs have been assigned to their respective grades, the problem of assigning rates still remains. Solutions are provided through negotiation or wage survey, but the use of both methods is preferable. If negotiation provides the solution, one method would be to negotiate the rates for the lowest and highest classifications and then, by dividing the spread between the high and low classifications by the number of grades minus one, to determine the spread between the grades. For example, if the rate for grade one was negotiated at 95 cents and for grade eight at $1.65, then the total spread of 70 cents divided by seven would result in 10-cent steps between the grades. Using such a method, however, presupposes equal differences in relative job worth between grades, a supposition that may be incorrect.

Another method of negotiation would be to negotiate a rate for each classification. Pressure on both sides of the table being equal, the result might better reflect true differentials between grades; but if the pressure is unevenly balanced, the negotiated rates might tend to favor certain large or small groups or perhaps to favor the highest or lowest grades, depending on what best suited the side exerting the strongest bargaining pressure.

The locality wage survey can be used with excellent results. The jobs selected for use in making the survey are assigned their proper classifications or grades in accordance with the new classifications. The rates determined from the survey for jobs assigned to each grade are tabulated, and the mean rate of each group is used as the rate for the grade; all jobs falling in the grade receive the same rate. It is assumed, of course, that single rates rather than rate ranges are used. Rate ranges are the subject of a later discussion.

It is altogether possible, after the results of the wage survey have been applied, to negotiate the rate adjustments, which would raise the general level of the scale. The union thereby preserves its zealously guarded prerogative of negotiating the general wage level, while management maintains the relative position of jobs on the scale.

Factor Comparison and Point Rating
Conversion Lines

The Scatter Diagram.—It is the usual practice under the factor comparison and point rating methods to construct a scatter diagram. This is done as soon as the jobs have been evaluated and the point or other worth values are known. Such a diagram readily reflects the relative positions within the framework of the rate structure of all jobs that have been evaluated and tells at a glance how rational or irrational the wage structure is.

Under the point system of evaluation, the diagram is constructed by plotting the position of each job, the point values along the abscissa and the rates in cents per hour up the ordinate. Figure 7–1 is a scatter diagram showing the plotting of the jobs recorded on the summary rating sheet (Fig. 7–10). The rate scale used may be derived from the locality wage survey, collective bargaining, or the present scale, depending on the circumstances. Ordinarily, it is derived from the present scale but later adjusted to reflect the results of the locality wage survey, negotiation, or both.

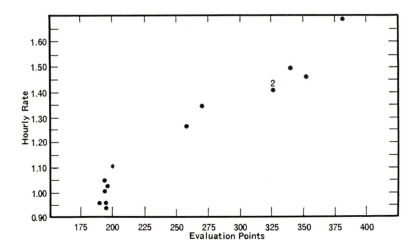

Fig. 7–1.—Scatter diagram — plot of evaluated jobs.

Under the factor comparison method, the scatter diagram is drawn in somewhat the same way as for point rating, in that the vertical scale or ordinate is the present money scale; but it differs in that the abscissa is a scale of evaluated rates. To plot a job on the diagram, it is necessary to count out on the horizontal scale an amount equal to the evaluated rate and then, from that point, to count up an amount equal to the present rate and to plot the point. Plotting all jobs in such a manner provides a picture of the present rate structure (Fig. 7–9).

High-Low Conversion Lines.—A line connecting the top and bottom jobs plotted on a graph is the simplest type of conversion line, but it is neither the most common nor the most satisfactory. Such a line frequently fails to reflect a true wage curve and results in an excessive number of jobs falling below the line. It is doubtful whether only two points should be permitted to determine the slope of the conversion line. One of the many possible errors that may creep into the evaluation of either the high or the low job or unbalanced collective bargaining pressure, might throw the slope off its true course.

There are certain dangers connected with using such a trend indicator. Those experienced in job evaluation, who have a few known figures at their disposal, plus vision and judgment, may be in a position to control the results of the program. As an example, if it is known that the present maximum and minimum rates are not to be changed as a result of a job evaluation but that all jobs falling below the line will be brought up to it, then by first evaluating the highest and lowest worth jobs, locating these points on the graph, and drawing a line to connect the two, such a line will be very close to the conversion line. Pressure can then be brought to bear to evaluate the remainder of the jobs so that they fall at a point on the line calling for a rate equal to or less than the present scale. Such a procedure has been used in instances where circumstances permitted, but it defeats the entire purpose of job evaluation by perpetuating inequities. If a straight line connecting the high and low jobs is to be used, the rates for the two jobs should be negotiated or adjusted to reflect a wage survey after all the jobs have been evaluated.

Figure 7–2 shows a simple conversion line connecting the high and low negotiated rates. The two jobs connected by the line are the high and low jobs plotted on the scatter diagram shown in Figure 7–1. The relation of existing rates to the conversion line is shown in Figure 7–3 which superimposes the conversion line (Fig. 7–2) on the scatter diagram (Fig. 7–1). Those rates resting below the line will be increased and brought up to the line, while those above the line should remain where they are until a new operator takes over the job. At such time

the new worker will receive a rate decreased by the amount
necessary to bring it down to the line. The rates remaining

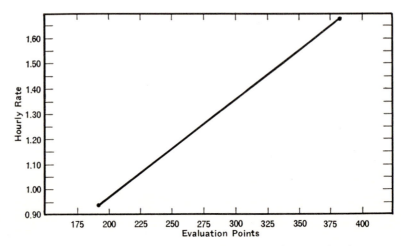

Fig. 7–2. —Conversion line connecting the high and low negotiated rates.

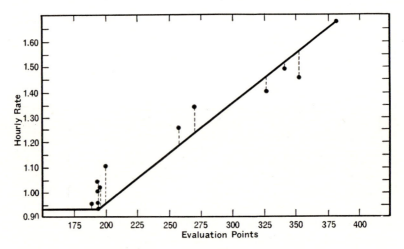

Fig. 7–3.—Relation of existing rates (•) to the conversion line connecting
the high and low negotiated rates.

above the line are usually termed "red circle" or "ringed" rates.

a) Adjusting the Line.—The high-low conversion line is
the one most commonly negotiated. As will be seen later, the

least squares conversion line is the one used for a defensible redistribution of an inequitable wage structure, is arrived at by
a mathematical process, and cannot remain at a true slope if the
position of either end of the line is negotiated. Figures 7–4 to
7–7, inclusive, illustrate the effect of various changes in the
high-low conversion line which may result from negotiation.

Figure 7–4 illustrates the effect of raising the minimum rate.
This course would benefit the lower skilled occupations but
would give little recognition to the higher skilled jobs. Such a

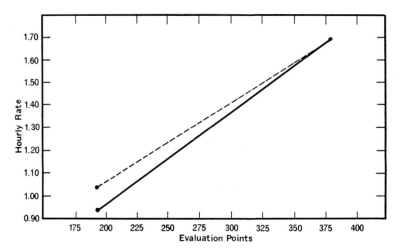

FIG. 7–4.—Effect of increasing the minimum rate by 10 cents, shown by
broken line.

revision in the line might easily result from the continued pressure of a rising cost of living or from a desire to attract unskilled labor.

On the other hand, Figure 7–5 illustrates the result of raising
the maximum rate without changing the minimum rate. This
revision of a line's slope will usually be the result of efforts to
attract skilled labor by bringing the rates up to a point equal to
or above those reflected in a wage survey. Very seldom will
unions ask for such a change in the rate structure unless for
purposes of adjusting the differential between high and low skills.

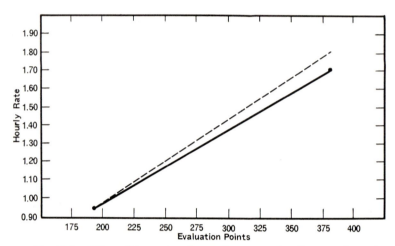

Fig. 7–5.—Effect of increasing the maximum rate by 10 cents, shown by broken line.

The most prevalent type of negotiated revision of the high-low conversion line, particularly during a period of increasing wages, is the straight or constant money increase. This affects the top, bottom, and intermediate rates by the same amount, as may be seen in the relation of the two lines in Figure 7–6.

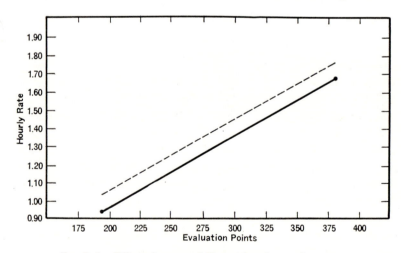

Fig. 7–6.—Effect of a general 10-cent hourly rate increase.

A general increase of this kind maintains the relationship between the jobs resulting from an evaluation. On the graph, the same result can be attained by raising the money values on the vertical scale by an amount equal to the increase.

Figure 7–7 shows the result of a constant percentage increase. Such an increase benefits the higher skilled more than the unskilled worker and is very seldom negotiated during periods of increasing wages. There being a desire on the part of most

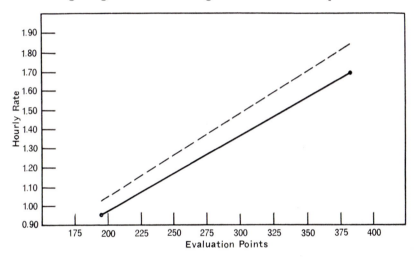

FIG. 7–7.—Effect of a general 10 per cent rate increase.

unions to further the financial cause of those comprising the majority of their membership, it is altogether possible that in periods of declining wage rates percentage decreases will be negotiated as a means of lessening the impact on the low-skilled workers who form this majority.

Factor Comparison Conversion Line.—Under the factor comparison method, the simplest approach to a conversion line is the plotting of the position of key jobs and connecting such jobs by a line, as shown in Figure 7–8. Because the present hourly rates for key jobs are identical with the evaluated hourly rates, the line will be straight. After constructing the line, the re-

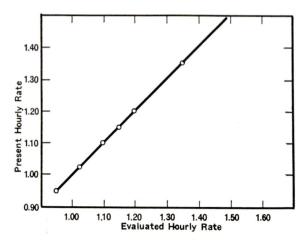

Fig. 7–8.—Line connecting the key jobs (o), showing conversion under the factor comparison method.

maining jobs are plotted as shown in Figure 7–9 and their relation to the line noted.

Least Squares Method.—The method of least squares will show the trend line of a badly distorted wage structure. It is a com-

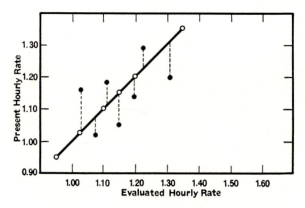

Fig. 7–9.—Position of jobs relative to the conversion line connecting key jobs under the factor comparison method. Key job (o); present rate (•).

monly used method of drawing a conversion line and is preferred by many authorities on job evaluation. Rather than enter into a discussion of the mathematical derivation of the method, a practical example is cited which should be sufficient to acquaint the reader with its application to job evaluation conversion lines.[1]

a) Application to Point Rating.—For purposes of comparison, the same group of jobs listed in the summary job rating sheet (Fig. 5–2) will be used as examples. The step-by-step procedure of computing and constructing a least squares method conversion line follows:

1. After the jobs have been evaluated, they are listed along with their point totals as in Figure 7–10. Point totals are entered in the X column. In the Y column are entered the hourly rates for the respective jobs. In the XY column is entered the point total X multiplied by the hourly rate Y; in the X^2 column the point totals are squared.

2. Next, the four columns are totaled and the number of jobs counted. The totals are:

$$\begin{aligned} X \quad \text{total} &= 3,617 \\ Y \quad \text{total} &= \$16.98 \\ XY \text{ total} &= \$4,612.06 \\ X^2 \text{ total} &= 1,003,345 \\ N \text{ (number of jobs)} &= 14 \end{aligned}$$

3. The above figures are then applied to the formula:

$$C = \frac{XY - \dfrac{XY}{N}}{X^2 - \dfrac{X^2}{N}}$$

or

$$C = \frac{4{,}612.06 - \dfrac{3{,}617 \times 16.98}{14}}{1{,}003{,}345 - \dfrac{3{,}617 \times 3{,}617}{14}} = \frac{225.16}{68{,}867} = 0.00327.$$

For an explanation of the mathematical derivation, consult any standard text on statistics, such as Arkin and Colton, *An Outline of Statistical Methods*, (New York: Barnes & Noble, 1939).

DEPARTMENTAL SUMMARY SHEET — JOB RATING
202 ___ DEPARTMENT
8-1-48

OCCUPATION	SKILL — EDUCATION D	P	EXPERIENCE D	P	INITIATIVE AND INGENUITY D	P	EFFORT — PHYSICAL DEMAND D	P	MENTAL AND VISUAL D	P	RESPONSIBILITY — EQUIPMENT OR PROCESS D	P	MATERIAL OR PRODUCT D	P	SAFETY OF OTHERS D	P	WORK OF OTHERS D	P	JOB CONDITIONS — WORKING CONDITIONS D	P	HAZARDS D	P	TOTAL X	AVG. HOURLY RATE Y	XY	X²
ASSEMBLY BENCH	2	28	2	44	2	28	2	20	3	15	2	10	2	10	1	5	1	5	2	20	2	10	195	1.00	195.00	38,025
AUTOMATIC SCREW MACHINE SETUP MAN	3	42	4	88	4	56	2	20	4	20	3	15	2	10	3	15	3	15	3	30	3	15	326	1.40	456.40	106,276
CARPENTER A	3	42	4	88	4	56	3	30	3	15	2	10	2	10	3	15	3	15	3	30	3	15	326	1.40	456.40	106,276
CRANEMAN	1	14	2	44	3	42	3	30	4	20	4	20	4	20	5	25	1	5	3	30	4	20	270	1.33	359.10	72,900
DRILL-PRESS OPERATOR	2	28	2	44	2	28	2	20	3	15	2	10	2	10	2	10	1	5	2	20	2	10	200	1.10	220.00	40,000
ELECTRICIAN A	4	56	4	88	4	56	2	20	3	15	3	15	4	20	3	15	3	15	3	30	5	25	355	1.45	514.75	126,025
HELPER, TRADES	1	14	1	22	2	28	4	40	2	10	2	10	1	5	3	15	3	15	2	20	3	15	194	0.95	184.30	37,636
INSPECTOR-TESTER	2	28	2	44	2	28	2	20	3	15	2	10	2	10	1	5	1	5	2	20	2	10	195	1.02	198.90	38,025
JANITOR	1	14	1	22	2	28	3	30	2	10	2	10	2	10	1	5	1	5	4	40	4	20	194	0.93	180.42	37,636
LABORER	1	14	1	22	1	14	4	40	2	10	1	5	2	10	3	15	1	5	4	40	3	15	190	0.95	180.50	36,100
MACHINIST A	4	56	4	88	4	56	2	20	4	20	2	10	4	20	3	15	2	10	3	30	3	15	340	1.48	503.20	115,600
PLATER	1	14	3	66	3	42	3	30	2	10	2	10	2	10	2	10	2	10	4	40	3	15	257	1.25	321.25	66,049
TOOL AND DIE MAKER	4	56	5	110	5	70	2	20	4	20	3	15	5	25	3	15	3	15	2	20	3	15	381	1.68	640.08	145,161
TRUCKER, ELECTRIC	1	14	1	22	2	28	3	30	3	15	3	15	2	10	4	20	1	5	2	20	3	15	194	1.04	201.76	37,636
TOTAL																							3,617	16.98	4,612.06	1,003,345

D = DEGREE
P = POINTS

FIG. 7–10.—Rating sheet showing the computations necessary for constructing a least squares conversion line.

4. The same figures are then applied, where appropriate, to the following two formulas:

$$X \text{ value of midpoint} = \frac{X}{N} = \frac{3,617}{14} = 258$$

$$Y \text{ value of midpoint} = \frac{Y}{N} = \frac{16.98}{14} = 1.213.$$

5. Next, the trend points of Y_1 and Y_2 are computed. To do this, two evaluation point totals are chosen at random,

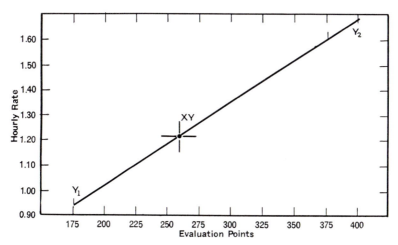

FIG. 7–11.—Least squares method conversion line showing midpoint (XY) and points (Y_1, Y_2) that determine the slope.

one more and the other less than 258 (X value of midpoint). In the following example, 375 and 175 are used:

$$Y_1 = 1.213 - 0.00327\ (258 - 175) = 1.213 - 0.273 = 0.94$$

$$Y_2 = 1.213 + 0.00327\ (375 - 258) = 1.213 + 0.383 = 1.596.$$

6. The next step is to plot the points as illustrated in Figure 7–11. The midpoint is at the intersection of a line drawn perpendicular to the abscissa at 258 points and a line drawn perpendicular to the ordinate at 1.213 per hour. Points

Y_1 and Y_2 are plotted similarly at 175 and 375 on the horizontal scale and values 0.94 and 1.596 on the vertical scales. The straight line connecting Y_1 and Y_2 and passing through the midpoint is the conversion line.

b) Application to Factor Comparison.—The least squares method is also used for establishing conversion lines under the factor comparison method. The same procedure is used except that in place of evaluation points on the abscissa, as in point rating, the rates evaluated under the method are used.

c) Adjusting the Conversion Line.—The slope of the line of conversion established by the least squares method is determined on a mathematical basis. It is difficult to substantiate a change in the computed slope because of the application of human judgment in the process of negotiation. Therefore, if the conversion line established on the basis of the least squares method is to be changed, the change should not affect the slope but the position of the line on the scatter diagram (Fig. 7–1). The horizontal base is fixed in accordance with the evaluation plan used, and the evaluation points cannot be changed without endangering the entire worth relationship between jobs. It may be concluded, therefore, that the change of the position of the line on the diagram may best be affected by altering the vertical, or money rate, scale. In short, if a new conversion line is to be negotiated, it should be negotiated on the basis of a constant money increase or decrease.

In a substantial number of cases it will be found that the slope of a least squares conversion line is so abrupt that to apply the conversion line would be impractible. In such cases other types of conversion lines must be used.

Figure 7–12 illustrates the relationship between the line connecting the negotiated high and low rates and the least squares method conversion line. It should be noted that the bottom of the least squares conversion line is above while the top is below the other line. This is because the jobs having a higher than the negotiated minimum rate are concentrated at the lower end of the scale. Such a concentration indicates a badly distorted wage structure. In the example, the truest line is the one arrived at through the least squares method, although this will not always be the case.

Lines by Inspection.—Very often the conversion line is drawn in by eye or by what is commonly referred to as "inspecting in a line." Such a line may be used where the location of jobs on the scatter diagram reflects a fairly narrow and regular dispersion and can be inspected-in with reasonable assurance

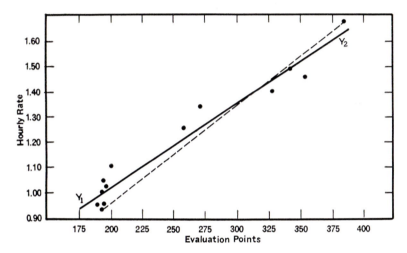

Fig. 7–12.—Relation of existing rates (•) to the least squares conversion line (solid) and the line connecting high and low negotiated rates (broken).

that it is a true indication of trend. Another circumstance under which the conversion line may be used is where a company feels that a straight line does not represent their true trend but that their line is a geometric progression. Regardless of why the line is used, it is usually open to criticism because of the judgment factor involved; for this reason it should be fairly well substantiated by wage survey data.

It is not to be concluded, however, that geometric progression is without foundation, for it can be reasoned that as the required degree of mental development, skill, responsibility, etc. increases the number of workers capable of meeting the requirements rapidly decreases. Another recognition of the geometric principle is in Weber's "law of discrimination" which states that an arithmetic relationship of sensations or responses is a geometric series of corresponding stimuli. However, where a union is involved, the inspected-in or geometric progression line will, in all probability, be negotiated, as it should be if successful administration of the evaluation project is expected.

A line drawn by inspection is shown in Figure 7–13. To those drawing such a line, it may be a satisfactory indication

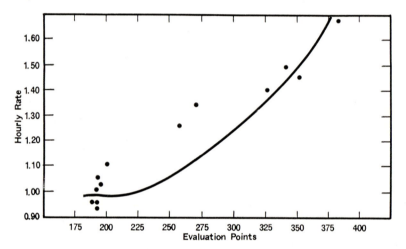

Fig. 7–13.—Relation of existing rates to the line of best fit drawn in by inspection.

of what they think the trend is, or it may be a negotiated compromise. In any event, the illustrated line indicates a trend which is far from that indicated by the line connecting the high and low negotiated rates or from that constructed under the least squares method; the comparison of the three lines is shown in Figure 7–14. Such a wide variation between the inspected-in and other lines is not often the case if those drawing the line have had much experience in the use of the least squares method, for with experience they are better able to visualize the effect of concentrations of jobs.

While the conversion line may show the trend of rates . within the wage scale, its construction still leaves many steps to be taken. A number of fundamental issues must be decided; and most of them, where a union is involved, must be decided through negotiation. It must be decided whether a single rate or a rate range will be applied to each job; whether or not jobs will be grouped by worth ranges or by labor grades; and, if such grouping is to be effected, whether there will be a single rate or a rate range for each group. It must also be decided to

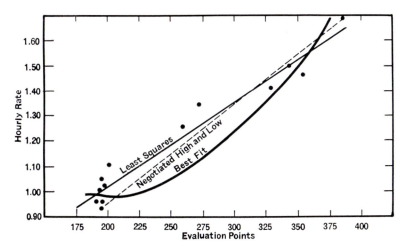

Fig. 7-14.—Comparative relation of existing rates to: line of best fit; line of least squares; line of negotiated high and low.

what jobs the scale is to apply—manual, clerical, or both. The question of age and sex differentials may also call for a decision.

Rates for Individual Jobs

The use of a single rate for each job poses the many problems fostered by an unwieldy rate structure. It is not unusual to find as many as 500 jobs evaluated in a single plant; and if single rates for each job were used, there would very likely be as many rates as there were cents in the spread between the top and bottom rates. Some jobs would be paid 89 cents, some 90 cents, and some 91 cents. It can hardly be expected that group judgment will be able to differentiate between jobs to such a minute degree; and what is more illogical is to expect workers and their supervisors to accept explanations of why such a multitude of rates should exist.

It is also possible to apply a range of rates to each individual job. Under such circumstances one job might have a rate range of 89–94 cents; the next, 90–95 cents; the next, 91–96 cents; and so on up the scale. Such ranges might be used to reward seniority or extra effort, or they might be used with a system of merit rating. Use of such a basis of compensation has all the disadvantages of applying single rates to jobs, and in addition to making the structure more unwieldy, it introduces the added difficulties of explaining and justifying the complexity of excessive rate range overlap.

Companies resorting to individual job rates or to rate ranges as a means of compensation will undoubtedly encounter enough difficulties to make it almost mandatory to effect a change. The number of rate grievances will approach a maximum, and there will likely be a constant pressure for cent-by-cent increases. Requests for such increases will be hard to refuse, because an explanation of one-cent differentials will be extremely difficult. The multiplicity of grievances will cause dissatisfaction among workers and supervision, and the months of time and effort spent in analyzing and evaluating the jobs may turn out to have been wasted. Timekeeping and payroll procedures will become more involved, and the complexities of cost accounting and budgetary and cost control are bound to multiply.

Labor Grades

In order to circumvent the difficulties encountered in the use of individual rates, worth ranges or labor grades are used. Labor grades are nothing more or less than worth bands or brackets to which jobs are assigned. For example, a company having four hundred evaluated jobs might segregate the jobs on the basis of point totals, or it may place the evaluated jobs into sixteen groups or labor grades, each of which would carry a single rate or rate range. Thus, the number of rates to contend with would be reduced to as few as sixteen if single rates were used.

The number of labor grades used varies considerably in actual practice, but ordinarily it ranges from ten to sixteen. The number of jobs falling into a grade and the difference in rates between grades will vary inversely with the number of labor grades used, and the number of rates will vary directly

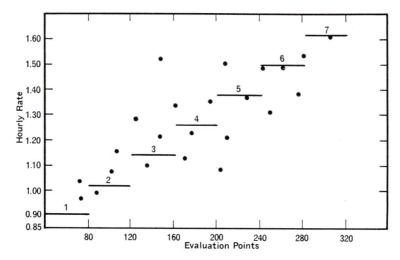

FIG. 7–15.—Relative positions of jobs with respect to seven labor grades.

with the number of labor grades used. Because of this, adjustments in the rate structure will be affected by the number of grades decided upon.

By altering the number of grades, it is possible to manipulate a large number of jobs from one grade to another. Figures 7–15 and 7–16 illustrate the effect of altering the number of labor grades. Figure 7–15 reflects the relative position with respect to labor grades when seven grades are used. The grades are so placed that eleven jobs fall above and twelve jobs fall below the lines. However, as a study of Figure 7–16 brings out, by increasing the number of labor grades to nine, the number of jobs falling above the line is increased to fifteen while the number falling below the line is reduced to eight. It may be assumed, then, that because the number of labor grades used will have an ultimate effect on the wage structure

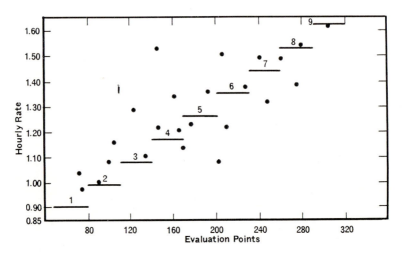

FIG. 7–16.—Relative positions of jobs with respect to nine labor grades.

the matter will be subject to negotiation where a union is participating in the installation.

Table 7–1 sets forth a distribution of sixteen labor grades as used in a clerical evaluation point plan. As shown in the

TABLE 7–1

LABOR GRADE EVALUATION POINT RANGES

Labor Grade	Range of Evaluation Points	Labor Grade	Range of Evaluation Points
1...............	Up to 894	9...............	1,385–1,454
2...............	895–964	10...............	1,455–1,524
3...............	965–1,034	11...............	1,525–1,594
4...............	1,035–1,104	12...............	1,595–1,664
5...............	1,105–1,174	13...............	1,665–1,734
6...............	1,175–1,244	14...............	1,735–1,804
7...............	1,245–1,314	15...............	1,805–1,874
8...............	1,315–1,384	16...............	1,875 and up

table, there is a constant 70-point range for each labor grade
Constant point ranges are not always the case, however, as
arbitrary, arithmetic, or geometric progressions may be used.
Where a more even distribution of jobs between grades is desired but cannot be accomplished through the use of constant
ranges, a progression may be used. Trial and error and negotiation usually dictate the number and progressions of ranges
to be used. Table 7–2 illustrates a progressive distribution of
points to labor grades which was used with a point rating plan
in a plant where the union had considerable say in the forma-
tion of the wage structure.

TABLE 7–2

PROGRESSIVE DISTRIBUTION OF POINTS TO LABOR GRADES

Labor Grade	Range of Evaluation Points	Extent of Point Range
1	Up to 224	. . . . . .
2	225–242	18
3	243–262	20
4	263–284	22
5	285–308	24
6	309–334	26
7	335–362	28
8	363 and over	. . . . . .

Single Rates versus Rate Ranges for Labor Grades

In most instances the answer to the question of whether a
single rate or a rate range is to be applied to each labor grade
is provided when it is known whether or not a system of merit
rating is to be incorporated into the system of compensation.
Merit rating is discussed in detail in a later chapter. There are,
however, other factors that may have to be considered, such as
the attitude of the workers as reflected in collective bargaining,
past company practice, present industry and area practice, the
type of incentive plan used, if any, and budgetary and cost
control and cost estimating procedures.

Single Rates.—Where a single rate is assigned to a labor grade, all jobs falling into that grade automatically receive the assigned rate. For example (Fig. 7–15), the second labor grade will carry the single rate of $1.02, and all jobs falling directly above or directly below the second labor grade line will receive $1.02; any other jobs which in the future evaluate out at between 80 and 120 points will receive the same rate.

With the use of a single rate for each labor grade, the number of rates in effect at any one time may sometimes be governed by the number of labor grades. However, there are very few cases where this is absolutely true, for there are above-the-line or "ringed" rates which may not be eliminated for a considerable period of time. It must be recognized, however, that the use of a single rate does tend toward maximum simplicity of the wage structure. A minimum of rates heips to ease the timekeeping and payroll jobs. Because there is greater assurance of rate stability, cost and price estimating is simplified and becomes more reliable. The single rate is particularly advantageous where standard costs and budgetary control are concerned, for the cost standards and budgeted control limits are more accurately and easily established and variances more easily analyzed.

An added advantage of the single rate for each labor grade is the tendency toward eliminating favoritism and pressure by employees who have aggressive sales personalities. Two often claimed advantages of job evaluation are its ability to reduce wage rate favoritism to a minimum and its ability to render the advertising ability of the employee impotent. If the claims are justified, then it appears that a single rate for each labor grade aids in accomplishing a mission of job evaluation. As for favoritism on the part of supervision, it should be recognized that rate increases are not the only means of favoring employees; if such a tendency exists, other means can be found.

Rate Ranges.—If a rate range is assigned to each labor grade, all jobs falling into a particular grade will carry the rate range of that grade. Thus, if the range of rates for a labor grade having a point range of 309 to 334 points is from $1.35 to $1.50, then all jobs evaluated at between 309 and 334 points will fall in the $1.35 to $1.50 rate range and employees holding such jobs will receive a minimum of $1.35 but not more than $1.50 per hour.

There is little advantage in applying rate ranges to labor grades other than that it enables management to reward an employee for factors not recognized in either job evaluation or wage incentives. Any claim to popularity must evolve from the desire of some managements to employ a system of merit rating. Therefore, if management can assure itself that the advantages of merit rating outweigh its disadvantages, some advantage will accrue through the application of rate ranges to labor grades.

Because there will be more than one rate for each labor grade, the number of rates handled by timekeeping and payroll personnel may prove to be somewhat cumbersome. Because identical operations may receive rates embracing the entire rate range, the problems of estimating costs and of cost and budgetary control become more complex. For example, if a cost standard is to be set for purposes of pricing or cost control, the question will arise as to what rate, within a rate range, should be used in arriving at the standard. If the top rate of the range is used, there will invariably be a favorable labor price variance, for rarely will all employees receive the top rate; conversely, the variance will be unfavorable if the bottom rate is used. While use of the middle rate of the range may appear to be more logical, it could easily happen that the trend in variances would be from favorable to unfavorable, indicating a trend of increasing laxity on the part of supervision in properly utilizing labor when, in reality, such a trend would not be an actual fact but the result of automatic increases in rates within the range. In budgeting, the same problem is posed.

There is nothing in the application of rate ranges that is deterrent to favoritism in passing out wage increases except perhaps the top limit placed on the range. Further, constant pressure of organized groups or aggressive individuals will have a tendency toward forcing the rates upward within the range with the possible result that eventually all the rates will be at the range ceiling. Under such conditions, differentials cease to exist as does the excuse for rate ranges.

Number and Limits of Rate Ranges

The Number.—The number of rate ranges will depend upon the number of labor grades. Therefore, because the number of labor grades will have an effect on the shape of the wage structure, the matter of the number of rate ranges will be a subject for collective bargaining; however, if there is no employee representation, the sole judgment of management will determine the number of grades. It is possible, however, that, after an agreement has been reached on the number of labor grades to be used, some adjustments will have to be made if the number agreed upon was conducive to unsatisfactory money increments between grades causing excessive or insufficient money range overlap.

The Extent.—The extent of the rate range will, for the most part, be determined by what is judged to be a sufficient amount of incentive as required by the system of merit rating in use. Too extensive a rate range, however, may render it difficult to determine, within a satisfactory degree of accuracy, just where within the range a particular employee belongs. As in the case of wage incentives, the use of an incentive in merit rating of less than 20 per cent is generally recognized as a poor practice. The usual policy is to employ a money range of 15 to 25 per cent of the minimum rate applied to the labor grade. For example, assuming a 20 per cent range to be satisfactory, if a labor grade has a minimum rate of 90 cents, then the rate range for the labor grade would be 18 cents.

Consideration must be given to the extent of the rate range of one labor grade in relation to the range of another labor grade. Such relations will usually be determined by negotiation of the limit lines and the influences of industry practices and company customs. Limit lines may be set in any one of a number of ways, the most common being the constant or the variable percentage. An error is sometimes made in applying constant money limits to each labor grade. In such instances the limit lines run parallel to the conversion line as in Figure 7–17. Depending on the extent of the limits established, such a practice will penalize the jobs at one end of the scale or apply excessive ranges to those at the other end. In the example, it will be seen that the 16-cent constant range between limit lines

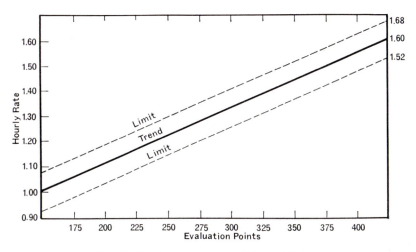

Fig. 7–17.—Constant money (16 cent) limits.

amounts to a range of 16 per cent for the first labor grade but to only 10 per cent at the top of the scale. This would be tantamount to setting relatively loose incentive rates for low-skilled jobs and to tightening rates progressively up the rate scale.

Figure 7–18 illustrates a more commonly used and equitable procedure for establishing limit lines, namely, the constant percentage limits method. This method permits the same percentage range at both ends of the scale but, as will be brought out later, is conducive to an undesirable amount of rate range overlap. Another solution, which reduces the amount of overlap, is the use of variable percentage limit lines

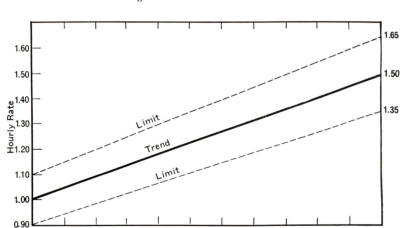

Fig. 7–18.—Constant percentage (20 per cent) limits.

that converge near the lower end of the scale. Lines of this type are illustrated in Figure 7–19.

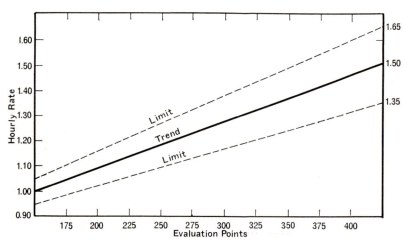

Fig. 7–19.—Straight trend with varied percentage limits; 10 per cent at bottom, 20 per cent at top.

Inspected-in Lines.—Limit lines having constant money, percentage, or variable percentage spreads may also be applied to inspected-in or logarithmic trend lines. One such example is reflected in Figure 7–20 illustrating a logarithmic trend line with varied percentage limits.

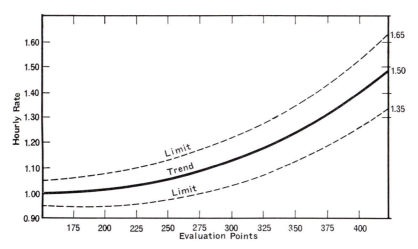

Fɪɢ. 7–20.—Logarithmic trend with varied percentage limits; 10 per cent at bottom, 20 per cent at top.

Overlap.—Connected with the use of rate ranges as applied to labor grades is the problem of the amount of money range overlap. Primarily, some overlap is required for the support of merit rating; but it is also desirable for flexibility in the limits within which employees may be moved where transfers are expedient. On the other hand, excessive overlap is apt to lead to a chaotic rate structure and defeat of the primary objectives of job evaluation. The problem of overlap is usually solved through trial and error and negotiation, and, as a result, management will probably arrive at its own policy in covering the matter. Figure 7–21 depicts rate ranges as applied to labor grades having equal evaluation point values. The ranges are confined to the limit lines established on the basis of constant percentage limits. It will be noted that the overlap is excessive, ranging from 80 to 84 per cent.

Overlap is lessened where a varied percentage is employed as in Figure 7–22; however, even in this case the overlap is

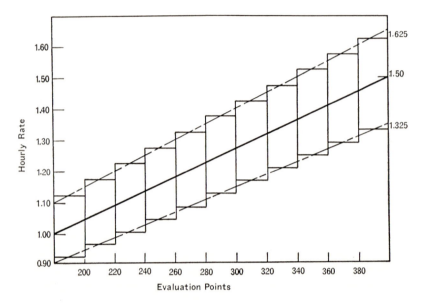

FIG. 7–21.—Rate ranges with excessive overlap based on constant percentage limit lines and equal worth ranges.

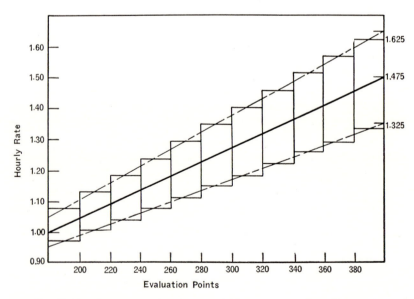

FIG. 7–22.—Rate ranges based on variable percentage limit lines and equal worth ranges. Overlap is excessive.

excessive, being 60 per cent in the first labor grade and pro-
gressing upward until it reaches 83 per cent in the top grade.
A means of further adjusting the overlap is to alter the number
of labor grades. Figures 7–21 and 7–22 show the same number
of labor grades and the same point ranges, the differences in
overlap being the result of the alteration of limit lines. Figure

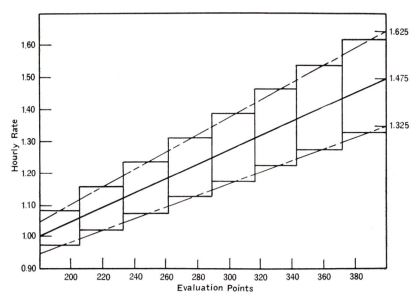

Fig. 7–23.—Overlap reduced, as compared with Figure 7–22. Eight rather
than eleven labor grades are used with variable percentage limit lines and equal
worth ranges.

7–23 reflects the same trend and limit lines as in Figure 7–22
but uses eight rather than eleven labor grades of equal worth.
The resulting overlaps range from 47 per cent at the lower end
of the scale to 70 per cent at the upper end. Still another
method of altering the amount of overlap is shown in Figure
7–24. The same trend limit line is used as in Figures 7–22 and
7–23, but the labor grade point ranges increase progressively
as the top grade is approached. The use of ten grades pro-
gressing in point worth results in overlap ranging from 65 per
cent at the lower end of the scale to 60 per cent at the upper end.

The application of proper rate ranges to labor grades, then, involves considerable experimenting with variations in the number of labor grades, their point values, and the relative position of limit and trend lines. It will be found that the use of expanding worth ranges, limit lines of varying percentages, and limit lines perhaps raised somewhat at the lower end of

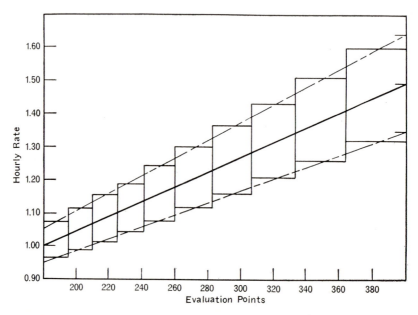

Fig. 7–24.—Rate ranges based on variable percentage limit lines and worth ranges.

the scale will provide the most satisfactory solution to maintaining money range overlap at a point where in no instance will there be an overlap between more than two successive labor grades.

Preliminary Considerations in Applying Money to Labor Grades

After constructing conversion lines and determining the number and ranges of labor grades, there remains the matter of assigning the money rates. Prior to solving the problem, consideration must be given to certain controversial subjects which have direct bearing on the shape of the wage structure, such as the incorporation of age and sex differentials, whether the same scale will apply to both manual and clerical jobs, whether the present scale of rates is satisfactory, whether a labor survey should be made to guide in the establishment of a new scale, and if such a survey is made what policies the company will pursue toward maintaining a specific relationship between its rates and the rates prevailing in the locality. In addition, study should be made of the relation of labor to other costs, the financial condition of the company, living costs, past policies and practices regarding area wage rates, and what effect collective bargaining will have on the assigning of money values to labor grades.

Age and Sex Differentials.—Tradition has been the underlying force behind the attitude of industry toward paying women less than men for the same work. Despite the increased application of the principles of job evaluation to wage structures and the pressure of collective bargaining, there still are many concerns which use different wage scales for men and women employees.

If the principle of evaluating the job and not the man is adhered to, there appears to be little justification for such differences in rates. Claims of justification usually rest on the economic fact that women are available at rates lower than those paid to men. It is frequently argued, however, that even though men and women may be working on the same job, they will rarely do the same amount of work, for women are not capable of the same physical exertion as men. Where there is proper delineation of jobs within a plant, such differences in job requirements will be recognized and the jobs evaluated accordingly; therefore, if jobs are properly identified and described, there will be little need for sex differentials to be arbitrarily established. In the face of a sound program of job evaluation, the adoption of industrial relations policies calling for like treatment of all employees in like situations, collective bargaining agreements, social justice, and legislation, it has become increasingly difficult to find justification for sex differentials.

There also appears to be little more foundation for paying boys and girls less than men and women for the same work than there is for employing sex differentials. Age should have no bearing on the wage structure to be used. Any peculiarities of a job which might require consideration of age should be set forth in the identification and description of the job and the job evaluated accordingly, thus rendering age differentials unnecessary.

Same Scale for Manual and Clerical Jobs.—Before arriving at a decision as to whether or not the same wage scale is to be used for both manual and clerical jobs, the reasons advanced for using different scales should be deliberated. As in the case of sex differentials, tradition has dictated the practice of compensating clerical employees on a lower scale than that of manual workers. Whatever reasons may exist for the differences, they are becoming more difficult to justify; and, because of this, continuation of the practice has been instrumental in the unionization of many clerical forces.

It has been possible in the past to hire clerical employees at lower rates primarily because of the certain privileges and advantages which accrue to office jobs, such as vacations, sick leave, an element of security that tradition decrees is available only to office personnel, the greater social prestige attached to clerical occupations, better working conditions, and the fact that manual jobs require a greater expenditure of physical effort. If such are the reasons advanced for the use of different wage scales, some of them are rapidly disappearing while others can be recognized in the job evaluation plan.

Such privileges as vacations and sick leave are now available to the shopworkers of many plants as a result of liberalization of management policy, union effort, and some governmental action. The differences in social prestige disappeared somewhat during World War II when large numbers of white-collar workers transferred their efforts to manual jobs. The vocational training courses offered by many public schools are also doing much to fill the social gap between the clerical and manual worker. While there is little doubt but what the clerical worker enjoys better working conditions and that his job is not as physically tiring as that of the manual worker, it must be realized that a job evaluation plan which is developed to cover both manual and clerical jobs should, if properly designed, recognize the factors of physical effort and working conditions regardless of whether or not the same wage scale is used in compensating both types of jobs.

Considerations before Eliminating Differentials.—The arguments for maintaining a manual-clerical differential no longer appear to be defensible; however, there are certain practical considerations to be reckoned with before eliminating an existing differential. One such consideration would be the cost and the effect of the cost increase on the company's profit picture. Not only must the direct cost be considered but also any cost which may result from the adjustments that might have to be made in administrative and executive salaries and from the possibilities of equalizing employee benefits. Other considerations would be the effect the elimination of the differential might have on the available supply of clerical labor and the intangible morale benefits that might accrue. Likely pressure of collective bargaining should also be weighed.

Wage Level Policy.—In the previous chapter it was stated that management is frequently guilty of going through all the motions of a job evaluation only to forget that what has been accomplished may not be of value if the evaluation is applied to an inadequate wage scale. Merely accepting the top and bottom rates of the present scale as correct and inserting rate ranges and labor grades within the top and bottom limits is very apt to defeat the many advantages of the project. Any wage scale in which inequities have existed is subject to investigation even though the jobs have been evaluated and their worth relationships established. It is advisable, therefore, for management to secure the necessary facts by conducting a wage survey and upon analyzing the results, to determine what position in the labor market the company wishes to maintain.

a) Policy of Average Position.—The most logical and satisfactory circumstance for the majority of companies is to maintain an average position in which the base and average earned rate curve is identical with that of the area and industry and where the average minimum hiring rate and miscellaneous additions to income are also the same.

b) Policy of Low Wage Scale.—Certain circumstances, however, may prevent assuming such an average position. Companies in which poor management has depleted capital, new companies having limited capital, companies engaged in marginal undertakings, or companies under management of personnel who mistakenly believe that low wage scales are conducive to increased profits will be those most likely to pursue policies of lower-than-average wage scales. Such policies usually make for difficulty in securing an adequate labor force, increased labor turnover, and a resulting increase in training and break-in costs.

c) Policy of Leadership.—There are, of course, those companies who believe that a policy of leadership is the best one to pursue. However, before deciding on such a course of action, the long-term possibilities should be investigated; for while such a policy may facilitate employment and be desirable during periods of rapid expansion, labor scarcity, or both, the position of leadership may become unenviable as well as difficult to withdraw from. Another point to regard is whether the policy will attract better-than-average producers. Such a claim may be hard to substantiate.

Factors Influencing Policy.—The fundamental aspects of business management preclude formulating any policy of labor market position without first considering the effects of the course of action. The results of changes in labor costs on the pricing structure, sales volume, relationship of labor cost to other costs,

financial status of the company, fiscal policies, and past practices should be examined prior to reaching a decision on the
matter. The influences of social and economic legislation must
be considered in conjunction with the changes in wage level
policy, and union negotiations must be given due weight inasmuch as the general wage levels are a joint consideration of
union and management. In recent years, cost of living trends
have been given serious weight in many wage scale adjustments; and they, too, should be considered prior to taking a
definite stand on the position to be taken in the labor market.

Assignment of Money to Labor Grades

Up to this point, evaluated jobs have been plotted on the
scatter diagram; a conversion line has been drawn and adjusted
to reflect the negotiated money scale, the wage rate survey, or
both; the number and worth of labor grades has been determined; and, when used, the extent of rate ranges has been
decided. There remains the problem of assigning money values
to the labor grades; a problem which can be easily solved by
following a simple procedure.

The procedure involves plotting the final wage curve on a
sheet of graph paper large enough to permit reading off rates
to the nearest cent. Along the abscissa of the graph, the midpoint of each labor grade is marked, while up the ordinate,
the money scale is marked off. From the midpoint of each
labor grade, lines are drawn perpendicular to the abscissa and
extended upward until they meet the wage curve. From the
point of intersection with the curve, the lines are continued at
right angles and parallel with the abscissa and extended to meet
the ordinate or money rate scale. At the point where the line
intersects the money rate scale, the rate for the labor grade can
be read. See Figure 7–25.

If rate ranges are used, the single rates determined will be
increased and decreased according to the percentages determined for each labor grade. Thus, if a 5 per cent increase and

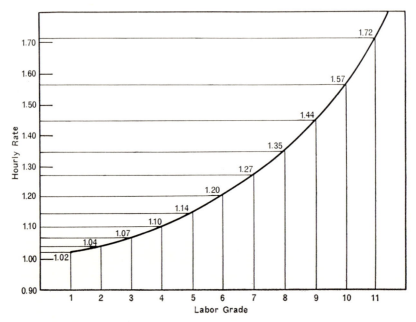

Fig. 7-25.—Determination of rates to be assigned to labor grades.

decrease is applied and the rate for the first labor grade is $1.00, then the range will be between 95 cents and $1.05.

QUESTIONS

1. What is meant by a "high-low conversion line"? What are your criticisms of the use of such a line?
2. When adjusting a high-low conversion line, who would benefit by raising the upper end of the line? The lower end? Under what circumstances would such adjustments take place?
3. What is the difference between a constant money increase and a constant percentage increase? What effect does each have on maintaining the relationship between jobs resulting from an evaluation?
4. How should a least squares conversion line be adjusted? Why?
5. Under what circumstances would a line by inspection be used?
6. What is your criticism of a single rate for each job? A range of rates for each job?

7. What is a labor grade? How many are ordinarily incorporated into the rate structure?

8. What effect can manipulating the number of labor grades have on the wage structure?

9. What are the advantages of applying single rates for labor grades? Under what circumstances are rate ranges applied to labor grades?

10. What determines the number of rate ranges? The extent of the rate ranges?

11. What is your criticism of the application of constant money limits to each labor grade?

12. What is meant by "overlap"? What type of limit lines tend to reduce overlap? How can overlap be adjusted?

13. What are some considerations preliminary to the application of money to labor grades?

14. How do you justify paying women less than men for the same work? The use of a different wage scale for manual and for clerical workers?

15. Explain the policy of average position; policy of low wage scale; and policy of leadership. What factors influence the formulation of such policies?

CHAPTER 8

SELLING JOB EVALUATION

S ELECTING the most vital phase of job evaluation is difficult, for each successive task involved in an installation is important to the success of the project. If any one phase is to be singled out as being most imperative, it will probably be selling the idea; even the basic purpose cannot be accomplished until the persons concerned with the results are convinced of the benefits that can be achieved through a sound application of job evaluation.

The Sales Program

Sales organizations spend thousands of dollars and months of time preparing for sales campaigns. With job evaluation, the campaign differs in the degree of preparation but is as important to the ultimate outcome of the program as the outcome of a sales manager's strategy is to the resulting sales volume. If, as is widely believed, sales are the blood stream of a business enterprise, then companies contemplating job evaluation should find little excuse for not receiving the co-operation of workers and supervisors through an intensive sales campaign. Is not the value of the required support worthy of planned strategy?

Since job evaluation has so many acceptable and desirable features, it can be sold to the employee, his union, and his supervisors just as easily as any other merchandisable article. However, it cannot be assumed that, because of its salability, the worker will rush to the bargain counter to buy a program for erasing rate inequities or that he can be easily sold with careless, slipshod methods. Only by approaching the worker, his union, and supervision in a manner similar to our way of approaching a valuable customer can we expect to close a deal with them. This does not mean that cajolery or emotional sales appeal has to be employed. It does mean placing before them a very down-to-earth program that will show the benefits of co-operation.

Before an attempt is made to sell a program, therefore, management must have at its disposal all the facts relating to the advantages of job evaluation. These facts should be assembled so that they can be directed toward those from whom the strongest resistance can be expected. Contrary to prevalent belief, the most difficult job, in many cases, is not selling the employee or his union but selling supervision. Supervisors have enjoyed the prerogative of setting rates by fiat for a much longer time than unions have enjoyed the prerogative of setting rates by collective bargaining, and, such being the case, supervision will have to be presented with irrefutable arguments before their resistance can be overcome.

Selling a program of job evaluation, then, requires that the data presented be properly organized, methods and techniques of presentation determined, and the sales plan forcefully executed. This chapter is devoted to the subject of organizing and presenting a program for selling job evaluation to those whose co-operation is so vitally important to a successful installation. The matter is presented through a discussion of the following topics:

1. Delineation of policy.
2. Employee participation.
3. Meeting with the union.
4. Meeting with supervision.
5. Organizing a training program.
6. Publicizing the program.

Delineation of Policy

Very often employees and supervisors will not be so much interested in the technicalities of the installation as in how they will be affected by it. Their interest will frequently be reflected in innumerable questions which can be answered through a clear, concise, and sincere expression of job evaluation policies. In many instances such an expression will be demanded by union representatives and will be in written form, either in cluded in or appended to the union-management agreement. Policies concerning who are to be the participants in the plan, what employees are to be included, how out-of-line rates are to be handled under numerous and varying circumstances, when the project is to be completed, and who is to administer the plan are among those which employees and supervisors must be familiar with and agree to before they can be expected to accept a proposal.

Of utmost importance will be management's policy in putting the idea across. Here enters the all-important question of employee participation as well as the problems of securing the co-operation of supervision and unions, training affected personnel in the application of job evaluation, and the steps to be taken to publicize the program. There must be absolute agreement on such policies, for the soundness with which they are formulated will determine to a considerable measure the success of the undertaking.

Employee Participation

The amount of employee support that a job evaluation program receives usually varies directly with the extent of employee participation in developing and executing the program. From its inception, plans must be made for taking the employees into management's confidence. Job evaluation is worked by no secret formula, and to treat it as such can result in it becoming an employee's guessing game. Keeping the worker in ignorance breeds confusion, suspicion, and rumor. News travels fast through plants and offices, and, unfortunately, what starts as fact usually ends as fiction unless the facts are made known before the guesswork has had an opportunity to do its damage.

Sudden alterations of practices and procedures, or changes in policy, confuse the rank-and-file worker; and he is resentful of things he does not understand. On the other hand, if he is prepared for the contemplated changes and logical explanations are given for the new undertaking, he will have an entirely different psychological reaction. The best way to acquaint the worker with the program is to allow him to be a part of it. To do so makes him feel that, no matter how humble his station, his co-operation and understanding are necessary, and this satisfies in him his craving for a feeling of importance.

A number of methods of employee participation are discussed later in this chapter. The important thing, however, is not the manner in which employees participate but the extent to which they are made to feel that it is their program.

Meeting with the Union

Probably the first step to be taken where a union is involved is to meet with the business agent or another official of the union, for he will have a deciding vote in approving the project. It will be necessary to learn his attitude toward job evaluation, what the general policies of the international union regarding rate inequities are, and whether he is free to approve the program without the consent of others. How the meeting is conducted will contribute greatly to the success of the program. Many such meetings have failed because of management's efforts to force a premature decision without giving the union representative an opportunity to study the proposal and its effects on the union membership. Unions are still young and distrustful of management innovations and are unwilling to buy a "pig-in-a-poke." There is no hocus-pocus about straightening out wage rate maladjustments; job evaluation as a method to solution can stand on its merits, and pressure tactics are not required to sell it.

At the first meeting with the union, there is one fundamental point that should be agreed upon and that is: which prerogatives concerning the administration of wages belong to the union and which belong to management. Reaching an agreement on this matter will lead to smoother relations in future meetings, in addition to pointing out the union's objections to job evaluation. At the preliminary meeting, details are not usually discussed. The plan to be used, how the wage curve is to be established, labor grades, and merit rating can be discussed at a later date, after the general idea has been approved. Presenting a full program for approval too early in the series of conferences may cause resentment by the union at not having been invited to participate in the project at its inception; also including too many details at this time may confuse the major issue for which the meeting was arranged.

After the first meeting with the union, and assuming favorable union reaction, the next step is to discuss the project details. In advance of these discussions, the subject matter should be well prepared and organized and include the plan to be used and the reasons why it was chosen, citing, if possible, other companies using it with success; methods of preparing job descriptions; who is to participate in the actual work of evaluating jobs; and a well-defined, frank statement of company objectives and policies.

At this time the matter of conducting meetings with union members can also be decided upon. Many union officials do not have sufficient knowledge of job evaluation to present it to their membership clearly, and they might welcome the assistance of someone who does.

Meetings with the membership, however, are frequently more successful if handled by consultants experienced in such matters, for employees are less dubious about the project if it is presented by impartial authorities. Another subject that should be considered is the advisability of holding training sessions for union stewards who may be called upon to participate in the preparation of job descriptions and the evaluation of jobs. This, of course, presupposes the decision of management to invite the union to take part in the program.

These meetings, then, are organized for the primary purpose of securing union co-operation through a frank explanation of what job evaluation is, what it involves, its advantages to those concerned, and company objectives and policies. Too many managements have learned too late that failure to secure union co-operation means failure of the program.

Meeting with Supervision

Having received satisfactory indications of union acceptance of job evaluation, management should prepare the organization for carrying out the program. The first approach should be through meetings with supervisors, for it is they who will be expected to assure the success and continuance of the program. Without such assurance, top management can expect no more favorable outcome than if they had failed to secure the co-operation of the employees and their representatives. Meetings should be held with groups numbering not more than twenty persons, if possible; however, a larger number can be invited to the first meeting when only generalities but no details are presented. Small groups are more conducive to open discussion and to a better understanding of the subject matter.

Where a preliminary meeting composed of all supervision is held, an officer or major executive of the company should open the meeting with appropriate introductory remarks stressing, for the most part, the desire of management for maximum co-operation from supervision. If a consultant has been engaged, the meeting may then be turned over to him. Some companies invite employee representatives to attend these meetings so that they will be assured that the same information is dispensed to all concerned. Where this has been a policy, the results have been extremely favorable.

One, and perhaps the most important, objective of these meetings is to explain the reasons for the program. A clear, concise announcement of the company objectives should be presented along with a statement of what the program is expected to accomplish. Factual data on reasons why other companies have instituted similar programs may be injected into the discussion. The fundamentals of job evaluation may be explained at this time, but the meetings should not take the place of the training conferences to be held at a later date when complete plans have been agreed upon.

Throughout these meetings, expressions of attitude toward job evaluation should be encouraged. Some of those present will undoubtedly challenge the feasibility of installing the plan, feeling that it will not accomplish all that is claimed for it. Here, the experiences of other companies in attaining the desired objectives may dispel many misgivings. Data on grievances resulting from rate inequities should be presented as a means of strengthening interest in the program. The use of job descriptions as instruments to be used in hiring, transferring, and promoting employees may have strong appeal to supervision.

Among those in attendance, a few, if not many, will be conscious of the potential loss of their prerogative of setting and manipulating wage rates. When such an attitude exists, and it usually does, it should be made clear that supervision will continue to have a voice in setting rates; they will be asked to participate, in many instances, as job evaluation committee members; their recommendations will receive due consideration; and they will contribute much of the information embodied in the job descriptions used in the evaluation process. In addition, they will no longer be suspected of favoritism in setting or manipulating rates. Supervision may be inclined to worry over union objection. However, if meetings are held after consent of the union has been received, their concern will be groundless; furthermore, the extent of union participation in the entire program should be outlined. These meetings have added value in that management will receive indications of who is most qualified to participate as committee members.

Co-operation must be a keynote of all the meetings. Because some will feel that they are to be divested of long-standing prerogatives, there will be some reticence toward working with the program to its successful conclusion. It is vitally important that supervision answer the questions of the analysts in an unbiased manner. There have been many instances where foremen have belittled a job by not giving due credit to all job characteristics only to find a dissatisfied employee after the newly evaluated rates have been announced. Co-operation with analysts should be stressed at these meetings.

It is altogether possible that some changes in job content should be made prior to the time the job is analyzed and evaluated in order to alleviate future disagreements and misunderstandings. Also, an employee may be assigned a low job classification but may be performing work of a higher classification. In such a situation the employee's classification should be changed or the employee should be instructed to do only the work required by the lower classification. This is an important step in preparing for the program, and supervision should be advised on the matter during these meetings.

Organizing a Training Program

Subsequent to the conferences with supervision and union representatives, a series of training sessions should be started. All plans should be definitely formulated, for those in whose hands responsibility for training is placed must be able to offer a well-organized program for imparting the necessary information within the allotted period of time. In planning the training sessions, attention should be focused on the matters of who shall conduct the sessions, who shall attend, subjects to be covered, schedule of meetings, and training aids to be employed.

It is imperative that those conducting the classes be well versed in all phases of job evaluation. This indicates that the person responsible for directing the job evaluation program may not necessarily be the one who will conduct the training sessions. If there is no one among the company personnel capable of effectively presenting the subject matter, it may be necessary to retain the services of a reliable consultant. The person selected for the task should be able to command attention, thus indicating an executive of the company; however, knowledge of the subject and a forceful presentation are more important than executive ability.

In attendance should be the supervisors down to and including the level of foremen or the equivalent, union officials who may be interested, and union stewards. Whether union representatives and supervisors attend these sessions together or as separate groups is a question of management policy. Attendance together may have the disadvantage of reducing the amount of classroom discussion because of a dislike for bringing up controversial union-management issues; however, there is little reason why any question concerning job evaluation should not be discussed openly. On the other hand, attendance at the same classes should help to improve the relations between supervisors and stewards and the workers' attitude toward management and to expedite the employees' understanding and acceptance of the company's wage administration policy.

The schedule of classes will depend on such circumstances as the number of personnel comprising each class, the capabilities of instructors, and the time available. When there are approximately twenty persons in each class, ten one-hour, daily sessions should be adequate for coverage of the subject matter. When classes are larger or instructors less competent, the number or duration of sessions may have to be increased. The most satisfactory classes are those held during working hours, preferably in the morning between nine and eleven o'clock when the mind is most receptive to instruction. Classrooms should be located on the company premises to facilitate practical demonstrations and to conserve time.

Meetings held prior to the start of the training sessions should serve to indoctrinate the trainees with the general concepts of job evaluation. Training sessions expand upon the generalities and treat the details in such a manner as to eliminate any notion of mysticism from the minds of those who are actually to participate in the installation. Management must rely, to a considerable extent, on supervisors and stewards to sell job evaluation to the rank and file, and these classes should equip them with the information necessary to do a selling job.

Subject matter of the training course should include such topics as why job evaluation is being used and what it is expected to accomplish; why a particular plan was selected and others considered but discarded; what the company policies with respect to job evaluation are; how jobs are analyzed and descriptions written; what the factors and their degree definitions mean, and how they are applied during the evaluation process if the point rating system is used; and how point and rate ranges and wage curves are established. Briefly, the course should be as extensive as time permits, leaving as little to the imagination of the students as possible. The last five to ten minutes of each session might be used for written "true or false" examinations. This has been done with excellent results.

Where the point rating system is to be used, the last two one-hour sessions might be devoted to establishing bench marks for each degree of each factor. If students are told ahead of time that they will be asked to submit names of jobs which they believe fit the various degrees of the factors, these sessions devoted to bench marks will prove to be the most enlightening of all. The instructor will know how well some of the theories taught in class have been applied; inconsistencies and misunderstandings can be ironed out; and, when group judgment is brought into agreement, certain bench marks can be permanently established for use during the evaluation of jobs.

Use of training aids should be made to the fullest extent possible and reading matter kept to a minimum. A copy of the job evaluation manual should be given to each person in attendance to be read during leisure hours. A list of texts might also be furnished those who are interested in further study. Many companies prepare booklets for distribution to all employees for the purpose of acquainting them with job evaluation. These might be used as classroom texts, provided the subject matter is expanded upon by the instructor; but such material does not, as a rule, go sufficiently into detail for training purposes. Large-scale reproductions of forms to be used should be made available to instructors whenever possible; for attention can then be focused on one point, and narrative explanations are easier to follow.

One of the most effective training aids is a motion picture or a series of slides. (Fig. 8–1.) These are particularly good if accompanied by a sound narrative. When the job evaluation program was instituted in the city-wide Y.M.C.A. of Chicago, comprising approximately 2,000 employees, the supervisory and other key personnel were shown a series of slides explaining job evaluation with excellent results. Many large companies are equipped to handle this method of presentation as are a number of the better-qualified management consulting organizations.

Publicizing the Program

Up to this point, the discussion of selling job evaluation has centered around contact with supervisors and union representatives; little has been said about selling the employee whose job is to be evaluated and who will be most directly affected by the program. Management should have in mind its methods of approaching this problem at the time the first conferences are held, and the machinery should be set in motion as soon as an agreement is reached with the union and the supervisors. Proper timing is imperative. Premature publicizing of the program may have crippling, if not fatal, consequences in the meetings attended by antagonistic elements; and, if publicity reaches the employee too late, rumor may have spread with harmful effect and agitators may have had their opportunity to organize disruptive campaigns. It is well to have all employees well informed prior to the time the analysts enter the offices or shops, for unless the analysts are evasive, they will spend considerable time explaining what the information they are seeking is to be used for. If employees know what job evaluation is, there is likely to be less rumor and more co-operation with analysts.

Many managements are prone to disregard the effects of social changes that have taken place during and since the thirties, and, therefore, they do not recognize the extent to which workers are demanding and receiving a voice in the policy-making that affects their wages, security, and working

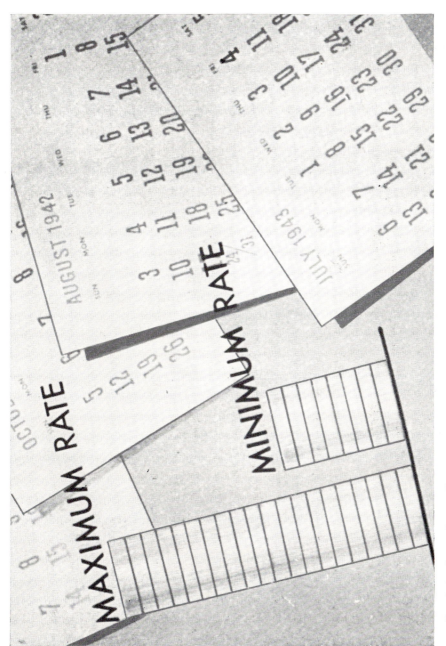

Fig. 8-1.—Scenes from a film strip used in a job evaluation training lecture. (Courtesy of Thadene Hayworth & Associates, Hollywood, California.)

conditions. Employees have always wanted to be told in advance of contemplated changes affecting them; now they demand this information. If, in the past, companies had pursued the practice of imparting information to their workers, they would not have been forced into it. Where job evaluation is concerned, the difference between the informed and misinformed employee is reflected in his attitude on the matter and in his reluctance to accept rumor as fact. Therefore, not only because they usually expect and want to be told but because rumor can be squelched and understanding bred, employees should be informed of the contemplated program. The method employed will be governed by the individual circumstances, but whatever it may be, it should be simple and understandable. However, certain systems of job evaluation—the factor comparison method, for example—are not easily described to employees and are not conducive to effective publicity.

One of the most effective and widely used media for introducing job evaluation to workers is a letter addressed to the employees and signed by an officer or executive of the company, preferably the president or general manager. One such letter is reproduced in Figure 8–2. It brings out two important points that employees are interested in, namely, it stresses management's support, and it assures the worker that his wages will not be reduced as a result of the program. The letter may be posted on bulletin boards, distributed by foremen and/or stewards, or mailed directly to the employee's home. The latter method has the advantage of the letter reaching the reader at a time when the contents can be more readily absorbed. Such a means of communicating the idea also tends to impress the recipient with the importance of the program and with his importance as a part of it. The results attained are well worth the time, effort, and postage involved. The least effective method of calling attention to the letter is by posting it on a bulletin board, for many workers will rarely evince enough interest to stop and read it.

Effective results have been attained through the publication and distribution of booklets which explain in some detail

THE YOUNG MEN'S CHRISTIAN ASSOCIATION *of* CHICAGO

G E N E R A L   O F F I C E S

19 SOUTH LA SALLE STREET
CHICAGO 3, ILLINOIS
C E N T R A L   6 7 8 7

January 25, 1947

To: All Employees

Your employer, the Y.M.C.A. of Chicago, has decided to carry
out a study of all jobs and positions in various departments
throughout the city for the purpose of establishing the proper
relationship of work assignments and compensation between such
jobs and positions.

As a means of insuring impartial results through this study, we
have employed the firm of_____
to make the necessary analysis of the duties and characteristics
involved in your jobs and positions. Their reputation for fairness and competence in such work is well established, and we
are confident that they will accomplish the task quickly and
effectively. However, we fully realize that the success of their
efforts is largely dependent upon the cooperation they receive
from all of you. Therefore, we ask that you do your best to
provide them with complete and accurate information about your
jobs. Some of you will receive questionnaires to fill out about
your work; others will be interviewed on the job by the_____
_____firm's engineers. In either case, your co-
operation is important.

No employee will suffer a reduction in compensation as a result
of this study, and it is probable that the final results may
enable some to benefit by redistribution of work assignments
and compensation on an equitable basis.

Should you have any questions about the project as it proceeds,
please feel free to bring them to the attention of the_____
_____personally, or
through your supervisor.

J. L. Nelson
Executive Secretary

FIG. 8-2.—A letter introducing the job evaluation program to employees.

the general principles of job evaluation. The American Seating
Company, the Cooper-Bessemer Corporation, and the Thompson
Aircraft Company are among those who have explained their
wage structures to their employees in this manner. The Ameri-

PHYSICAL HAZARD . . .

the possibility of injury in any form to which the employee may be exposed in the performance of his job . . . *this not only includes the number of hazards, but also how severe they may be.*

JOB CONDITIONS . . .

a measure of the disagreeableness in the performance of the work . . . *such as heat, cold, humidity, dust, grease, paint, or other similar conditions.*

SAFETY OF OTHERS . . .

a measure of the care that must be exercised to avoid accidents to other employees . . . *what is the possibility of the operator on this job injuring others and the seriousness of the injuries.*

FIG. 8-3.—A page from the American Seating Company's booklet *You and Your Wages.*

can Seating Company booklet, *You and Your Wages,* (Fig. 8-3) not only explains job evaluation but merit rating and wage incentive as well. It is simply written, implemented with clever illustrations, and covers such topics as what job evaluation is, how it developed, how it works, the factors, factor definitions, and the application of factors. Many publications of this kind have one easily corrected weakness in that not enough space is devoted to the declaration of management's job evaluation policies.

Another media often used for the publicizing of wage administration policy changes is the house organ (Fig. 8-4). This method has the advantages of good distribution and of coverage of the employees; it is usually read at the employee's leisure and is conducive to informality of presentation of subject matter. The Stewart-Warner Corporation of Chicago, and Sharp & Dohme, Incorporated, of Philadelphia, are examples of companies using house organs for the purpose of taking personnel into their confidence on contemplated changes in wage administration practices.

There are other means of accomplishing what letters, booklets, and house organs can do. However, regardless of methods, due consideration should be given to discussing them with union representatives; for here, too, an opportunity presents itself to seek union participation in the program.

QUESTIONS

1. What are some of the policies employees and supervisors will want to be informed about before they can be expected to accept a program of job evaluation?

2. Give your reasons for believing or for not believing that employees should participate in a job evaluation program.

3. Do you believe that employee participation in a job evaluation program interferes with management's right to manage its business?

4. Why is a meeting with union representatives an important first step in selling a job evaluation project? What is one fundamental point to be agreed upon at the first meeting with the union?

5. What are the purposes of the meetings with supervision? What should be the keynote of such meetings?

Here's How Job Evaluation
Was Used to Set New Rates

The new wage schedule which went into effect last week as a result of the wage agreement signed yesterday, is based upon a scientific job evaluation survey which required the work of five highly trained men working for more than a year to properly study and rate the 750 different jobs performed by S-W employees.

This program directly affects every S-W employee. In order that all may better understand what job evaluation means and how it operates, the following article which was prepared by R. J. Muldoon, chief of the job evaluation section of the Personnel Department, and which appeared originally in the March 20th issue of your plant paper, is being reprinted:

There is no mystery or secrecy about job evaluation. It is simply a systematic method of comparing the requirements of one job with those of another.

Job evaluation is nothing more or less than an additional way of making certain that our wage policy is applied fairly over the entire organization.

It does NOT set rates.

It DOES make sure that a value is set upon each job in fair proportion to the value of every other job in the plant.

It does NOT measure YOUR abilities.

It DOES measure what the JOB requires of you.

Naturally, you want to know how a value was set on your particular job, and this article will attempt to answer that question.

In determining the worth of your job, certain factors which are common to all jobs are considered. These are Skill, Effort, Responsibility and Job Conditions. These major factors are so large that it is impossible to accurately review them as a whole. The most logical procedure then, is to analyze each of the elements which go to make up the major factors.

These elements are as follows:

SKILL:

1. Education: This element appraises the schooling or technical training which is ordinarily required to learn a job.

2. Experience: This element appraises the length of time usually required by an individual with the specified education or trade training to learn to perform the work satisfactorily.

3. Initiative and Ingenuity: These elements deal with the independent action, exercise of judgment, making of decisions or the amount of planning which the job requires.

EFFORT:

4. Physical Demand: This element appraises the amount of physical effort required.

5. Mental and Visual Demand: Alertness required, concentration and coordination of manual dexterity with mental attention are considered in rating this element.

Fig. 8–4.—Explaining job evaluation to employees from the house organ *The Stewart Warnerite* of Stewart-Warner Corporation.

RESPONSIBILITY:
6. For Equipment: This element appraises the responsibility for preventing damage to the equipment or process used in the performance of the job.
7. For Material: This element appraises the responsibility for preventing waste or loss of raw material or partially finished products through carelessness.
8. For Safety of Others: This element appraises the care which must be exercised to prevent injury to others.
9. For Work of Others: This element appraises the responsibility which goes with the job for instructing or directing the work of others.

JOB CONDITIONS:
10. Working Conditions: This element appraises the surroundings or physical conditions under which the job must be done and the extent to which those conditions make the job agreeable.
11. Hazards: This element appraises the accident hazards connected with or surrounding the job.

Each of the above elements is broken down into five different degrees, and each degree assigned a specific number of points. For example, under the education factor the toolmaker's job would require a four-year apprenticeship and receive 56 points, while the simpler or laboring job would only require the ability to read and write and receive 14 points.

In rating the various jobs, every effort is made to insure the greatest possible degree of accuracy and impartiality. Briefly, the procedure is as follows: Two men from the job evaluation group tour a department accompanied by the department head or foreman and observed the various types of work being done, the equipment used, the effort required and the working conditions. Additional information, such as education and experience required for the job and responsibility for equipment and materials is obtained from the department head.

The jobs are then written up by one of the men, checked by the other, reviewed by the Job Evaluation group as a whole, and rechecked by the head of the group. If there is any question as to the correctness of the rating of any particular job, other members of the rating group observe the job and the correct rating is determined.

After a point rating was established for each job according to the above procedure, all the jobs in the plant were then divided evenly into groups or labor grades, according to their point value. Minimum and maximum rates based on the prevailing rates for the various types of work in the Chicago area as found by the War Labor Board were then set up and progressive rates worked out for each labor grade in proportion to its point value, allowing for progression within the labor grade.

From this outline it will be apparent that the job evaluation plan gives each worker the satisfaction of knowing that his job is in the same classification and carries the same rate of pay as other comparable jobs elsewhere in the plant, and that the rates of pay provided in all classifications are comparable to or above the rates being paid for similar work in other plants.

FIG. 8–4.—*Continued.*

6. Who should conduct job evaluation training sessions? Who should attend them? How many sessions should there be?

7. What training aids are useful in explaining job evaluation?

8. Why is it so important that employees be told in advance of a job evaluation program?

9. What do you believe to be the most effective media for publicizing a job evaluation program?

CHAPTER 9

THE COMMITTEE

THE hasty forming and improper staffing of committees has, in many instances, resulted not only in unsatisfactory job evaluation installations but in poorly administered programs as well. Before appointing a committee, due consideration should be given to such matters as its functions, responsibilities, authority, composition, and size. This chapter is devoted to a discussion of these matters.

Because of the unscientific nature of job evaluation, it is necessary to rely, to a considerable extent, on human judgment. The judgment of the individual varies from day to day, may be easily warped by a slight change in mental or physical condition, and in general lacks the consistency required by job evaluation. In order that inconsistency in judgment may be averaged out, group judgment is resorted to. This is the primary reason why a committee is used during most phases of job evaluation. However, committees have advantages in other respects.

One benefit of a committee is that it enables participation in a program by management, supervision, and employees or their representatives, thus permitting the necessary co-operation between the various groups affected by a job evaluation project. The possibility of one person having a knowledge of all the jobs to be evaluated is somewhat remote, but a committee that includes a rotating representative for each department will be more likely to have at hand information on any job to be considered.

Functions and Responsibilities

In too many cases the committee is set up for the sole purpose of evaluating jobs. If the evaluation procedure was the only phase of the program requiring group judgment, such a policy might be condoned; but there are other problems that cannot be safely judged by an individual. The weighting of factors, the clarity of factor and degree definitions, the choice of the plan, the factors to be used, and the number of degrees to be used for each factor are all problems that are more accurately solved through group rather than individual application. Not only is it advisable, from the standpoint of consistency of results, to have the committee pass judgment on these problems but also because the best-qualified group and the one which will produce the best results within the shortest span of time is the one that is thoroughly acquainted with each and every phase of the project.

The functions and responsibilities of the committee will depend on the extent to which management is willing to delegate the work required in executing the program. Some committees are assigned the single task of analyzing jobs and preparing job descriptions; others confine their efforts to the evaluation or ranking of jobs; still others may be appointed for the purpose of selecting or devising a plan, for conducting a wage survey, or perhaps for establishing the wage curve and determining the number and extent of labor grades and rate ranges, if employed. (See Fig. 9–1.)

In larger companies it is often the practice to establish a steering committee to which is delegated the responsibility for executing that portion of the program which management believes should be handled by a group. This body may, in turn, appoint subcommittees to handle specific phases of the project, such as devising a plan, making a locality wage survey, or evaluating certain types of jobs. Such a procedure is advantageous to large companies in that it permits a number of phases of the program to be worked on at one time, the work being co-ordinated by a central body. Considerable time can be saved, for example, by having the committee assigned the task of preparing job descriptions begin their work far enough in advance to keep the committee doing the evaluating well backlogged with descriptions; while both of those committees are busy, a third might be conducting a wage survey to be completed in time for use in establishing the wage curve.

Where smaller companies are engaged in job evaluation, a single body will suffice, provided the chairman is a capable director and co-ordinator. Proper guidance is of utmost im-

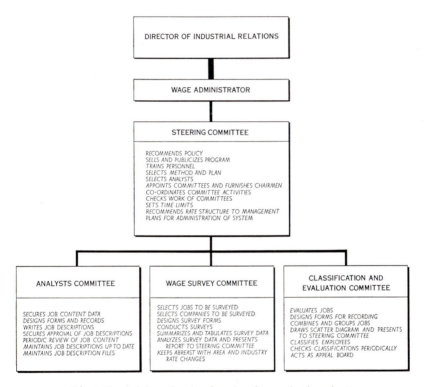

Fig. 9–1.—A job evaluation functional organization chart.

portance to the successful functioning of a committee. If the efforts of the group are to be effective, a strong, level-headed person, familiar with all phases of job evaluation and having at least a fair knowledge of the content of the jobs to be evaluated, should be designated as chairman.

In most instances it will be found that the only person who can fulfill these requirements is the individual who has been responsible for the completion of many of the early phases of the project, that is, the chief job analyst. In the event that this person's personal characteristics do not measure up to the requirements, it may be necessary to select a member of the executive staff to direct the committee's activities. In any case, the matter of committee guidance must be given full consideration if the group is to function and to meet its responsibilities in a satisfactory manner.

In Chapter 10 the functional responsibility of executing and maintaining the job evaluation is discussed. It is stated that the duties of the person in whom authority is vested for carrying out the program are largely administrative and that the committees are charged with handling the necessary details for executing the plans. It is logical, therefore, that the committee be responsible and report to the person it is to assist. This may be the director of labor relations, the wage administrator, employment manager, or some other person responsible for the administration of wages and salaries.

Composition of Committee

Determining the number of personnel to serve on the committee is not a routine matter. The circumstances involved vary with the size of the company, the presence or absence of a union among employees, and with the group of employees whose jobs are being evaluated. The two major principles to be observed in determining committee size are that there be a sufficient number of persons to permit reliance upon their group judgment and that the number be small enough to work closely together to avoid confusion and unwieldiness.

Steering Committee.—Where a company is large enough to use a steering committee, such a committee does not necessarily have to be large; in fact, the smaller committee will probably be more effective in co-ordinating the efforts between members. The steering committee, if small, might consist of the wage and salary administrator and the chief job analyst representing management, two union members, preferably officers, representing the employees, and an impartial fifth member. Expansion in the size of this committee might be accomplished through the addition of department superintendents and key members of the union.

Union Participation.—Opinion is divided on the question of equal participation of union and management. Union personnel may object to the selection of what they deem to be a top-heavy committee composed of from five to seven representatives of management and only two representatives of the employees. Normally such an objection might be very serious, but the principle of operation of an evaluation committee is similar to that of a jury. Each member should be free to express his opinion and, if possible, to sway the opinion of others; but there should be final agreement among the group, or the result is of little benefit to anyone.

One large union objects to its members participating in any part of the work of evaluation committees. The union's objection is based on the fear that its members may be bound by a mistake of their representatives; and its leaders prefer to be in a position to criticize the evaluation without being reminded that they have agreed to a certain job value or principle of the plan being used. Fortunately, however, many local officials have come to realize that a spirit of co-operation between the union and the management will produce better over-all results, even though one or two union members might be required to accept a decision with which they are not in complete agreement.

Analyst's Committee.—In the large majority of job evaluations, a single committee handles all phases of the installation. This is done because most companies are not large enough to require more than one committee and there is usually a lack of qualified personnel. The single group is most often referred to as the analyst's committee and is delegated the task of studying jobs, preparing descriptions, and evaluating or ranking jobs. Such a committee should rarely exceed seven members but should include, for practical purposes, equal participation between management and the union. A suggested membership for this type of committee is as follows:

1. The chief job analyst.
2. A second job analyst.
3. The foreman.

4. An officer of the union local.
5. The chief union steward.
6. The department union steward.

The foreman and department steward should be rotating members, representing the department in which the jobs are being observed and evaluated. When the work in one department is completed, the foreman and steward return to their department and the foreman and steward of the next department to be worked in take their place on the committee. Such a procedure has the advantage of keeping the size of the group down to an efficient size, educating each foreman and steward in many of the principles of job evaluation, and assuring the inclusion of personnel who have a wide store of knowledge concerning each specific job.

The suggested committee assumes the presence of a union. If the employees whose jobs are to be evaluated are not organized, the idea of employee representation need not be abandoned; for even though the employees cannot be bound by the action of informally selected representatives, their confidence in the program will be enhanced by the knowledge that some of their number have been selected to participate in its formulation. The decision as to whether there shall be employee representation in the absence of a union depends on the attitude of management and the status of employer-employee relations within the company.

When only salaried positions are involved, the committee should include representation similar to that required for the evaluation of hourly paid factory jobs. However, the executives and the person responsible for the personnel function should be selected from the office rather than from the factory executive staff.

Regardless of how many committees may have a hand in the program, the analyst's committee should be the one that is set up on a permanent basis. After completion of the program, the system must be maintained and administered; and the logical body to handle the evaluation of new jobs, or jobs whose content has changed, is the same body that evaluated the other jobs. For this reason it is inadvisable to include executives as permanent members of the analyst's committee. Their positions rarely permit being absent for protracted periods, and reliability of attendance is required of the group membership. Executives are usually confined to rotating or steering committee membership.

Qualifications of Members.—When selecting members for committees, management and union alike should exercise care in choosing personnel who have the proper qualifications. The fact that a person holds a responsible executive position with the company or union does not necessarily mean that that person will make a satisfactory committee member. Each individual should have a reputation for fair dealing and be respected by management and employees. With the exception of employee participants, the members' earnings should be above the general earnings level of the jobs being evaluated. Analytical ability and a high degree of reasoning power are essential, particularly to those who are members of the steering committee, thus indicating executives as members of that body. At least one member of the steering committee should be closely allied with the industrial relations policies, problems, and function.

While neither management nor the union is in a position to select the entire body of the analyst's committee, the responsibility rests with each of those groups to select their own representatives. In selecting such a representative, it is necessary to bear in mind what his job consists of and the qualities essential to the performance of the task. An analyst of jobs must possess mechanical comprehension so that he can ask questions intelligently of operators and analyze mechanical processes. He must be able to comprehend the magnitude of the executive's problems and to understand the clerical routines of the office worker. He must be an inquisitive individual, possessing a flexible, curious, and analytical mind so that, regardless of the number of different types of jobs confronting him in any one day, he will be able to break them down and to analyze them.

As a writer of job descriptions, the analyst should possess a good vocabulary, well stocked with clear, concise, and understandable terms. He must possess literary ability, for it is essential that he be able to express in writing what he has learned about a job through observation and discussion, or from a questionnaire.

As an evaluator of jobs, he must possess excellent practical judgment, for he is the one who will determine to what degree a characteristic or factor is prevalent in a job. He must be able to match the job content against the factor degree definitions so that proper point values will be assigned to the job. He must use good judgment in approaching the workers to discuss and to observe their jobs. In addition, the analyst should have some knowledge of trend line computation and distribution curves.

In brief, a person qualified to sit on the analyst's committee should possess higher than average mentality, excellent practical judgment, the ability to get along with people, aptitudes for and/or interests in the mechanical, computational, literary, and clerical fields, and better-than-average analytical ability.

Selecting Analysts

Analysts may be selected from within the ranks of employees, or they may be secured from outside sources through the regular recruitment channels. When possible, and without sacrificing requirement standards, personnel should be selected from within the company. Use of this source has the advantage of enabling management to select from a group of employees having some knowledge of operations, processes, and policies, an acquaintance with personnel, and whose work habits and dependability are known.

On the other hand, using such a source without regard for essential requirements, can endanger a job evaluation program. One company almost completely sabotaged their job evaluation program by insisting on using, as analysts, unqualified personnel drawn from the employee's ranks. The union was also guilty of the same practice, for it appointed two union officers having few, if any, of the essential requirements for participating as members of the evaluation committee.

When analysts are recruited from sources outside the company, they should be required to have had previous practical experience in all phases of job evaluation in addition to the other necessary attributes. When selection is to be made from within the company's ranks, the personnel may be chosen from a group submitted by the personnel department, by supervision, or both. Management may also call for volunteers by publishing notices or by making such requests through the department heads.

Personnel Testing.—Regardless of what source furnishes the applicants, they should be thoroughly screened and interviewed; and those who appear to be the most desirable should be given a battery of tests to determine their fitness for the position of analyst. Many companies have their own testing facilities, but those that do not can resort to the services of a reliable personnel testing laboratory, or perhaps to the industrial psychology department of a near-by university.

Carl F. Bracken, an authority on personnel testing, believes that in addition to actual job knowledge the aptitudes, personality characteristics, and vocational interests of the individual should be carefully evaluated and measured against the requirements of the position. This can best be done by supplementing an objective, diagnostic interview with psychometric measurement. Bracken does not advocate the use of tests as a substitute for the interview but stresses their value as a refining instrument in the selection procedure. From his extensive experience in the selection of key personnel, both staff and line, he has been able to establish accurate means of psychometric measurement which, when used in combination with an interview, have materially improved the ratio of selection accuracy. With specific reference to the position of job analyst, he states:

The requirements of this position call for an individual with keen analytical ability and a strong degree of social intelligence. He must be practical and possess a good vocabulary so that he can express

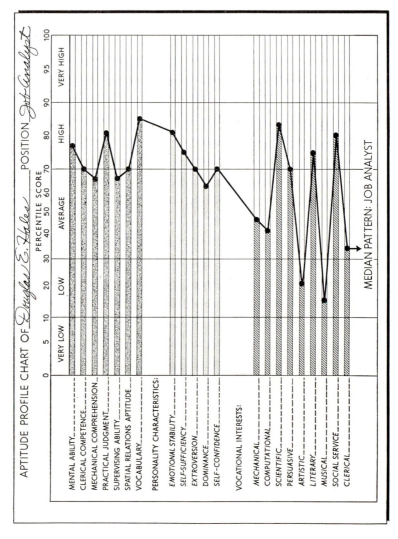

APTITUDE PROFILE CHART OF _Douglas E. Hales_ POSITION _Job Analyst_

PERCENTILE SCORE

| VERY LOW | LOW | AVERAGE | HIGH | VERY HIGH |

MENTAL ABILITY
CLERICAL COMPETENCE
MECHANICAL COMPREHENSION
PRACTICAL JUDGMENT
SUPERVISING ABILITY
SPATIAL RELATIONS APTITUDE
VOCABULARY

PERSONALITY CHARACTERISTICS:

EMOTIONAL STABILITY
SELF-SUFFICIENCY
EXTROVERSION
DOMINANCE
SELF-CONFIDENCE

VOCATIONAL INTERESTS:

MECHANICAL
COMPUTATIONAL
SCIENTIFIC
PERSUASIVE
ARTISTIC
LITERARY
MUSICAL
SOCIAL SERVICE
CLERICAL

MEDIAN PATTERN: JOB ANALYST

FIG. 9–2A

NAME: _Douglas E. Hales_   AGE: _34_

POSITION: _Job Analyst_   COMPANY:_____

TEST	RAW SCORE	PERCENTILE SCORE
MENTAL ABILITY_____		76
CLERICAL COMPETENCE_____		70
MECHANICAL COMPREHENSION__		65
PRACTICAL JUDGMENT_____		80
SUPERVISING ABILITY_____		65
SPATIAL RELATIONS APTITUDE___		70
VOCABULARY_____		82
PERSONALITY CHARACTERISTICS:		
EMOTIONAL STABILITY_____		80
SELF-SUFFICIENCY_____		75
EXTROVERSION_____		70
DOMINANCE_____		60
SELF-CONFIDENCE_____		70
VOCATIONAL INTERESTS:		
MECHANICAL_____		45
COMPUTATIONAL_____		40
SCIENTIFIC_____		85
PERSUASIVE_____		70
ARTISTIC_____		20
LITERARY_____		75
MUSICAL_____		15
SOCIAL SERVICE_____		80
CLERICAL_____		35

FIG. 9-2B

himself effectively. To a large extent, the results of his work will be reduced to writing, hence the importance of a good vocabulary. While it is not necessary for him to be mechanically inclined, he should have at least an average understanding of mechanical functions and relationships because many elements of jobs he will evaluate are of this nature.

From the standpoint of personality, the job analyst should be emotionally stable, poised, and self-confident. He must possess an ability for working with people because of the need to gain their confidence and co-operation.

. . . . I have found that vocational interests are of primary importance in measuring the long-range stability of an individual because of a basic need for obtaining job satisfaction. When the individual has an outlet for his dominant interests, he has made a good vocational choice and can be counted upon as a dependable employee. Conversely, he will soon become dissatisfied and a problem employee if the duties of his position do not provide such outlets.

In Job Analysts I have found, from experience, that their dominant interests lie in the mechanical, computational, persuasive, literary, and social service fields.[1]

An aptitude chart and a test scores sheet used in personnel testing are shown in Figure 9–2, A and B.

QUESTIONS

1. Why are committees used during most phases of job evaluation?
2. What are the functions and responsibilities of job evaluation committees other than the evaluation of jobs?
3. What is meant by a "steering committee"? Why is it advantageously used by large companies?
4. To whom should the committees report?
5. If you were a union official, would you or would you not object to members of your union participating as members of a job evaluation committee? Why?
6. As a member of management, where no union is involved, would you or would you not request employees to participate as members of a job evaluation committee? Why?
7. What qualifications do you believe a job evaluation committee member should have? A job analyst? Do you believe you would make a good job analyst? Why?

---

[1]From a personal interview by the authors.

CHAPTER 10

JOB EVALUATION ADMINISTRATION

THERE is frequent inclination on the part of management to feel that if a plan is well installed it will be self-perpetuating. Such an attitude induces inadequate administrative arrangements leading to a high mortality among job evaluation plans; and in instances where failure is not complete, the effectiveness of the plans is considerably reduced. A well-chosen or devised plan, excellent job descriptions, sound evaluations, and painstaking locality wage surveys can reap maximum benefit only if the program is effectively administered. The fundamentals of job evaluation administration are discussed in this chapter.

Administrative Functions

After a system has been put into operation, a multitude of problems and tasks will arise that, if success of the system is to be assured, must be handled with speed, fairness, and consistency. The handling of such problems and tasks embraces four broad administrative functions, namely, (1) planning, (2) maintaining interest and satisfaction, (3) control, and (4) routine operations.

Planning

One of the basic requirements of job evaluation administration is that those charged with the administrative responsibility receive day-to-day information regarding the functioning of the system. This is particularly important in light of the fact that many of the controversies attached to the program will not be known until the plan has been in operation for a number of weeks or perhaps months. Planning requires a study of the functioning of the system so that its weaknesses may be ascertained, corrective action formulated, and improvements recommended. Only after experiencing the results of weaknesses in the plan will it be possible to foresee and to forestall the future difficulties which will confront those responsible for administering the system.

Information on the day-to-day functioning of the system will emanate from innumerable sources; but where a union is involved, the success, or lack thereof, with which the system is operating will be reflected primarily in the number of grievances resulting from the evaluation. If no grievance procedure is embodied in the agreement between the union and management, an appeal procedure should be established; statistical records reflecting the number of appeals handled will indicate how satisfactorily the plan is working.

Other sources of information are: foremen and supervisors, union stewards, employees, personnel department exit interviews, and industrial relation and wage administration departments. Maintaining the necessary close liaison with all such sources of information is, except in the case of very small companies, a task of considerable difficulty. This is particularly true in companies having decentralized operations, for liaison cannot be accomplished unless the responsible party receives the necessary assistance.

Maintaining Interest and Satisfaction

Chapter 8 emphasized the necessity of selling job evaluation to all concerned if the program is to succeed in accomplishing the desired results. Selling the idea must not cease however, after the system is placed into operation but must continue if the plan of maintaining an equitable wage structure is to endure. Continued interest and confidence in the fairness and value of the program are acquired through a continuing educational process and constant close contact between the administrators, on the one hand, and management, supervision, and employees and their representatives, on the other. Keeping the affected parties sold on job evaluation is a problem closely allied with the study of system weaknesses, for the elimination of such weaknesses is conducive to a greater degree of satisfaction with the plan. For that reason the continued maintenance of interest in and satisfaction with the plan are usually the responsibility of the same person responsible for the planning.

Satisfaction with the system is best maintained by anticipating the grievances of employees and the criticisms of supervision. Very frequently the administrators, knowing that an inequitable rate exists, will make no attempt to admit an inequity and correct it of their own volition; instead, they will wait until the aggrieved employee submits a grievance. When the grievance is settled, the employee has probably lost confidence in the system, feeling that management uses it only for its own benefit; and once the result of the grievance is learned by others, they too will lose confidence in the value and fairness of the plan and, perhaps, precipitate an avalanche of unjustified grievances. Definite attempts must be made to continually convince the employees of management's desire to perpetuate a sound, equitable wage structure.

Interest in the program will lag if the employees and supervision are not kept constantly appraised of the continued application of the system. Letting the employee know that his job and classification are reviewed periodically without his requesting it, keeps his interest alive; likewise, the dissemination of information concerning rates that have been increased, without union pressure, as a result of a review of the job will do much to sustain employee interest in the plan. Any opportunity to publicize the advantages accruing to the employee or supervisor should not be neglected.

Control

One of the basic objectives of job evaluation is the centralization of control over wage and salary rates. A fundamental purpose of such centralized control is to preserve the plan through the elimination of arbitrary and haphazard rate changes or of failures to make needed changes. Controls should be instituted and defined at the time the plan is established, and the necessary control forms and records should be designed and available at the time the controls are effectuated. Control provides a means of setting forth the requirements for approving new or revised rates, and, therefore, it furnishes a guide to the administration of the company's wage and salary policies.

Where a company's operations are centered at a single location, the problem of a unified control is simplified, because control vested in a single group or individual is more effective. Even under such circumstances, however, it may be desirable to establish salary controls which are separate from wage controls and perhaps to separate the controls for rates subject to union negotiation from those not subject to such negotiation.

Where a company's operations are decentralized, the problems of co-ordination and control become more complex. When more than one plant is involved. one of them should be designated as the control plant and the evaluations of the other plants correlated with those of the control plant. In some plants different groups may be represented by different unions, a condition conducive to further complexities of co-ordination and control.

Problems induced by multiplant, multi-industry, and multi-union operations complicate the maintenance of a consistent wage structure and resolve into problems of setting up a workable internal administrative organization and a system of adjustable controls to meet the varying external conditions. Solution of the problem requires that the absolute consistency sought in centralized control be sacrificed to some extent to the need for flexibility to permit the local administration to adjust the program to local conditions and requirements.

Records and Statistics.—The administrators of the job evaluation program and the management will want information on the effects of the program as it progresses and develops. Such information can be furnished in a few simple forms and charts which show at a glance the number of employees in each labor grade and the average rate for each department.

Figure 10–1 is a form designed for statistical presentation of the number of employees in a department assigned to each labor grade. Each time a count is made of the number of persons assigned to each grade in a department, the payroll department should pass this information on to the wage ad-

	NUMBER OF EMPLOYEES BY LABOR GRADE									
DEPARTMENT:										
DATE	NUMBER OF EMPLOYEES									AVG. RATE
	1	2	3	4	5	6	7	8	TOTAL	

Fig. 10–1.—Record of the number of employees in each labor grade used for control over the upgrading tendency.

ministration department so that the figures along with the average hourly rates can be entered. The form provides period-to-period comparison of the number of persons in each grade and of the average hourly rates. During the early stages of the program, the figures should be compiled and entered about every three weeks; later, after the wage structure has stabilized, every six to eight weeks should be sufficient.

Figure 10–2 is a graph that might be used to augment the statistical record. The trend of the average hourly rate can be plotted, using the abscissa to represent the dates the counts were made and the ordinate to represent the average hourly rate. A study of Figure 10–1 will show whether or not the department is growing in size and, if it is expanding, in what labor grades the expansion is the greatest. Further study may bring out sudden increases in one labor grade with correspond-

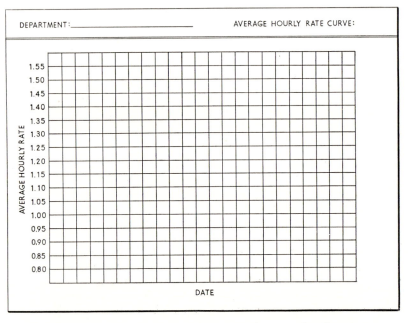

Fɪɢ. 10–2.—Graphic form for plotting trend of average hourly rates.

ing decreases in others and perhaps an abrupt reversion to a normal distribution of employees. Such study will, therefore, give rise to innumerable questions which the administrators of the job evaluation system must be prepared to answer. The figures may reflect an upgrading or downgrading tendency which, if not arrested, could throw the company's wage structure out of balance.

The graph shown in Figure 10–2 gives an instantaneous reflection of the effectiveness with which the pay rates have been

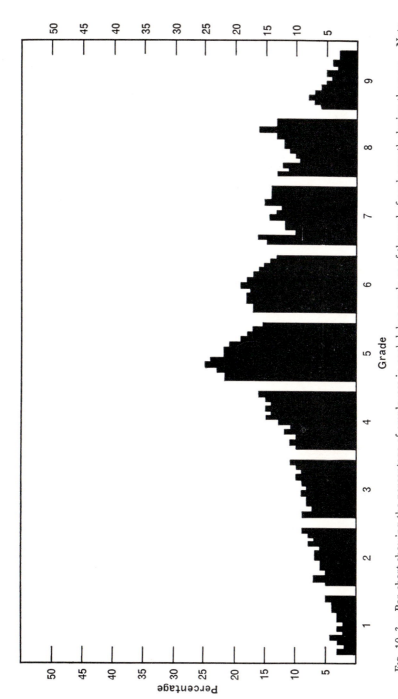

Fig. 10–3.—Bar chart showing the percentage of employees in each labor grade as of the end of each month during the year. Note the increase in unskilled and decrease in skilled employees.

controlled and is, therefore, a partial reflection of the figures
entered in Figure 10–1. In some instances the use of bar graphs
gives a quicker portrayal of the fluctuations in the number of
employees assigned to labor grades. Such a bar chart is constructed by marking off along the abscissa a section for each
labor grade. The ordinate is a scale representing the percentage of jobs falling into each labor grade. Vertical bars are

RINGED RATE RECORD					
4–WEEK PERIOD ENDING:_____					
DEPT.	NUMBER OF EMPLOYEES			HOURLY COST		
	THIS PERIOD	+ OR – LAST PERIOD	+ OR – 9-10-48	THIS PERIOD	+ OR – LAST PERIOD	+ OR – 9-10-48
TOTAL						

Fig. 10–4.

then drawn within the proper section and to the proper height
on each date that a count is made. Figure 10–3 (p. 231) is an
example of such a chart.

A measure of the effectiveness with which a job evaluation
project is administered is the number of "ringed" or "red
circle" rates in effect at any given time. Such rates are those
in excess of the evaluated rate for a particular job. Accordingly,
a control frequently used is the ringed rate record shown in
Figure 10–4. Such a record reflects by departments the number
of employees having wage rates in excess of those resulting from

the evaluation. Comparisons between the current and past periods and the date of the original evalution indicate the effect of efforts to eliminate ringed rates. In addition, the cost per hour comparisons show management what it is costing to maintain the ringed rates, and this may afford an insight into the reasons for unfavorable variations from standard costs. The ringed rate record illustrated is compiled from a listing of

RECORD OF RINGED RATES							
DEPT.							DATE
CLOCK NO.	NAME	JOB CODE	RATE			RINGED RATE ELIMINATED	
			EVAL.	PRES.	DIFF.	DATE	REASON

Fig. 10–5.—Form for listing employees having ringed rates.

employees showing the employee's name, clock number, current rate, and evaluated rate. Such a listing (Fig. 10–5) frequently accompanies the ringed rate record when it is distributed to supervision.

The use of these controls and their accurate interpretation presupposes the maintenance of workers' qualification standards. Favoritism on the part of the supervisor, salesmanship on the part of the employee, and pressure on the part of the union are largely responsible for the tendency to upgrade jobs to the higher grades. However, upgrading without due cause may render the control statistics ineffective.

Routine Operations

While the over-all control of the system is usually centered in one person or committee, the details or routine operations requiring frequent attention are usually handled by assistants acquainted with the fundamentals of job evaluation. Such routine operations include: defining job detail and job description meaning, maintaining job descriptions, establishing rates for new jobs, reviewing correctness of established rates and rates of individuals, and conducting periodic wage surveys.

Defining Job Detail.—It is assumed that, when job descriptions are written originally, a conscientious effort will be made to accurately define all phases of the work comprising the job. Not until the plan has been in operation for some time, however, will most of the controversies over definition of job detail become known; for some arguments, particularly concerning new or specialized jobs, will result despite the care exercised in the preparation of descriptions. Some controversies will have arisen during the assignment of jobs, but in order to get the system into operation quickly, they may have been only partially settled. Because more time is available after the system has been placed in operation, it is then that more thought can be applied to the questions in dispute.

The defining of job detail is for the most part a matter of clarification of job duties. This may be accomplished by the addition or deletion of a few words, the rewriting of ambiguous sentences, or perhaps a very complete study of the job and an operational analysis. The extent of clarification required will be determined only when the parties concerned are satisfied that no further clarification is necessary.

Defining Description Meaning.—Although a job may be accurately described as to the duties involved, very often a controversy will arise over the meaning of the description itself. Such controversies are usually the result of a lack of semantic precision and are, for the most part, settled during the course of the evaluation. It is entirely possible, however, for all members of the evaluation committee to be in complete accord on the meaning of certain descriptive words and phrases which may be misunderstood by others. At times, words that can be interpreted in a manner different from the intended meaning are used as part of a strategy to deliberately upgrade undeserving classifications. For this reason, partially at least, the difficulties are most apt to center about those occupations to which many employees have been assigned. Such words and phrases as "difficult," "minor adjustments," "fairly complex blueprints," "variety of operations," and "considerable effort" are subject to multiple interpretations and may be the cause of considerable controversy. When job descriptions are phrased to provide a promotional series for the purpose of giving the lower classed workers an objective, an opportunity may be presented to confuse the matter of classification by interpreting a certain phrase to mean that all employees doing a specific part of a higher rated job should be upgraded regardless of whether they can do the entire job or not. To alleviate these difficulties, job descriptions will have to be rewritten in such a manner as to clarify the meaning of such phrases and words without destroying the meaning of the job content itself.

Assurance that job descriptions are being maintained can best be gained through a systematic control procedure. The most important advantage to be gained from close control over maintenance of job descriptions lies in the fact that such maintenance requires periodic review of all jobs, thus enabling the company to foresee many possible grievances, to take the necessary corrective action, and to keep alive the employees' interest in the program.

Certainty that new jobs will be described can be gained by establishing a policy prohibiting the hiring or transfer of employees to jobs that have not been analyzed and evaluated and by prohibiting the issuance of pay checks to employees assigned to new jobs unless such jobs have been evaluated.

Changes in Job Content.—The problem of changes in job content will, if it is to be handled in a manner conducive to satisfaction with the plan, require co-operation on the part of the foreman to notify the proper persons when changes in job content occur. Where a union is concerned, the union stewards will keep management informed of many changes in job content; but usually they confine their information to changes that will indicate upgrading, being somewhat reticent about reporting anything that might lead to a reduction in the rate of an employee. Employees also will be more likely to report reasons for a rate increase, leaving the reasons for a decrease to be reported by the foreman.

Figure 10–6 is a suggested form to be used by the foreman, employee, or steward for reporting changes on job content. It should be made out in triplicate, the original being sent to the wage administrator, one copy being retained by the foreman, and the other copy retained by the employee. The form can also be used as a request for a review of a job, even though no change in job content has occurred. When a job has been reviewed, the information should be recorded on the job description held in the master file; and if changes are made in the description, copies of the old and new descriptions and of the job review request should be retained together in the master file.

As a means of maintaining control over job review frequency, a record can be kept of the number of jobs reviewed periodically and of the results of such reviews. Figure 10–7 is a form to be used for recording the activities of the job evaluation department in maintaining job descriptions. It affords an insight into the work accomplished during the week as well as a record of the status of the descriptions, the amount of work ahead of the job evaluation department, and the sources of requests for job reviews. A separate form may be used for each department and for hourly paid and salaried employees, if closer control appears advisable.

Review of Rates.—As soon as a description of a new job has been prepared, one copy, or several, if desired, should be forwarded to the evaluation committee where appropriate action will be taken to evaluate the job. Because jobs are usually reviewed for the purpose of adjusting the wage rates, any job whose content has changed—and such change noted in the

JOB REVIEW REQUEST

TO: *JOB EVALUATION DEPT.*

JOB TITLE:_____ JOB NO.:_____

DEPARTMENT:_____ DATE:_____

REASON FOR REQUEST:_____

_____

_____

_____

_____

_____

_____

_____

_____

☐ EMPLOYEE   ☐ STEWARD

REQUESTED BY: ☐ FOREMAN   ☐ _____

SIGNATURE:_____ FOREMAN'S O. K.:_____

DISPOSITION OF REQUEST

JOB REVIEWED BY:_____ DATE:_____

                   SIGNATURE

RESULT OF REVIEW:_____

_____

_____

_____

_____

_____

_____

_____

_____

DATE EMPLOYEE NOTIFIED:_____ DATE FOREMAN NOTIFIED:_____

Fig. 10–6.

description—will be subject to re-evaluation by the committee. Assurance that the rates for new jobs are being established should come as a result of a payroll control, as heretofore mentioned. Revisions of rates resulting from re-evaluation of jobs should be announced by the wage and salary administrator to the foreman, who informs the employee either directly or through the union steward.

JOB REVIEW AND DESCRIPTION STATUS REPORT WEEK ENDING 8-9-48		
JOB DESCRIPTIONS ON FILE BEGINNING OF WEEK:		
CHECKED WITHIN LAST 3 MOS.	114	
CHECKED WITHIN LAST 3-6 MOS.	99	
NOT CHECKED FOR OVER 6 MOS.	23	
TOTAL	236	
JOB DESCRIPTIONS CHECKED DURING WEEK:		
NEW JOBS	2	
JOB CONTENT CHANGES	11	
NO CHANGE	12	
ELIMINATIONS	6	
OTHER	–	
TOTAL	31	
JOB DESCRIPTIONS ON FILE END OF WEEK:		
CHECKED WITHIN LAST 3 MOS.	126	
CHECKED WITHIN LAST 3-6 MOS.	89	
NOT CHECKED FOR OVER 6 MOS.	17	
TOTAL	232	
REVIEWS AS A RESULT OF:		
REQUEST OF EMPLOYEE	2	
REQUEST OF FOREMAN	4	
REQUEST OF STEWARD	2	
REQUEST OF OTHERS (J. E. Comm)	3	
ROUTINE CHECK	20	
TOTAL	31	
JOBS FOR WHICH NO DESCRIPTIONS HAVE BEEN WRITTEN	3	
SIGNED: W. F. Best J. E. DEPT.		

Fig. 10–7.

Wage Surveys.—Another problem facing those administering a job evaluation system is that of keeping informed on the comparative industry and area wage rates. This matter was discussed in detail in Chapter 6.

Administrative Structure

A well-qualified administrative staff is essential to the success of any job evaluation system. The number of specialists required to administer a plan depends upon the plan itself, the number of jobs involved, the geographical location of the company's plants and offices, and the administrative organization structure. One full-time analyst appears to be the minimum for even a small plant. Another essential of a successful program is the maintenance of executive participation; however, too great a claim on the executive's time may cause some resentment of the system. For this reason it is advisable to provide executive administrators with a sufficient number of staff assistants having specialized knowledge of job evaluation.

The Small Company.—The small single-plant, single-industry company has the simplest administrative problem. Under such conditions, responsibility for the entire administration of the evaluation program is usually placed on the shoulders of a single executive who is provided with an assistant to handle the details of maintaining the rate structure. Such an administrative structure should suffice for plants having less than one hundred employees. Companies of that size rarely have personnel devoting their entire time to such functions as industrial relations and industrial engineering; and for that reason the person handling the details of the system may assume the job evaluation duties in addition to those of personnel manager or industrial engineer. The very small plant, however, is not likely to initiate a formal job evaluation plan, primarily because the managements of such companies have been able to maintain fairly close control over their relatively simple wage structures or because, being small, their rate structure is governed by the competition of the larger plants and offices in the locality.

When a company having only twenty to thirty employees has felt the need of some form of job evaluation, administration of the system is usually found to be very simple. In the first place, point rating or factor comparison methods would not be warranted because of the time and effort involved to properly create a plan. As a result the job ranking method and its attendant simplicity will very frequently afford satisfactory results. Another circumstance that makes administration less complex is the frequent impracticability of written job descriptions. In many small organizations, the jobs must be exceedingly wide in scope, for the volume of work required in one occupation is not enough to warrant the full time of one employee. For example, in a small office one employee may act as cost accountant, stock record clerk, billing clerk, purchasing agent, bookkeeper, and office manager; he may fire the furnace in the absence of the janitor, and in his spare time, he may do some selling. A written description of such a job would hardly be of use for purposes of job evaluation. If all requirements of the job were mentioned, it would be a somewhat cumbersome document; and if reduced to practical size, it would probably be too general for an accurate appraisal of the job. Therefore, in very small companies, job evaluation formality will usually be tempered with practicality.

The Large Company.—It is usually the case that companies employing a large number of personnel have the greatest need for a job evaluation plan. In the single-plant company, the chief line executives—controller, treasurer, or office manager—supervisors, personnel and industrial engineering departments, and, if the plant is unionized, union stewards are all involved in the operation and installation of the plan.

As the size of the company increases, the problem becomes more complex, particularly if the operations are decentralized. Large firms having more than one plant may have their main job evaluation staff located at a central office, its primary function being the correlation and co-ordination of the work of the local staffs administering the plan or plans at the local plants. Other firms, however, may allow each plant and office complete autonomy over its job evaluation administration, maintaining an interest only in the general wage and salary administration policy. The administrative structure to be employed under multiplant and multioffice circumstances will depend a great deal on the amount of flexibility required to meet local industry and union conditions and local legislation. The pressure of localized collective bargaining, locality wage differentials, possible differences in union representation, differences in operations, and the possibility of not having identical plans in all plants are among the factors conducive to granting autonomy in administration.

While responsibility for the over-all successful operation of the system is centered in one executive or committee, specific aspects of the administration are usually delegated to staff assistants. The preparation, clarification, and maintenance of job descriptions are usually done by job analysts assigned to the industrial engineering or wage administration departments; the evaluation of jobs usually rests with the evaluation committee, while the analysts are ordinarily given the task of conducting the wage surveys. However, it rests with the person having the over-all responsibility for the system to plan and to maintain interest in the program and to see that the necessary controls are established.

Appeal Procedure

Job evaluation deals with all kinds of individuals; and such being the case, management will be confronted not only with the weaknesses of job evaluation but with human behavior as well. Casual handling of employees' complaints is not practical in the light of the need for keeping the program sold; and for this reason a standard appeal procedure should be established to expeditiously handle misunderstandings, disagreements, errors in evaluation or classification, and cases of hurt feelings, emotion, or downright cussedness.

Procedure Essentials.—The type of appeal procedure used will be governed to some extent by such factors as the administrative structure, number of unions to be considered, grievance procedures embodied in union agreements, size of the company, and whether operations are centralized or decentralized. There are, however, certain essentials which should be incorporated into any good appeal procedure. They are:

1. Speed in processing cases and in rendering sound judgment.

2. Simplicity to the extent of permitting all persons concerned to easily understand the procedure.

3. A preliminary review of the appeal as a means of settling as many cases near the source of trouble as possible.

4. Freedom from technicalities and ramifications that may confuse employees.

5. Careful selection of personnel who are to render the decisions.

6. A complete and accurate set of appeal records, including case histories and references, statistical tabulations, processing records of original complaints, and transcriptions of proceedings.

Procedure Details.—Without careful incorporation of the above essentials, the appeal procedure, no matter how well considered, may be of little value in accomplishing the desired purpose. The details suggested in the following paragraphs are generally applicable to most circumstances but are by no means to be considered as the only solution. The details of the procedure must fit the individual circumstances of the company.

a) Initiating Complaints.—Dissatisfaction with an evaluation or a classification may be expressed by either an employee or his supervisor. In cases where the employee expresses dissatisfaction, the complaint should be discussed with the supervisor; and if both agree that the complaint is justified, a job review request (Fig. 10–6) is filled out and the case automatically referred to the job evaluation department. However, if the supervisor and employee do not reach an agreement, the complaint goes directly to the review board, the case being initiated by the supervisor. If the case goes to the job evaluation department, as a result of accord between the employee and his supervisor, and the department approves the request, the case is closed.

b) Formal Appeal.—On the other hand, if the department refuses the request, a formal appeal must be made to the review board, the case being initiated by the employee. Denial of a

---

BOARD REVIEW REQUEST

EMPLOYEE'S NAME:_____ CLOCK NO:_____ DEPT.:_____
JOB TITLE:_____CODE:_____
JOB DUTIES:_____
_____
_____
_____

REASON FOR REQUEST:_____
_____
_____
_____
_____

I WILL BE REPRESENTED BY:_____ OF DEPT.:_____

DATE:_____ SIGNED:_____

TO BE FILLED IN BY CHAIRMAN OF REVIEW BOARD

DISPOSITION:_____
_____
_____
_____
_____
_____
_____
_____
_____
_____

DATE:_____
FILE REF.:_____

SIGNED:_____
CHAIRMAN

Fig. 10-8.—Employee's request for board review.

request should always be accompanied by a statement of reasons for the denial. A form similar to Figure 10-8 is filled in, the statement of the case filled in by the complainant and the rebuttal by the other party. The form is then passed on to the review board.

The composition of the board will vary with the circumstances. Where a union is involved, the employees and management should have equal representation and elect an additional member to act as chairman and conciliator. Provision should be made for some members to form subcommittees to investigate cases preliminary to the hearings as a means of speeding up the hearing procedure. Where no collective bargaining agency is involved, the employees should be given an opportunity to appoint their own representatives. Under such circumstances, a permanent chairman, having a reputation among all concerned for fair and impartial dealings, is advisable. Also, the possibility should not be overlooked for using the job evaluation review committee, where such is available, to handle the work of the review board. This possibility applies regardless of the presence or lack of a collective bargaining agency.

c) Investigation of the Case.—When the review board receives the statement of complaint, the first step is to appoint a subcommittee to make a preliminary investigation of the case. The investigation may uncover facts so conclusive that the case can be disposed of without a formal hearing, as a result of either party withdrawing their complaint or rebuttal. If the facts are not conclusive, however, the subcommittee should prepare its report in writing and attach it to the statement of complaint.

d) Board Hearing.—The hearing should be announced in ample time for all parties to be prepared. In attendance, in addition to the interested parties, should be someone capable of recording the proceedings. Hearings should be conducted by the chairman along the accepted principles of procedure. The case should be clearly stated and agreed upon and both sides given equal opportunity to present, question, and cross-question witnesses and to present admissible evidence. Periods should be allowed for rebuttal after each side has presented its side of the story. When the case has been completely heard and all discussion terminated as a result of mutual agreement or majority vote, the issue will, it is assumed, be clear; then the committee, in open session, will discuss the matter, reach a decision, and inform the complainant of the decision. This decision is usually later verified in writing.

At the time an employee is informed of the decision, the chairman should ask whether the employee wishes to appeal the case to a higher authority. If an affirmative answer is forthcoming, the complete record of the case should be forwarded to the office of the higher authority who will review the record, make a decision, and inform the parties in writing of the result of the appeal. A copy of the letter should be incorporated in the record.

QUESTIONS

1. What are the four broad functions of job evaluation administration?
2. What are the sources of information concerning how well a job evaluation program is functioning?
3. What are some measures that can be taken to maintain interest in and satisfaction with a job evaluation program?
4. What is the fundamental purpose of centralized control as provided by job evaluation?
5. What are some of the routine operations involved in the administration of a job evaluation program?
6. How can you be assured that all changes in job content are brought to the attention of the proper persons?
7. There are certain essentials that should be incorporated into any appeal procedure. What are they?

CHAPTER 11

JOB EVALUATION PROBLEMS AND FAILURES

A SURVEY conducted by Princeton University, the results of which were published in 1947, revealed that of sixty-eight job evaluation plans established, twenty or approximately 30 per cent were reported by the surveyed companies to have been unsatisfactory.[1] A mortality rate of such proportions indicates a need for acquainting those considering a job evaluation installation with the pitfalls that may be encountered, not only during the installation but during the administration of the system as well, and with the reasons for job evaluation failure. This chapter is devoted to a discussion of the internal and external conditions affecting the effectiveness of systems and the primary causes of their failure.

Internal Conditions

Lack of Experienced Personnel.—Personnel well versed in job evaluation principles, practices, and procedures have been at a premium since formal methods of erasing wage rate inequities became known. The reason for the lack of qualified personnel lies in the fact that job evaluation, as a tool of wage administration, is still in its infancy and that the number of personnel having experience with it, at least up until World War II, has been limited. The increased use of job evaluation during the war did not provide, as might be expected, a proportionate increase in the number of people with satisfactory experience. Unfortunately, much of the experience gained during the war years has been detrimental to the future of job evaluation; for

---

[1] *The Operation of Job Evaluation Plans: A Survey of Experience* (Princeton, N. J.: Princeton University, Industrial Relations Section, Department of Economics and Social Institutions, 1947)

during that time, numerous plans were placed in effect solely as a means of circumventing emergency wage legislation and no end of tricks and subterfuges were perpetrated under the guise of job evaluation in order that companies maintain their positions in the labor market. Organized labor was willing to go along if it meant wage increases. Such practices bred many bad habits which still remain. While many claim to have had experience with job evaluation, a relatively small number can honestly claim that they have had a sound experience. As long as the supply of qualified specialists remains at a low level, management must face the problem squarely. It is no more logical to try to install and to maintain a sound system of job evaluation with untrained personnel than it is to place a junior ledger clerk in charge of a complicated accounting system.

One answer to the problem of a lack of qualified personnel is the retention of a reputable consultant. Such a solution, however, may provide only a partial remedy unless, during his engagement, he thoroughly trains the staff appointed to perpetuate the system. The retention of a consultant to install a plan only is a waste of time, effort, and funds unless he provides the knowledge of how to carry on when his services terminate. In short, before an attempt is made at a job evaluation, management must assure itself that it is, or will be, properly staffed with trained personnel.

Lack of Executive Participation.—This is an internal condition which usually emanates from a failure to sell executives on the advantages of job evaluation and to keep them sold. It should not be expected that executives devote a disproportionate amount of time on job evaluation to the detriment of their regularly assigned responsibilities but that the time necessary to be given be given willingly. As a project gradually assumes a more routine nature, there may be a tendency to gradually reduce the number of participating executives and the time each spends in participation. Such a retirement from active participation may be desirable for a number of reasons, but it is done at the risk of reducing interest in the plan unless proper steps are taken to keep the executives sold. Executives must be convinced that job evaluation is a continuous process, not a self-operating system.

Changes in Key Personnel.—Another internal condition affecting the continuity of a program is the turnover of key personnel. An installation may have the full backing of top management at the start, but changes in key personnel at a later date may result in new personnel who are unacquainted or in disagreement with job evaluation having a voice in its administration. The possibility of changes in key personnel indicates that management must be prepared to indoctrinate new employees with the job evaluation practices and principles of management and with the benefits to be gained from the program. Union officials and stewards should also be subject to the indoctrination policy; however, the unions may have their own ideas along such lines. One means of indoctrination is a job evaluation manual that includes an explanation of the plan and the policies, practices, and procedures to be followed in its installation and administration.

Pressure against Rate Ceiling.—Of concern to wage administrators working with job evaluation plans are the out-of-line or ringed rates. Such rates result, first, from assuring employees that their rates will not be lowered as a result of the evaluation and, second, from the pressure on the part of employees for increases in rates above the maximum called for by the job. The former reason poses fewer problems than the latter, but there is an increasing tendency to incorporate into union agreements provisions that make the elimination of ringed rates almost an impossibility. Some agreements provide that employees with ringed rates will not be allowed to participate in any general wage increases; such provisions, however, are difficult for the employee to accept in the light of increasing living costs.

The second reason for ringed rates results from the laxity on the part of supervision to resist employee requests for individual increases, the failure of unions to support the program by resisting unwarranted pressure on the part of employees who seek upgrading, and the failure to promote employees who are capable of handling higher rated jobs. The ringed rate problem is one that can be solved almost wholly through education in the basic principles of job evaluation and classification.

One pitfall those contemplating job evaluation should be cautioned against, is limiting the amount to be spent on the elimination of inequities. In two instances, one involving a company that is a leader in a basic industry, the other involving a large equipment manufacturer—both, however, having agreements with the same international union—the respective managements and the union agreed that inequities in the wage structures existed. Agreements were signed by the parties to provide for job evaluation. However, the agreements stipulated that the cost to the companies would not exceed a certain amount stated in terms of an average cost per hour per employee.

In the case of the large equipment manufacturer this stipulated figure was two cents. When the jobs had been evaluated and a least squares conversion line computed and drawn, the resulting cost to the company amounted to 5.8 cents. The company, being unwilling to accept the burden of the excess cost, negotiated with the union and reduced the cost to approximately 3.5 cents. Negotiation consisted primarily of reviewing the evaluted jobs with the president of the local union and reducing the point values in a somewhat arbitrary manner. The job evaluation committee was not consulted during the review. The adjusted evaluation was finally agreed to, and a supplementary agreement was signed. At a later date, however, the union claimed that the evaluation was not a true one, citing as a basis for its claims the arbitrary adjustments which had taken place. On the basis of that contention, the union refused to use the evaluation as a guide in evaluating new jobs or those requiring re-evaluation because of changes in job content. As a result each new evaluation tended to throw the rate structure out of line owing to inconsistencies, and the wage rate inequalities increased.

While the contention of the union had merit, the union was equally guilty with management in originally agreeing to hold the cost of the evaluation down to any set figure. An evaluation subjected to revisions to keep it within limits can hardly be a reliable instrument for measuring relative job worth. In both cases the final evaluations were unreliable.

Methods Changes.—A job evaluation program that does not make satisfactory provisions for re-evaluating jobs substantially altered due to technological changes will result in a condition whereby each improvement in method will tend to establish wage rate inequalities. Routine maintenance of a system requires, among other things, that job descriptions keep abreast with all changes in job content. The division of gains resulting from job simplification has long been a matter of controversy between unions and management, and the fear that job evaluation would be used to deny the right to bargain for a share of such gains has been the basis for opposition to job evaluation on the part of many unions. If methods changes are introduced, the job should be re-evaluated to reflect the changes. If job evaluation is to be conducted on the basis of sound judgment, horse-trading of evaluation points or of relative ranking position over the collective bargaining table does not appear to be consistent. Where a job is downgraded, the employee on the job should be reclassified as soon as possible into a position requiring the skill he has developed. Technological improvements will serve society better if the skill they replace can be utilized elsewhere. Downgrading as a result of methods changes will be a threat to job evaluation unless the unions modify their opposition to re-evaluation on the basis of methods change and unless management is willing to make an honest effort to utilize the skills developed in the employee.

Union Attitudes.—Many unions have expressed dissatisfaction with formal job evaluation plans. A mere knowledge of the union's attitude, however, will accomplish little unless management has a desire to make use of the knowledge to eliminate evident union discontent. Many labor organizations express a traditional distrust of anything in the way of a management technique. As for job evaluation, the following excerpt from a letter written by the director of research of a large labor organization expresses fairly well the general attitude of organized labor:

> Job evaluation plans are under suspicion in unions because the techniques were developed by company unions in connection with the so-called "American Plan" after the First World War. The company unions were proposed, of course, by the corporations as a substitute for "bona fide" trade unions, and many of these company unions were regarded as at least a step in advance of no organization of workers. Then came job classification and job evaluation which were substitutes for collective bargaining, or at least a method of reducing the field of joint decision between union and management.
>
> The — — — — — has as yet not gotten past the stage of discussion of the implications of job evaluation, and feels that unless plans are jointly instituted and jointly agreed to and supervised jointly, they cannot keep the confidence of the workers. There is a very strong feeling among trade unions that have had some experience with the operation of plans that formulas have no claim to scientific basis and are less valid than decisions based on experience. Experience, of course, includes the best practices of the whole industry.

The expressed or implied attitudes of organized labor indicate some of the problems to be solved if collective bargaining is to be furthered rather than thwarted by job evaluation.

Union Participation.—Regardless of whether or not job evaluation is applied by management unilaterally, unions will ordinarily have some voice in the program. In cases of bilateral programs, union participation should start with the selecting or originating of the plan to be used and should carry on during all the administrative phases. The bilateral program should work out most successfully if both parties are capable of and willing to apply the plan without bias. However, if such an application is not possible because of the attitude of the individuals concerned, then much time, effort, and expense will be spared by employing a unilateral program. Union policy may prohibit participation in the actual evaluation of jobs, permitting only a review and either acceptance or refusal of the overall results. In some cases both sides may conduct their own evaluations, compare results, and bilaterally evaluate those jobs over which there is disagreement. The latter method is, in effect, a bilateral evaluation which may prove to be faster, because the groups evaluating the occupations are smaller and discussion is lessened. Further, it is possible for the two groups to have differences in point totals for the individual jobs and still come out with identical wage curves, provided of course the evaluations are consistent.

Under unilateral evaluations, the amount of information given out to the union ranges from a complete job evaluation manual—explaining the plan, wage curve, and the practices and procedures followed and including a complete set of job descriptions, point totals, and conversion charts—down to a simple listing of jobs showing the old and evaluated rates. Problems arising out of the extent of union participation are the result not so much of a lack of participation but of the application of a plan without regard for the union's belief that any action relating to the establishment of rates is a subject for collective bargaining. Therefore, if a unilateral installation is necessary, every possible effort should be made to keep the union informed on the steps being taken and to secure approval on the day-to-day results.

Effect of Union Influence.—A union has unlimited opportunity to limit the application of job evaluation or to make it a successful undertaking. If hostility toward the adjustment of inequities or to a particular plan of operation prevails, the union is close enough to the employee's ear to easily discredit the system and to point out, if not magnify, its inconsistencies and other weaknesses if there are any. Many plans are never installed and many are abandoned because of union hostility. Such resistance, however, should not prevent the use of the system by management as a means of determining the rates for new jobs or as a guide in settling wage disputes.

While securing union participation may be an answer to the problem of union approval, there is no conclusive evidence to the effect that joint participation will assure the success of an installation. Reading through one of the periodicals devoted to reviews of arbitration cases gives convincing proof that joint participation does not of itself prevent administrative problems. Many plans, although jointly and successfully installed, failed later because the union found a multitude of technicalities around which to base grievances or did not abide by the standards of consistency it had helped to establish. In general, however, it has been found that the union exerts a better influence on a program under conditions of joint participation.

Sources of Union Dissatisfaction.—As the letter on page 252 indicates, many union officials are not satisfied that formal job evaluation is an acceptable means of wage rate determination. The greatest source of dissatisfaction probably lies in the fear of unions that job evaluation limits collective bargaining by the application of formulas. In addition to disliking the more or less rule-of-thumb methods of establishing rates, union officials feel that they are at a decided disadvantage at the bargaining table because of their lack of the technical training required to understand and to intelligently discuss job evaluation systems; this, they feel, reduces the effectiveness of their bargaining abilities.

Whether union participation or lack thereof is a source of general dissatisfaction among labor organization is a question that cannot be answered one way or the other owing to the divergence of opinion among union officials. On the one hand, Mr. William Gomberg, director of the Management Engineering Department, International Ladies Garment Workers Union (A.F. of L.) believes that "where the union refuses to participate in the actual formulation of the job evaluation plan but insists solely upon its right either to accept or reject the findings of the plan, it may find itself without any criteria to challenge management's position."[2] The opposite viewpoint is expressed in the United Electrical Workers (C.I.O.) guide as follows:

The local union should refuse to become a party to or be bound by any point rating system which management may use to establish job evaluations. It should not appear in the contract. As with time

[2] *A Labor Union Manual on Job Evaluation* (Chicago: Roosevelt College, Labor Education Division, 1947), p. 48.

studies, the U.E. lets the company use any method it pleases but under close union surveillance. If the result is satisfactory, well and good. If not, the company will hear from us.[3]

The latter viewpoint indicates that the union feels participation would be tantamount to a stamp of approval on results which may turn out to be unsatisfactory to its membership. Mr. Gomberg, on the other hand, apparently realizes that the collective bargaining strength of his union will be enhanced if the union closely follows the course of the installation and states its objections as inconsistencies and other weaknesses occur.

It should not be construed that all labor organizations disagree with the basic principles of job evaluation. What many of them do object to is the type of plan selected and the manner in which it may be presented. Point rating and factor comparison methods and the complicated charts that sometimes accompany such plans are often confusing. Joint participation should eliminate most, if not all, of such confusion; but where the particular organization refuses to participate, the solution to the problems lies in the education of the rank and file by the use of handbooks, company periodicals, movies, and other means of publicizing the program. Another objection, which can be met, partially at least, by joint participation, concerns administrative malpractices on the part of management. If union representatives assist in the administration of the system, the possibility of such malpractice will naturally be reduced.

Other sources of union dissatisfaction with job evaluation may include: the effect of job evaluation on wages when methods changes are effectuated; the focusing of attention of job content where little concern had been evinced before, thereby aggravating rather than reducing grievances; and the fundamental objection to the term "job evaluation." Generally, it will be found that the primary and most often voiced objection to job evaluation concerns its tendency to limit collective bargaining; all other objections are secondary. For this reason

---

[3]United Electrical, Radio, and Machine Workers of America, *U. E. Guide to Wage Payment Plan, Time Study and Job Evaluation*, Topic No. 49 (1947), p. 77.

management should take all possible steps to gain joint participation in the program.

External Conditions

Labor Market Conditions.—Job evaluation measures the differences in job content as a means of determining, in an unscientific but systematic manner, what, if any, rate differentials are justified. Therein lies a source of dissatisfaction and criticism that as yet has not been removed. Job content may be measured, but so far no way has been devised to measure the supply of and the demand for the skills required by the job and the willingness and ability of workers to accept certain responsibilities, exert effort of a certain degree, and work under certain conditions. Although the choice of factors and the application of weights may measure, to some extent, the relative demand for skills as of the date the plan is installed, no feature of the general type of plan now in use provides the flexibility required to reflect varying labor market conditions. As mentioned earlier in this text, the answer may lie in the use of a balancing factor which would permit adjustments of point values or of ranking position without actually disturbing the evaluation of the job content. The use of such a factor, however, would pose additional problems, particularly with regard to the application of judgment. Labor market wage surveys might be one answer, but too often a lack of comparison between jobs, conditions, and attitudes exists to permit reliance upon a wage survey.

Another point to be considered is the viewpoint of the individual worker. Where one employee would rather have a sense of security and uninterrupted employment at $1.25 per hour, another is willing to sacrifice security, seniority, and other considerations for a $2.00 per hour rate. An example of this situation existed in a southern Wisconsin industrial community in the spring of 1948. The evaluated rates for the highest classifications of carpenters and masons in a large plant in the area were $1.38 and $1.33 per hour, respectively, the evaluations arrived at under joint participation. However, on a large construction project within two miles of the plant, the rates paid for similar work were $2.40 and $2.10 per hour, respectively. Despite the opportunity for a substantial increase in earnings by offering their skills elsewhere, not one employee transferred his services to the construction project. When questioned as to their reasons for not taking advantage of the opportunity for increased wages, the employees stated that they were assured of continued employment at the plant, they wanted to preserve their seniority, and paid vacations, holidays, and group life insurance and hospital benefits had to be considered.

In the above case an external labor market condition was not bothersome to the particular company. Such was not the case, however, with many companies during the war years. The growing strength of unions and the growing submission to industry-wide bargaining induced widespread acceptance of general wage increases which, to a considerable extent, modified many balanced differentials that existed. This condition, along with the tremendous demands for certain skills, has created one of the most serious problems of current wage administration.

Many companies have found that by adhering strictly to their job evaluation systems they could not provide a satisfactory means of balancing the supply and demand among occupations. As a result some give and take has been necessary to bridge the gap between practical considerations of market conditions and a possible impractical strict adherence to job evaluation principles. This is particularly true during periods of full employment and other extreme conditions of economic environment.

Conflicts with Job Content as Measurement.—In Chapter 7 it was brought out that, before money values could be assigned to the rate structure, certain decisions were in order concerning sex differentials. The continued adherance to a policy of recognizing such differentials is inconsistent with the principle of job content as measurement, and the resulting conflict may undermine the operation of a plan. Certain competitive conditions may preclude the elimination of such differentials, making a problem difficult to solve and affording a basis for criticism of job evaluation objectives. There are, in addition to eliminating the differentials entirely, certain alternatives, namely, the use of multiple conversion lines—a different line for each sex, the exclusion of female occupations from the application, and the application of weights to factors in such a manner as to emphasize those characteristics that are most predominant in male occupations. The first two alternatives are objectionable because they defeat the object of sound job evaluation, and the third might be construed as being a manipulation contrary to the true intent of a system of measuring job content. While the trend is away from a recognition of sex differentials, many unions and many groups of rank and file resist the trend because of the traditions within certain industries.

Traditional differentials will offer a more difficult barrier to hurdle than any other element that conflicts with job content as a measurement of job worth. Employees and well-organized labor bodies, particularly the craft unions, often justify differentials purely on the basis of long historical standing. This basis of justification often makes it impossible and inadvisable to attempt a job evaluation installation except perhaps as a guide in establishing new rates. Further, cognizance should not be lost of the prestige value attached to some occupations.

Geographic differentials are not likely to create problems unless a plan is installed on an industry-wide, multiplant basis and the proper flexibility is not provided. Following the wage practices of the areas in which plants are located simplifies the problem, although there is the danger that the job evaluation may focus attention on geographic differentials which are difficult for many unions to understand. There is, therefore, a tendency in job evaluation to complicate rather than to simplify the problem of geographic differentials.

Industry differentials present a more complex problem. Where one company is engaged in more than one industry, it may be extremely difficult to justify in the minds of a single union the divergence in evaluated rates existing between the industries, even though the competitive conditions, tradition, and other factors may dictate the differentials. Uniform systems of job evaluation have been found by many multi-industry companies to be cumbersome and impracticable, particularly where a substantial degree of autonomy was not granted the individual plants. Conversely, the use of multiple systems has proven difficult to defend by some multi-industry companies. Because plans should be selected, altered, or devised to fit the local circumstances and conditions and because the circumstances and conditions generally vary between industries, the use of multiple rather than uniform systems is indicated; any decision, however, is guided by the peculiarities in the situation.

Primary Reasons for Failure

In the preceding pages of this chapter the most commonly encountered internal and external conditions affecting the successful operation of job evaluation systems were discussed. In some companies the conditions posed only minor problems, while in others the same conditions produced problems of such magnitude that job evaluation was not attempted; or if it was, near or complete failure resulted. The following, drawn from the experience of the authors and from discussions with management, union officials, and management consultants, summarizes the primary reasons for job evaluation failure:

1. Failure on the part of management to sell job evaluation to supervision, employees, union officials, and executives and to keep them sold during the life of the program.

2. Failure on the part of analysts to secure the complete set of facts required to provide a basis for sound evaluation, as a result of poor training or pressure to do a quick job without allowing sufficient time to secure a complete study.

3. Lack of or laxity in administration that permitted the plan to die, inequities to creep in, and pressure of groups and individuals to throw the wage curve off balance to an irreparable extent.

4. Failure of top management to support the plan, thus giving the impression to executives and to supervision that the system was unworthy of their attention.

5. Lack of trained, competent personnel to install and to administer the system and careless selection of consultants.

6. Resistance on the part of unions to encroachment upon collective bargaining and resistance because of traditional differentials.

7. Weaknesses in specific plans, including poor choice, weighting, and definition of factors.

8. Changes in key personnel that resulted in changes in top management's attitude toward the usefulness of the system.

9. Failure to invite joint participation in the program, thus causing resistance on the part of the union.

10. Failure to provide sufficient flexibility in the program to allow for multiplant, multi-industry, multiunion administrative requirements, unusual labor market conditions, and technological changes.

11. Lack of willingness to recognize factors other than job content in the determination of wages.

12. Use of the program as a subterfuge to gain a desired end of management, union, or both.

There are other conditions that might be called primary causes for failure, but the large majority of failures are directly traceable to one or more of the above, other conditions usually being minor but contributory factors.

QUESTIONS

1. To what can the lack of personnel qualified to install and to administer job evaluation programs be attributed?
2. What may be the cause for a lack of executive participation in a job evaluation program?
3. What precautions should management take against the turnover of key personnel who are involved in job evaluation?
4. What are "ringed rates"? How do they occur?

5. What is the danger in establishing a predetermined amount to be used in eliminating wage rate iniquities?

6. If a job is downgraded because of technological changes, what should be done with the employee on that job?

7. Some unions are distrustful of job evaluation. How do you account for such distrust?

8. Does union participation assure success of a job evaluation program? Why?

9. What are some of the sources of union dissatisfaction with job evaluation? How do you believe such dissatisfaction can be overcome?

10. What effect may the labor market conditions have on job evaluation?

11. What are some factors that may conflict with job content as a measure of job worth?

12. What, in your opinion. is the one factor most conducive to job evaluation failure? Why?

Chapter 12

MERIT RATING

U P TO this point the discussion has centered entirely around the methods and problems of determining relative job worth. Any consideration of personnel involved in the performance of the jobs was discouraged, for accurate appraisal of job content and determination of relative presence of worth determining job characteristics preclude evaluation of the individual. It is usually the case, however, that on identical jobs no two operators are of equal value to their employer owing to differences in personal traits. Between operators, the quality and quantity of work will differ; one may be more dependable than another; the amount of supervision required by one may be more or less than that required by another; or one operator may be continually disgruntled without justification while his co-worker may be characterized by an ever-cheerful attitude. Such personal traits are not measurements of job worth, but they are indicative of the relative worth of one employee as compared to another.

In recent years, particularly since World War I, many companies have recognized the value of methods whereby employees might be systematically, periodically, and, within the limits of human possibility impartially rated on matters concerning the performance on their jobs. Such methods or systems are most frequently referred to as "merit rating" and provide the subject matter of this chapter, which is discussed under the following topics:

1. Benefits and uses of merit rating.
2. Some disadvantages of merit rating.
3. Origin and present status.
4. Methods of merit rating.

5. Developing a plan.
6. Accuracy of ratings.
7. Merit rating administration.

Benefits and Uses of Merit Rating

The proponents of merit rating claim for it many benefits in addition to the fulfillment of its primary purpose which is assisting in the measuring of how well an individual worker performs his assigned duties. In other words, merit rating is a means of clearly differentiating between the employee who merely spends time on the job and the one who actually works. This is particularly true in the case of time-paid or daywork employees or where the incentive rates are exceptionally loose and do not reflect a true picture of the operator's effort. Merit rating, then, also affords a means of providing an incentive for employees who are engaged in occupations not adapted to other types of incentive.

While emphasis is usually placed on the benefits derived from having a systematic means of determining merit wage increases, there are other benefits and uses of merit rating which must be recognized as being of considerable value. Such other uses are concerned generally with: (1) promotions, (2) layoffs, (3) transfers, (4) employee guidance, and (5) employee and public relations.

Promotions.—The intelligent selection of employees for promotion has been a continuing management problem. The problem may be solved in part through the merit rating process which aids, by systematically analyzing each individual, in uncovering special or latent talent and capacity for added responsibility. Merit rating alone, however, should not be the sole determinant of promotions; it should be used in conjunction with other data, such as previous employment record, age, physical ability, attendance, schooling, and psychological tests in one form or another.

Layoffs.—Obviously it is to the benefit of management to retain on its payroll during periods of layoff those employees having the greatest ability. Not only does merit rating provide a measure of the worker's ability, but, when properly administered, also serves as a pattern to the worker for job performance standards and comparisons with other employees. In many organizations, particularly those in which the union so insists, seniority strictly determines the people who are subject to layoff. However, in many unorganized plants and in some unionized plants, seniority is the governing factor only when the skill and ability of employees are equal. Illustrative of this viewpoint is a clause taken from an agreement by a large local of the United Steel Workers of America (C.I.O.):

Sec. 4. It is understood and agreed that in all cases of:

(a) Promotion, (except promotions to positions excluded from the definition of "employees" in Section 1 of Article II hereof), the following factors as listed below shall be considered, however, only where factors "a" and "b" are relatively equal shall length of continuous service be the determining factor.
    a) Ability to perform the work.
    b) Physical fitness.
    c) Continuous service.

(b) Increase or decrease in forces—the following factors as listed below shall be considered; however, only where factors "a" and "b" are relatively equal shall continuous service be the determining factor.
    a) Ability to perform the work.
    b) Physical fitness.
    c) Continuous service.[1]

Transfers.—Many transfers, other than those made at the employee's request or for the temporary utilization of skills, are made for the purpose of adapting abilities to job requirements. Where such transfers are in order, records of the employee's background, results of vocational and aptitude tests, and merit ratings will lend considerable assistance to management in transferring the individual to the job where he is more likely to be successful and satisfied.

---

[1] *Agreement between Fairbanks, Morse & Co. (Beloit Works) and United Steel Workers of America (C.I.O.) and Local Union 1533 (Beloit, Wisconsin), July 1, 1947.*

Employee Guidance.—In a previous chapter it was stated that employees wanted to be told in advance of the changes in policy affecting their wages and well-being. The same statement applies equally well where the employee's performance is concerned. Too frequently employees are demoted or dismissed without first being warned of their deficiencies. In such instances employees are usually justified in complaining that supervision failed to let them know how they were getting along. Merit rating enables supervisors to talk to their men and to point out their good qualities as well as the less desirable ones. This tends to lessen the sting of criticism and helps both parties to reach an understanding. Merit rating properly applied provides employees and supervisor with a stimulus to self-analysis, self-improvement, and self-development.

Employee and Public Relations.—An employee is usually a satisfied and willing worker when he knows that he will not be sidetracked as a result of his supervisor's forgetfulness, that his good work will be recognized, and that his supervision will be understanding and intelligent. Periodic reviews of the employee's status should result in pay increases, promotions, or both for deserving and eligible employees. Employees should receive from supervision, as a result of a merit rating plan, analytical and constructive consideration and a greater degree of consistency in treatment and handling. As a result of improved employee relations, public relations for the company are bound to improve. Confidence is inspired in customers and in the public when it becomes known that the company's interest in its employees is expressed through carefully developed merit rating methods.

Some Disadvantages of Merit Rating

Merit rating, however, is not without some disadvantages and criticism. The criticism emanates, for the most part, from union officials who feel that merit rating affords supervision an opportunity to demonstrate favoritism toward individuals. Unfortunately, the criticism is justified in many cases where administration of the plan is weak or where raters have been improperly trained. Another union criticism is that merit rating, as in the case of job evaluation, tends to reduce the effectiveness of collective bargaining.

In a previous chapter the matter of single rates versus rate ranges was discussed and the statement was made that single rates for labor grades tended toward maximum simplicity of the rate structure. This fact was also cited as being one of the advantages of job evaluation. Merit rating, however, requires a range of rates for each labor grade in order to provide rate differentials for reflecting the differences in the merit of workers assigned to identical jobs. As a result the number of rates increase, thus making a more complex rate structure which in turn, complicates payroll procedures and makes budgetary control more difficult and financial forecasting and cost estimating less accurate.

Origin and Present Status

Formal merit rating enjoys somewhat the same status as job evaluation in that its application by industrial and commercial organizations on an extensive basis has taken place in recent years. Government agencies seem to have been the leaders in the use of merit rating. As early as 1915 some school teachers were merit rated. In 1916 the Bureau of Salesmanship was organized, and the following year it adopted a rating scale for salesmen. Meanwhile, the army adopted the Scott man-to-man system which by 1919 had been applied to all commissioned officers. Although the army later discontinued this method, it continues the use of efficiency ratings for all enlisted and commissioned personnel.

Further recognition was given merit rating as a method o measuring the ability of individuals when the Classification Act of 1923 was enacted. This act embodied the basic legislation covering employee rating procedures in the federal government. The following is quoted from the act:

The — — board shall review and may revise uniform systems of efficiency rating established or to be established for the various grades or classes thereof. . . .

The head of each department shall rate in accordance with such systems the efficiency of each employee under his control or direction. The current ratings for each grade or class thereof shall be open to inspection by the representatives of the board and by the employees of the department under conditions to be determined by the board. . . . .

There has been a steady increase in the application of merit rating during the past three decades. A survey conducted by the authors revealed that of 150 companies polled in May, 1948, the increase in the use of merit rating plans was as follows:

Year	Companies Using Merit Rating Plans
1918	7 or 5 per cent
1928	48 or 32 per cent
1938	66 or 44 per cent
1948	93 or 62 per cent

Methods of Merit Rating

In order to facilitate the process whereby supervisors may periodically judge the relative worth of their employees, most organizations employing merit rating have established procedures for the handling and recording of ratings. As with job evaluation, however, the forms used and the procedures established vary between companies because the plans are adapted to the specific needs of the organizations concerned. There is little or no assurance, therefore, that the system successfully employed by one company will meet the requirements of another. The most successful plans are those devised to attain the objectives and to suit the particular conditions and jobs of the individual company.

Generally, there are four basic forms of merit rating, but the numerous combinations of the basic systems account for the large number of variations in the plans now in use. The four basic methods and the order in which they are to be examined are: (1) man-to-man comparison, (2) ranking, (3) check lists, and (4) scales.

Man-to-Man Comparison.—The man-to-man comparison scale, often referred to as the "Army rating scale," was originally developed as a means for selecting salesmen and was later adopted by the United States Army for rating officers and prospective officers during the first World War. The plan called for a brief paragraph describing each of the five characteristics utilized, namely: (1) physical qualities, (2) intelligence, (3) leadership, (4) personal qualities, and (5) general value to the service. Each factor had five degrees, and each degree was assigned a numerical value. The description and degree values for "intelligence" are as follows:

II. INTELLIGENCE:

Accuracy, ease in learning, ability to grasp quickly the point of view of commanding officer, to issue clear and intelligent orders, to estimate a new situation, and to arrive at a sensible decision in a crisis.

Highest........................15
High...........................12
Middle......................... 9
Low........................... 6
Lowest......................... 3[2]

Use of the scale by the rating officer involved the following steps:

1. Selecting an officer of his acquaintance who exemplified each of the degrees of each factor.

2. Assigning to each officer subject to rating the numerical value of the officer on the scale most closely resembling him in the characteristic under consideration.

3. Adding the numerical values assigned each rated officer to arrive at the composite score for the individual officer.

4. Using each score as a basis of comparison for use in rating all officers considered.

While the man-to-man comparison scale afforded considerable improvement over the previously applied plans, it presented a number of difficulties that were instrumental in the almost total disappearance of the plan from use. The more serious difficulties were:

---

[2]Committee on Classification of Personnel, Adjutant General's Department, *Personnel Manual* (Washington, D.C.: U.S. Government Printing Office, 1919).

1. The acquaintanceship of many rating officers was so limited as to preclude the possibility of selecting officers who exemplified each of the degrees of each factor.

2. Even though the rater's acquaintanceship might be broad enough, the task of matching officers against appropriate factor degrees is tedious and cumbersome.

3. Difficulty in selecting the officers to be used in the scale is encountered because of the generalities involved in the definitions of the characteristics.

Ranking.—Merit rating by ranking is the simplest and least time-consuming method. It requires that the supervisor rank employees on the basis of their relative ability to perform their respective jobs. The ranking may be done on an over-all basis, or it may be refined by ranking employees under each of a number of characteristics, such as initiative, co-operativeness, and attitude. Another method of ranking is to establish grades and to place the individuals on the grade most descriptive of their degree of merit. Further refinement is afforded by ranking all employees within a certain grade, the best employees being placed at the top of the list. Each grade should be well defined and state the degree of merit required.

Although speed and simplicity characterize the ranking method, it has the following disadvantages:

1. Supervisors find it difficult to rank with certainty large numbers of employees, for as the number of employees increases the degree of differentiation between employees lessens. The supervisor may find himself in a state of confusion and lacking confidence in his rankings.

2. The method does not allow for a reflection of the degree of differences in merit between employees. It must be assumed under the plan that the differences in merit between employees is the same, an assumption likely to be erroneous, particularly where the extreme ends of the merit rating list are concerned.

3. The rankings are made by using one person as the basis for comparison of all the others being ranked, making it difficult to justify ratings questioned by employees.

Check Lists.—These are ordinarily lists of selected questions, statements, phrases, or words descriptive of the manner in which an employee might perform on the job. Some call for simple "yes" or "no" answers, while others provide a wider choice of descriptive words. In the latter case, the check list may become a simple scale. The rating process consists merely of placing a check mark after the appropriate answer. Figure 12–1 illustrates two types of check lists. It will be noted that the multiple choice type affords a more accurate expression on the part of the rater, while the "yes" and "no" type definitely limits the rater to a positive but frequently inaccurate answer; in fact, this type may prove to be of value only in rating employees who merit extremely high or low ratings.

The most serious problem connected with check lists is compiling a suitable list of questions or statements. A satisfactory plan requires not only the expenditure of considerable time and money but the employment of highly skilled statisticians and trained psychologists. It is because of the difficulty in developing a check list that the plan does not have wider acceptance.

Despite the difficulties of development, the check list that has been constructed by qualified personnel is an excellent method of merit rating because:

1. The tendency to rate an employee on the basis of the over-all general impression of the rater is lessened. This tendency, known as the "halo effect," is one of the dangers to be guarded against in merit rating.

2. The ratings become a matter of record and are more easily substantiated than if determined by ranking.

3. The check list is easy to follow and to score.

4. The criteria are very specific.

5. Employees of different departments can be compared.

6. The check list provides a set of specific points that can form the basis for discussions between supervisor and employee.

Scales.—Of the four basic methods of merit rating, the scale is the most widely used in industry. Under this method, each

TRAIT		
PRODUCTIVITY	UP TO 70%	☐
	70% TO 90%	☐
	90% TO 110%	☐
	110% TO 130%	☐
	OVER 130%	☐
ATTENDANCE	NO ABSENCES	☐
	1 TO 2 "	☐
	3 TO 4 "	☐
	5 TO 6 "	☐
	OVER 6 "	☐

CHECK LIST MULTIPLE CHOICE

TRAIT		YES	NO
QUALITY	ARE QUALITY STANDARDS REGULARLY MAINTAINED ?	☐	☐
	ARE HIS WORK HABITS ORDERLY ?	☐	☐
	DOES HE HANDLE MATERIALS ECONOMICALLY ?	☐	☐
	DOES HIS WORK REQUIRE EXCESSIVE CHECKING ?	☐	☐

CHECK LIST "YES" AND "NO"

FIG. 12–1.—Two types of merit rating check lists.

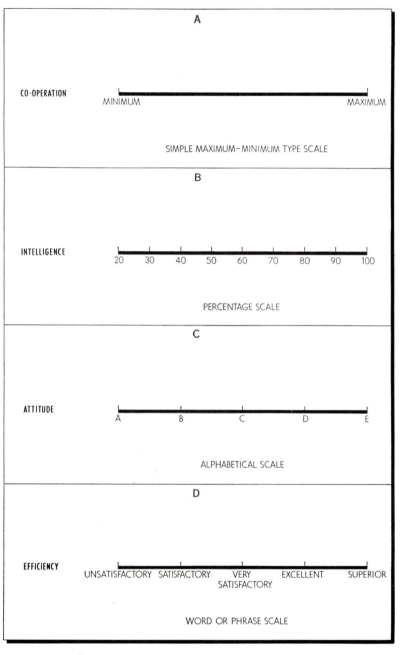

FIG. 12–2.—Four types of continuous type scales.

INSTRUCTIONS TO SUPERVISION

Make your rating an honest, accurate description of the employee being rated, basing opinions on job requirements and on performance of others in the same classification.

REMEMBER THAT YOUR OPINIONS ARE ALSO USED AS A MEASURE OF YOUR JUDGEMENT

1. Place a check (✓) in the space which expresses YOUR OPINION on each factor being rated
2. Place a check (✓) in the spaces at right of sheet to indicate changes in each rating factor.
3. Comment in space provided to clarify or substantiate your rating.

QUALITY OF WORK:

Consider neatness and accuracy of work regardless of volume.
Before checking, consult any production records maintained and compare the amount of his good work with that of others on the same job, and compare with standards which reasonably should be expected.

Work Almost Worthless	Frequent Errors	Normal Accuracy	Very Few Errors	Exceptionally Accurate, Practically No Mistakes		Has Improved	Little or No Change	Has Gone Back

Comment

QUANTITY OF PRODUCTION:

Consider the volume of work produced under normal conditions. Disregard errors.
Before checking, consult any production records maintained, compare his output with that of others on the same work and compare with standards which reasonably should be expected.

Very Slow Worker	Volume Below Average	Average	Turns Out Good Volume	Rapid Worker, Unusually Big Producer		Has Improved	Little or No Change	Has Gone Back

Comment

DEPENDABILITY:

Consider the manner in which he applies himself to his work, whether he does jobs on time, etc., and the amount of supervision he requires. Does he carry out instructions?

Cannot Be Relied Upon, Needs Constant Supervision	Conscientious But Needs Considerable Supervision	Fairly Reliable. Average Supervision Required	Applies Himself Well. Occasional Supervision Required	Justifies Utmost Confidence. Minimum Supervision Req'd.		Has Improved	Little or No Change	Has Gone Back

Comment

FIG. 12–3.—Section of a discontinuous type merit rating scale.

trait is accompanied by a scale similar to those illustrated in Figure 12–2 (p. 273). The rater simply checks along the scale the degree to which the employee being rated possesses the trait under consideration. Because of the almost unlimited variety of forms the scales may take, numerous variations in scales have been developed. Generally, however, most scale forms fall into one of two categories: continuous and discontinuous.

The simplest type of continuous scale consists of a straight line, the extreme ends of which are considered the maximum and minimum degrees of presence of a particular trait (see A, Fig. 12–2). The rater places a check mark at a point along the scale where he believes the degree of the trait most accurately describes the employee being rated. Because of a lack of guideposts along the scale, the rater receives a minimum of guidance. This has led to many modifications of the basic scale form, a few of which are illustrated by B, C, and D in Figure 12–2. It should be noted that in the scales illustrated it is possible to place a check mark at any point along the scale. This permits extremely fine discriminations, so fine, in fact, as to be beyond the scope of human judgment in many cases.

Because of the belief that the fine discriminations permitted by continuous scales are impractical, these scales are rapidly being replaced by the discontinuous type. This type of scale recognizes the limitations of human judgment, simplifies the rater's task, is easily understood by and sold to both supervisor and employee, and lends itself well to the training of raters. Figure 12–3 illustrates in part a discontinuous type merit rating scale. In discussing the development of a merit rating plan, the discontinuous scale type will be considered.

Developing a Plan

Any merit rating plan should be developed around the objectives for which it is being installed; in other words, management, before a plan is developed, must decide what the ratings are to be used for. If, for example, the ratings are to be used as a basis for promotion, the plan must be so designed as to reflect and to measure those traits necessary for promotion.

Merit rating may also be used as a means of control. For example, if absenteeism or scrap losses are a source of worry to management, such traits as attendance or quality can be emphasized when the plan is developed. However, efforts to devise a plan which serves too many purposes may result in the inclusion of an excessive number of traits, thereby making the rating a cumbersome and difficult process. The objective or purpose of the plan is to fulfill the primary consideration in its development.

Selecting Traits.—The first step in the development of a plan is to select the traits to be used. The choice of traits should be made only after due consideration has been given to such factors as the employees who are to be rated, the inclusion of objective items, and the significance and overlapping of traits. Professor Jucius sets forth four rules which, if adhered to, should result in excellent selections. They are:

a) Select traits that are specific rather than general, e.g., honesty is more definite than character.

b) Select traits that can be defined in terms understandable in the same way by all raters.

c) Select traits that are common to as many people as possible.

d) Select traits that raters can observe or be taught to observe in the day-to-day performance of employees.[3]

Employees to Be Rated.—There are, in most industrial organizations, five distinct groups of employees to be considered during the development of a merit rating plan, namely:

1. Nonsupervisory and noncreative shop and clerical personnel who are not required to contact the public.

2. Sales personnel or others who are required to meet the public.

3. Technical personnel, such as research engineers.

4. Supervisory personnel.

5. Executives.

Obviously, the traits applicable to one of the groups above may not be used to rate the employees in the other groups.

---

[3]Michael J. Jucius, *Personnel Management* (Chicago: Richard D. Irwin, Inc., 1947), p. 434.

The ability to meet the public is a vitally important trait in a successful salesman, but is of little concern in determining the worth of a draftsman, cost clerk, or blast furnace keeper. In general, the scales developed to rate those having little or no executive responsibility tend to place emphasis on such traits as skill, co-operativeness, ability to learn, and safety habits; while the supervisory level rating scales emphasize traits such as initiative, ingenuity, leadership, and tact. In short, a good merit rating plan must consider job definitions as obtained by job evaluation.

Objective Items.—Another problem that will confront those developing a plan of merit rating is whether or not objective items or traits should be used. Authorities on the subject of merit rating are somewhat divided in their opinions on the matter. Many feel that objective traits, such as productivity and attendance which are measurable by company records of one sort or another, should not be included in the plan. On the other hand, numerous successful plans have utilized objective traits because:

1. A trait may be objective in one department (where workers' productivity records are kept) but subjective in another (where workers' productivity cannot be measured).

2. Objective traits may measure the reliability of ratings of subjective traits.

3. Objective traits may be necessary in order to complete a record of the facts to be reviewed when employees are being considered for promotion, transfer, layoff, training, or other personnel transactions utilizing merit rating. If objective items are used, raters should be trained to make full use of all the records maintained concerning the items.

The following list of traits or work characteristics includes items that are objective, subjective, and in some instances both objective and subjective. Those items having no asterisk are definitely subjective; those having a single asterisk are objective; and those having a double asterisk may be either objective, subjective, or both, depending on the type of work performed and the records maintained by the company.

Ability to accept responsibility
Adaptability
Adjustment to job
Application to work
Attendance*
Attitude toward company
Attitude toward supervision
Attitude toward work assignments
Capable of handling better job
Capacity for advancement
Care of equipment**
Citizenship*
Conduct**
Co-operativeness
Cost-planning ability
Dependability**
Dependents*
Development
Health**
Honesty
Imagination
Industriousness
Initiative
Intelligence
Interest
Judgment
Knowledge of work
Leadership
Learning ability
Length of service*
Marital status*
Over-all performance
Personality
Personal qualities
Personal habits
Physical condition**
Quality of work**
Quantity of work**
Reliability**
Safety**
Self-confidence
Self-reliance
Speed at learning jobs
Supervisory ability
Work attitude

The above list is far from exhaustive but contains those items most commonly used. Most plans include the traits of quality of work and quantity of work, both of which may be either objective, subjective, or in some instances both. Co-operativeness and dependability were traits used in the majority of plans reviewed by the authors. With the increased use of personnel testing by personnel departments, there is a tendency toward an increase in the number of items in the objective category. Judgment, adaptability, learning ability, self-confidence, and initiative are a few of the characteristics that are being measured with considerable accuracy by means of properly applied test batteries.

Trait Significance.—When a trait is considered for selection, its significance as a characteristic of the work performed by the group of employees to be rated should be questioned. Rating a sweeper on personality is at best a questionable practice, even though that trait has been incorporated in some plans. Marital status, number of dependents, and citizenship are rarely, if ever, significant measures of employee merit. To be significant, the trait must be important for success on the job and identifiable with the work performed.

Overlapping.—Frequently, merit rating plans incorporate traits that are partially or wholly duplications of other traits used. For example, the trait "dependability" used in the same plan with "attendance" might easily be overlapping, for it may be assumed that a dependable person will have a regular attendance record. Such overlapping of traits only tends to confuse the rater and makes the job of rating more time-consuming. Further, overlapping results in a duplication of emphasis on certain traits by giving credit twice when the intent was to recognize the trait but once.

Number of Traits.—If proper consideration is given to plan objectives, to the employee group to be rated, and to the problems of trait significance and of overlapping, the number of traits embodied in the plan will be small. Of 150 plans reviewed by the authors, the majority utilized from five to nine traits, the average closely approaching seven. The maximum number utilized was twenty-three and the minimum three. The tendency in recent years has been toward a reduction in the number of measurement characteristics.

In general, the number will be governed by two fundamentals, namely:

1. What number of traits do the raters believe are necessary? Are they convinced that they can do a satisfactory job of merit rating with the number of traits placed at their disposal? If not, they are probably not sold on the plan.

2. What is the degree of complexity of the jobs held by those to be rated? The clerical or shopworker will not have as complex a job as his supervisor, and the scope of his abilities will not have to be as broad. Therefore, the number of characteristics required to measure the workers' abilities will not be as large as that required for supervisors and executives.

Weighting.—While care may be exercised in the selection of traits, all traits will not have the same degree of significance. There being no statistical or scientific method of determining the relative significance of traits, the problem is usually solved through the application of group judgment. The most satisfactory practice is to weight the items in accordance with the group judgment of those who are to do the rating.

Methods of applying weights vary, but usually the multiplier or percentage method is used. Use of the multiplier, sometimes referred to as a "weight factor," involves classifying the traits utilized as, perhaps, of primary importance, secondary importance, and minor importance and assigning a multiplier to each degree of importance. The maximum points assigned to each trait are constant, but the points awarded the individual are extended by the multiplier, thus weighting the trait. This method enables the use of the same set of traits and trait point values for somewhat different types of work by simply adjusting the multipliers. The percentage method requires that a percentage be applied to each trait, the same percentages applying to the degrees within the respective trait. The widely used National Metal Trades plan weights the six items utilized as follows:

Quality of work	25 per cent
Quantity of work	20 per cent
Adaptability	15 per cent
Job knowledge	20 per cent
Dependability	10 per cent
Attitude	10 per cent
Total	100 per cent

Trait Subdivisions.—After the selection and weighting of factors, a decision must be reached regarding the number of subdivisions into which each trait is to be divided. Of the 150 plans studied, 82 per cent used either four or five subdivisions. Actual practice, therefore, indicates the advisability of not endeavoring to secure too great a degree of accuracy. Too many subdivisions, which in reality are graduations on the rating scale, assume the rater's ability to make extremely fine discriminations. On the other hand, too few subdivisions make the desired degree of differentiation impossible. A restriction placed on the number of trait subdivisions is the fact that consistency in rating requires that each trait be clearly defined.

The possibility of defining degrees between minimum and maximum decreases as the number of degrees increases.

Another point to be considered in determining the number of subdivisions to be used is the inclination of raters to rate employees as "average" to an unwarranted degree. This is known as "central tendency" and can be partially reduced by the use of an even, rather than an odd, number of trait subdivisions, for the rater will be provided with no central subdivision to serve as a guide. Practice, the possibility of clear definition, and the problem of central tendency indicate the utilization of four trait subdivisions.

Scoring Ratings.—The uses and objectives of the merit rating plan will be fundamental factors in determining whether or not the ratings will be scored. If the primary function of the plan is to afford a basis of guidance and discussion for the employee, then a method of scoring may not be necessary or advisable. Some managements feel that it is impossible and undesirable to reduce human values to numerical terms, and for this reason they refrain from attempts to score ratings. However, if ratings are to be used for determining those employees to be promoted, transferred, or temporarily or permanently dismissed, then scoring may be advisable in that it affords a more explainable basis for any such action. The persons affected are more easily convinced because the scales have the appearance of fact. If ratings are to be scored, one of two type of scores will usually be used, although a compromise between the two is entirely possible. The two types are: over-all scoring and individual trait scoring.

a) Over-all Scoring.—These scores may be used as they are or may be grouped into categories, those employees falling into the same group who are considered roughly equal in merit. When over-all scores are used, the common practice is to assign a numerical value to each trait subdivision. Numerical values may be assigned on the basis of the pooled judgment of those who do the rating, although numerical values may also be assigned by more complicated methods based on the statistics of variability or "standard scores." Statistics of variability indicate that the greater the deviation of scores is from the average, the arithmetic expression of scores fails to reflect the true meaning of the deviation. Because of this, the standard scores unit is the standard deviation which may be interpreted to tell the amount by which a score deviates from the average score.

The danger of using raw scores lies in the fact that judgment alone does not permit a fine degree of discrimination. Ratings are no more precise than the judgments formulating them. Therefore, just as in job evaluation, where rate ranges rather than single rates are advisable, groupings or score ranges may be used in merit rating so that undue importance will not be attached to numerical scores and the inclination to regard scores as exact units of measurements will be lessened. An example of grouping or merit score ranges is seen in the National Metal Trades Association plan which provides for five groups as follows:

Group 1......................91 to 100 points
Group 2......................81 and under 91 points
Group 3......................71 and under 81 points
Group 4......................61 and under 71 points
Group 5......................60 points or less

b) Individual Trait Scoring.—There is the belief on the part of some organizations, however, that scoring on an over-all basis may cover up deficiences in important traits. Because of this, they resort to the use of an individual score for each trait. Such a procedure obviously makes the summarizing of rating results more difficult for supervision. It is claimed by exponents of the procedure, however, that such a disadvantage is offset by the fact that employees are assured due credit on some traits even though they may be very superior or inferior in others. Undue emphasis on trait scoring is no less dangerous than on over-all scoring and for the same reasons. Therefore, utilization of point groups should: (1) avoid overemphasis on numerical values, and, in addition, (2) tend to eliminate the practice of some supervisors of averaging all trait scores, the result of which may be a pseudo over-all score which is what the trait scoring method seeks to avoid.

Defining Terms.—Inconsistencies in ratings frequently are traceable to the failure of raters to consistently interpret the meanings of traits and of trait subdivisions. This is not surprising when such abstractions as "personality," "co-operation," and "attitude" are so prevalent in merit rating plans. As was brought out in the discussion of defining factors and factor degrees in job evaluation plans, words and phrases, if not carefully chosen, are likely to convey unlike meanings. The problem is particularly acute in the case of subjective traits, but there may be no problem at all if certain objective traits are used. For example, if the trait "quantity of work" is used and the scale is constructed to reflect productivity percentages, such percentages being a matter of accurate record, then there should be little or no problem of definition.

In general, definition of traits by means of a sentence or paragraph is the most satisfactory method, for it permits a wider latitude of expression than does definition by a single phrase, adverb, or adjective. In actual practice the majority of plans seem to define traits by name only and trait subdivisions by simple phrases. The best approach to solving the problem of how traits and trait subdivisions should be defined is to discuss the matter with the group who will do the rating. This will give greater assurance of mutual understanding of meaning and, therefore, of rating consistency. Briefly, then, the manner in which traits and their degrees are defined will best be determined by what the raters believe necessary for accurate ratings.

Rating Forms.—The basic information contained in any merit rating form consists of the traits, trait subdivisions, and necessary definitions; and if a system of scoring is used, provision is usually made for recording the scores. Such being the case, the variety of forms in use is almost unlimited owing to the wide divergence of opinion on such matters as the type, number, defining, weighting, and scoring of the traits to be used. Figure 12–4 illustrates one of the many forms now in use.

In addition to the basic information, certain supplementary facts are usually included in the form, namely:

MERIT RATING REPORT

Name _____ Clock No. _____ Date _____

Department _____ Job Classification _____ Grade _____

Duties:

DO NOT ALLOW PERSONAL FEELING TO GOVERN YOUR RATING. Do not be influenced by UNUSUAL SITUATIONS which are not typical. Check in block which seems best to fit above employee.

Knowledge of Work	Practically None ☐	Below Average ☐	Acceptable Knowledge ☐	Somewhat above Average ☐	Very well informed ☐
Effect on Workers	Often Breeds Trouble ☐	Sometimes causes Dissension ☐	No out-standing effect on workers ☐	Better than Average ☐	Promotes cooperation and Good-will ☐
Promptness	Always Tardy ☐	Must be reminded about Promptness ☐	Usually Prompt ☐	Never Late without good cause ☐	Almost never Late ☐
Responsibility	Careless and Negligent ☐	Not very reliable ☐	Accepts Resp. when asked ☐	Assumes Resp. without being told ☐	Accepts Resp. above Average Requirement ☐

Accuracy	Is highly inaccurate ☐	Is often inaccurate ☐	Makes Occasional errors ☐	Somewhat above Average ☐	Rarely makes mistakes ☐
Quantity of Work	Amount of work unsatisfactory ☐	Turns out just enough to get by ☐	Turns out fair amt. ☐	Always finishes alloted amount ☐	Turns out more than average amount ☐
Initiative	Must always be told what to do ☐	Needs considerable Supervision ☐	Needs Direction and help in cases ☐	Needs little Supervision ☐	Pushes work thru on own initiative ☐
Application	Indifferent and Lazy ☐	Tendency toward Indifference ☐	Average application ☐	Interested and Diligent ☐	Puts extra effort into work ☐

TOTAL _____

How long have you known this employee? _____ Do you consider this employee a prospect for upgrading? _____

How long under your supervision? _____

Yes _____ No _____ Now _____ Later _____ Rated by _____

Calculated by _____ Date _____ Committee Action _____ Date _____

Use back of sheet for additional information or remarks.

_____ Merit Rate Committee.

FIG. 12-4.—One of the many types of merit rating forms in use.

1. The name and clock or payroll number of the rated employee.
2. The employee's occupation and the department in which he works.
3. The name and title of the rater.
4. The name and title of the person reviewing and approving the rating.
5. The date.

In addition to the above, some forms provide spaces in which the rater may, in accordance with provided instructions, enter any comments he wishes to supplement the rating. Such comments may be of value in substantiating extremely high or low ratings. Another method used is that providing a series of questions concerning such matters as the raters' satisfaction with the employee and the employee's progress, suitability for the work he or she is performing, and general attitude. Regardless of how it is recorded, supplementary information will depend on such factors as: the information desired by top management, the objectives of the plan, the type of employees being rated, and the intelligence level of the raters.

Accuracy of Ratings

Inaccurate ratings are not only useless to management but can be harmful to employee morale, the status of industrial relations, and the acceptability of the merit rating program itself. Any program is incomplete unless a plan for testing the accuracy of ratings is provided. One such test is to check on the validity of the ratings; another is to check on their reliability. In general, validity refers to the accuracy of the ratings while reliability refers to the consistency of the rater.

Validity of Ratings.—Because guides or standards against which to compare ratings are frequently not available, the validity of ratings is often difficult to measure. Here again the question of whether the objective or subjective trait is most desirable enters the discussion. With the subjective trait there is little concrete or factual data upon which to base ratings, and, therefore, a test of the validity of the rating of that type of trait is in reality a test of the accuracy of judgment. The validity of the rating of an objective trait, however, can be tested by checking the rating against the factual data reflected in the records. The objective trait, therefore, appears to be more conducive to validity in rating.

In addition to comparing ratings with employment, performance, and other records, other frequently used methods of checking the validity of ratings are as follows:

1. Comparison of ratings with employee performance. For example, comparing personal traits of attitude, co-operation, and conduct with performance.

2. Comparisons of ratings with the results of psychological tests. For example, comparing the rating on judgment with the score attained on a practical judgment test.

3. Determining the existence of a "halo effect" by noting whether or not there is a tendency on the part of raters to rate all factors at approximately the same level as the first factor.

4. Comparing the ratings of the same employees made by two or more raters.

Reliability of Ratings.—The reliability of ratings can be and usually is checked by comparing periodically the ratings made by the same rater. For example, if a rater rates an employee the same today as he did three months ago, it can be assumed that the ratings are reliable—provided, of course, there has been no change in the ability of the employee. However, because employees do change from period to period, too much reliance on such comparisons is unwise; therefore, checks should be made to uncover changes that have taken place since the first ratings were made. Records reflecting the trend of employee performance can be used for such checks.

Distribution of Ratings.—Many authorities on rating methods apply normal distribution percentages as yardsticks for analyzing rating results. Such an approach has considerable merit, if the assumption is correct that the distribution of ratings follows the normal distribution curve. A normal distribution curve, graphically plotted, takes a bell shape, and any deviations from

normal result in skewing the curve. Figure 12–5 illustrates a
normal curve and the effect of a deviation from normal. In the

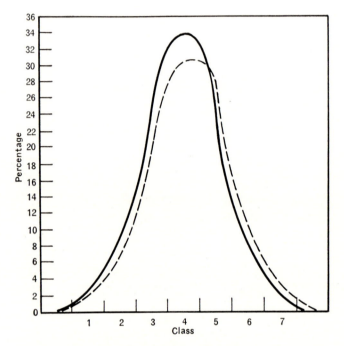

FIG. 12–5.—Plot of distribution of actual ratings (broken
line) against normal expectancy (solid line).

figure the normal distribution showed that the employees were
expected to be rated as follows:

Percentage of Employees	Class
2	lowest
8	second
23	third
34	middle
23	fifth
8	sixth
2	highest

Actually, however, the distribution of ratings (broken line) de-
viated from normal, causing the curve to be skewed to the right.
The actual ratings showed the following situation to exist:

Percentage	
of Employees	*Class*
2	lowest
6	second
20	third
30	middle
28	fifth
11	sixth
3	highest

The illustration reflects a situation that is not uncommon in actual practice. If the assumption of symmetrical distribution about the average is correct, then the deviation from normal might result in additional training sessions for raters or perhaps in replacements. However, while it is true that the characteristics of the employees tend to take the form of the normal distribution curve when they are graphically illustrated, there is no assurance that the curve will be normal if the number of employees rated is neither large nor random. Where merit rating is concerned, it is frequently the case in actual practice that the sample of ratees is not random; consequently, the curve is skewed to the right or in the direction of higher ratings. There are three fundamental causes of this tendency:

1. Standardizing of operations has advanced in many plants and offices to the point where only a small part of the employee's ability is required to meet quantity and quality requirements. As a result many of those who normally would fall in the low or middle classes are able to meet or to exceed normal requirements.

2. Modern selection and hiring methods which utilize aptitude, ability, and vocational interest tests result in the hiring of a higher proportion of employees having abilities greater than the average.

3. The instituting by many managements of systems of motivation, such as wage incentives. Merit rating itself will, if properly administered, cause many employees to seek self-improvement and thereby to lift themselves above the low or middle classes.

Because the assumption that ratings will follow a normal distribution curve is not entirely reliable, such curves should be used as checks on rating results only after the ratings have been tested. One method of testing would be to plot the ratings of a large number of raters and to compare the resulting curve with the normal curve. If the actual curve is closely identical with the normal curve, it will be safe to assume that the normal curve is satisfactory. If such is not the case, the actual curve can be considered as normal for those conditions but should be checked from time to time to spot any changes which may occur.

Merit Rating Administration

The administration of a merit rating program is most successfully carried out if those involved have been thoroughly sold on the benefits and uses of the program. The fundamental problems of merit rating and of equitable ratings and their proper utilization can be solved only if the co-operation of those charged with the responsibility for rating is secured. In Chapter 8 the necessity for selling job evaluation was emphasized, and in general the same points apply to selling merit rating. For a merit rating program to be successful, those vitally concerned must participate in the program to the fullest extent possible, and those who will be affected by the program must be educated to the benefits and advantages of merit rating by means of any and all media available. (See Fig. 12–6.) However, before a merit rating program can be sold, the basic policies concerning the program must be formulated. These policies concern the administration of the system and in most cases require decisions on the following matters:

1. Who shall do the rating?
2. How often shall employees be rated?
3. Should ratings be reviewed?
4. Who shall score the ratings?
5. Should ratings be discussed with employees?
6. How should raters be trained?

Who Shall Do the Rating?—Because merit rating involves the appraisal of an individual, it appears obvious that the person

DEPENDABILITY . . .

Can you be relied upon to carry
out all instructions and can your
supervisor "bank" on your being
on the job on time?

VERSATILITY

What jobs in
the plant, other
than your own,
can you handle
skillfully?

HEALTH . . .

Are your physical and
mental conditions good?

●

Each Seater has the privi-
lege of seeing his own
periodic merit rating. He
may make the request of his foreman, who will
show it to him in the presence of a representative
of the Industrial Relations Department.

FIG. 12–6.—Explaining and publicizing merit rating. A page from the
American Seating Company booklet *You and Your Wages.*

best acquainted with the personal traits of the employee to be
rated should receive first preference as a rater. It naturally
follows that the employee's immediate superior should head the

list of raters, for it is he or she who has had the closest contact with the employee and, therefore, who has been in the best position to make a fair appraisal. However, a greater degree of rating reliability can be expected if more than one person takes part in the rating. Therefore, every effort should be made to find additional raters.

In the small company the selection of additional qualified raters is a relatively simple task, because the members of the various levels of management tend to have closer contact with all personnel of the company. In large companies, however, such is not the case, and the problem may be rather difficult. The answer in the large companies may be found in one of the following suggestions:

1. Use only those persons as raters who are sufficiently well acquainted with the employees being rated to do a satisfactory job of rating. This approach may result in a single individual or in several persons doing the rating and in a wide variety in the number of raters between departments.

2. Have the member of the personnel department who is best acquainted with the employee do the rating in conjunction with the employee's supervisor. This suggestion has merit only if the personnel department member has had an opportunity to witness the employee at work.

3. Use a rating committee composed of a member of each of the several echelons of supervision. Such a procedure might have considerable merit in those cases where supervision has progressed up through the ranks and, on the way up, has had close contact with the employees being rated. The primary reason for employing a rating committee, however, is in the fact that at least two members probably will have had an acquaintance with employees being rated and they will be able, through open discussion and interrogation, to help the committee arrive at a fair rating.

4. Utilize the joint employee-management technique of having committees composed of supervision and employees. This method may have the advantages of complete employee participation and of having the raters well acquainted with the

personal traits of the ratees; it is seldom used, however, because of the prevalent opinion among management that merit rating is strictly a management function.

The number of raters to use depends on the available number of people who have had sufficient contact with the ratee to do an equitable job of rating. In the majority of cases this number is limited to one, namely, the immediate supervisor. Even where more than one rater is involved, the supervisor is, in the final analysis, the one who guides the judgment of the others; for he, in the absence of substantiating records, is the source of the information which is used as the basis for formulating opinions. In actual practice, the great majority of concerns use but a single rating for each employee.

How Often Shall Employee Be Rated?—The necessity for maintaining up-to-date ratings without placing undue burden on the raters fairly well establishes the maximum and minimum of rating frequency. Surveys show that about three-quarters of all ratings are made at intervals ranging from six to twelve months. In the final analysis the minimum frequency should be based upon the frequency of change in business conditions, the employee, and the relationship between the two. Such a frequency is at best difficult to measure if it can be measured at all. For this reason judgment may be the sole criterion of the maximum interval between ratings. One point, however, should be borne in mind, and that is: if intervals between ratings are too wide, there is the possibility of the rater and ratee losing interest in the project or forgetting that merit rating exists.

There are also more practical considerations in establishing the maximum frequency of ratings. Ratings made too frequently are apt to become mechanical and may not reflect noticeable changes in employees. Each successive rating, therefore, may be unduly influenced by the previous one. There is also a danger in overburdening supervision with ratings, for if merit rating absorbs too much of the supervisor's time, hurried and perhaps inequitable ratings may result. Further, too frequent ratings may cause them to become commonplace to the employee, and interest in the program may dwindle.

Probationary employees, trainees, and those taking short-term apprenticeship courses present a somewhat different problem. The progress of employees in these groups should be closely watched, and very frequent ratings may be advisable from the standpoint of guiding the employee in his efforts. Probationary and training periods of three to twelve months usually require ratings at monthly intervals, while periods of less than three months may require weekly or biweekly reports on employee merit for purposes of determining the degree of improvement being made by the individual.

Should Ratings Be Reviewed?—A review of ratings by persons other than the raters has considerable value in that it provides a check on consistency and tends to reduce the effect of favoritism and lack of understanding of the plan. A proper review of ratings, then, has the effect of increasing their validity and reliability. Ordinarily, where review procedures have been established, the immediate superior of the rater, a line executive or a representative of the personnel department, reviews the ratings. The practice of permitting the reviewer to change the ratings should be discouraged. It detracts from the prestige of the rater; and, if changes are excessive, it may result in the rater doing a halfhearted job, for he may feel that his efforts will bring little but criticism. The better procedure is to have the reviewer note discrepancies on the form and discuss them with the rater. This practice tends to maintain the authority, prestige, and self-confidence of the rater.

Who Shall Score the Ratings?—This is not a serious problem, provided the scores are not permitted to become generally known and are not likely to influence future ratings. In smaller companies raters often score their own ratings, and for this reason there may be a greater tendency toward perpetuating inaccuracies than is the case in the larger companies where scoring may be turned over to a clerical staff.

Should Ratings Be Discussed with Employees?—The consensus among administrators of merit rating seems to be that, theoretically at least, mutual benefits accrue through the discussion of ratings with employees. There are also those who disagree, sometimes violently, with the majority, and their reasons for disagreement are often well founded. One of the most forceful arguments on the affirmative side is based on the opinion that discussing ratings with employees forces an adherence to sound rating plans and to practices and care in ratings. If such deficiences as poorly selected traits, too many trait subdivisions, or poorly composed definitions exist in a plan, the rater may find it difficult to justify the ratings, and as a result corrective revisions will have to be made. Further, if a supervisor knows that he must talk over his ratings with his employees, he will want to be sure that he can substantiate them and will take greater pains in their formulation. Another consideration concerns the motivation of the employee toward self-analysis and improvement. Obviously, if an employee feels that he is entitled to promotion but is merely told that his record will not permit it, he may become frustrated and disheartened unless he is told in what particular trait he should bend his efforts toward improvement. In addition, most employees feel that they have a right to information regarding why they were eliminated from the promotion list, demoted, laid off, or transferred. Discussions, therefore, are a means of heading off and of reducing grievances, particularly where a union is concerned.

Those having a negative viewpoint on the matter of discussing ratings with employees frequently voice the following objections to the practice:

1. There may result a tendency on the part of supervisors to be lenient in their ratings in order to avoid discussing a justified low rating with an employee. There should be some doubt in such cases as to the advisability of maintaining that type of supervisor on the payroll; but, if necessary, the problem can be partially solved by a review of ratings by a higher authority.

2. Discussions may lead to arguments which in turn may lead to labor difficulties or perhaps to a loss of temper on the part of the supervisor and, consequently, to resentment on the part of the employee to the entire plan. Here the question seems to be not whether or not ratings should be discussed with employees but whether or not short-tempered supervisors inept at discussing merit rating should be permitted to discuss ratings with employees.

Regardless of what management decides on the matter, it will be found that sooner or later some employee will feel that he or she has been unjustly rated and a grievance will result. Where merit ratings are used to determine wage increases, promotions, layoffs, transfers, and demotions, unions will usually require that the employees be given a right to appeal the ratings which they believe to be unjust. Whether the appeal is made through an appeal procedure similar to that used in job evaluation or through a grievance procedure incorporated into the union agreement, a discussion of the rating with the employee is bound to result. Frequently, therefore, management may have little say in the matter of whether or not ratings will be discussed with employees.

How Should Raters Be Trained?—An ideal plan may be developed, management, supervision, and employees may be thoroughly sold on objectives and principles, and excellent merit rating administrative policies may be formulated, but all will be of no avail unless the ratings are fair, equitable, and used constructively. Proper ratings and their constructive use, it is generally agreed, are best accomplished by the proper training of raters. Much of the training is, or should be, accomplished when the raters are assisting in the development of the plan. Most often, however, little is learned of the actual mechanics of rating during this period; and it falls within the scope of responsibility of the administrators of the project to provide the necessary training in the process of actually rating employees and of constructively using the ratings.

Training in the mechanics of rating is best accomplished through the application of direct contact methods, such as training classes similar to those used on job evaluation projects or individual coaching of supervisors by qualified instructors. Such direct contact methods can be effectively augmented by use of the more indirect training manuals, slides, sound films, and other applicable types of training aids. Practice in actually rating employees should also be emphasized during the training period. Personal contact is most effective in training in the constructive use of ratings. Sound movies are an excellent but less direct method. The conferences should provide for actual practice in praising and assisting the employee and in reviewing ratings.

Conclusion

This chapter has been devoted to a discussion of systematic methods of determining man differentials—methods of merit rating that afford management a tool for appraising the relative worth of individuals. Previous chapters examined systematic methods of determining job differentials—methods of job evaluation that afford management a tool for appraising the relative worth of jobs. Merit rating and job evaluation are alike in that they can both function in accordance with predetermined procedures and can be impartial. However, merit rating is personal and follows the hiring of the employee, while job evaluation must be impersonal and precedes hiring of the employee. Where management is equipped with defensible means of impartially appraising both the worth of the job and the worth of the employee on the job, the source of many of labor's openly expressed grievances will be eliminated.

QUESTIONS

1. How does merit rating differ basically from job evaluation?
2. How does the employee benefit from merit rating? How does management benefit?
3. What are your criticisms of merit rating?
4. What are the difficulties encountered in the man-to-man merit rating method?
5. What are the advantages and disadvantages of the ranking method of merit rating?
6. Why do merit rating check lists not have wider acceptance?
7. Why are discontinuous type scales more satisfactory than the continuous type?
8. Around what should a merit rating plan be developed? Explain.

9. What are the considerations in selecting the traits to be used in a merit rating plan?

10. Differentiate between an objective and a subjective trait.

11. How many traits should be used in merit rating? Why? How many trait subdivisions would you advise using? Why?

12. What do you believe to be the most satisfactory manner of defining traits and their subdivisions? Why?

13. How would you check on the validity of your merit ratings? How would you check on the reliability of your merit ratings?

14. Who would you suggest do the merit rating? Who should score the ratings? Who should review the ratings?

15. How often should an employee be rated?

16. Would you, as a supervisor, discuss your ratings with the employees involved? Why?

BIBLIOGRAPHY

BIBLIOGRAPHY

AMERICAN IRON and STEEL INSTITUTE. *Merit Rating of Employees.* 1938.

ARKIN and COLTON. *An Outline of Statistical Methods.* New York: Barnes & Noble, 1939.

BALDERSTON, C. CANBY. *Wage Setting Based on Job Analysis and Evaluation,* Monograph No. 4. New York: Industrial Relations Counselors, 1943.

BENGE, BURKE, and HAY. *Manual of Job Evaluation.* New York: Harper & Bros., 1941.

BENGE, EUGENE J. *Job Evaluation and Merit Rating.* National Foremen's Institute, Inc., 1941.

BURTT, HAROLD E. *Principles of Employment Psychology.* New York: Harper & Bros., 1942.

FORD, ADELBERT. *A Scientific Approach to Labor Problems.* New York: McGraw-Hill Book Co., Inc., 1931.

GENERAL ELECTRIC COMPANY, Appliance and Merchandise Department. *A Description of the Hourly and Salary Rating Plans.* Bridgeport, Conn., 1939.

GILLETT, ALBERT H. *How to Evaluate Supervisory Jobs.* National Foremen's Institute, Inc., 1945.

GOLDEN and RUTTENBERG. *The Dynamics of Industrial Democracy.* New York: Harper & Bros., 1942.

GOMBERG, WILLIAM. *A Labor Union Manual on Job Evaluation.* Chicago: Roosevelt College Press, 1947.

GREEN, E. B. *Measurement of Human Behavior.* New York: Odyssey Press, 1941.

HAY, EDWARD N. *Business Ideas for Increasing Profits.* New York: Prentice-Hall, Inc., 1940.

HILL, R. L. "Efficiency Ratings," *Personnel Journal,* Vol. XV, No. 9 (1937).

HOLLINGSWORTH, H. L. *Judging Human Character.* New York: D. Appleton-Century Co., 1922.

JENKINS, J. G. *Psychology in Business and Industry.* New York: John Wiley & Sons, Inc., 1935.

JOHNSON, BOISE, and PRATT. *Job Evaluation.* New York: John Wiley & Sons, Inc., 1946.

JUCIUS, MAYNARD, and SHARTLE. *Job Analysis for Retail Stores.* Columbus: Ohio State University, Bureau of Business Research, 1945.

JUCIUS, MICHAEL J. *Personnel Management.* Chicago: Richard D. Irwin, Inc., 1947.

KRESS, A. L. "How to Rate Jobs and Men," *Factory Management and Maintenance*, Vol. XCVII, No. 10 (October, 1939).

LOTT, MERRILL R. *Wage Scales and Job Evaluation.* New York: Ronald Press Co., 1926.

LYTLE, C. W. *Job Evaluation Methods.* New York: Ronald Press Co., 1946.

LYTLE, C. W. *Wage Incentive Methods.* New York: Ronald Press Co., 1942.

MILLS, F. C. *Statistical Methods Applied to Economics and Business.* New York: Henry Holt & Co., Inc., 1938.

MOORE and HARTMANN. *Readings in Industrial Psychology.* New York: D. Appleton-Century Co., 1931.

RIEGEL, JOHN W. *Salary Determination.* Ann Arbor: University of Michigan, Bureau of Industrial Relations, 1940. Also *Wage Determination*, 1937.

SCOTT, CLOTHIER, MATHEWSON, and SPRIEGEL. *Personnel Management.* New York: McGraw-Hill Book Co., Inc., 1941.

SMYTH and MURPHY. *Job Evaluation and Employee Rating.* New York: McGraw-Hill Book Co., Inc., 1946.

STIGERS and REED. *Theory and Practice of Job Rating.* New York: McGraw-Hill Book Co., Inc., 1942.

UNITED ELECTRICAL, RADIO, and MACHINE WORKERS OF AMERICA. *U. E. Guide to Wage Payment Plan, Time Study and Job Evaluation.* 1943.

U.S. DEPARTMENT OF LABOR. "Digest of State and Federal Labor Legislation," *U.S. Department of Labor Bulletin 63.* Washington, D.C.: U.S. Government Printing Office, 1944.

VITELES, MORRIS S. *Industrial Psychology.* New York: W. W. Norton & Co., 1932.

WALTERS, J. E. *Personnel Relations.* New York: Ronald Press Co., 1945.

WATKINS and DODD. *The Management of Labor Relations.* New York: McGraw-Hill Book Co., Inc., 1938.

WAUGH, A. E. *Elements of Statistical Methods.* New York: McGraw-Hill Book Co., Inc., 1943.

WEED, D. W. "Job Evaluation by Point Ratings," *American Machinist,* Vol. XXCIII, No. 9 (May 3, 1939).

WESTINGHOUSE ELECTRIC CORPORATION. *Industrial Relations Manual.* 1934.

WORTHAM, MARY HARPER. *Rating of Supervisors.* Pasadena: California Institute of Technology Press, 1944.

YODER, DALE. *Personnel Management and Industrial Relations.* New York: Prentice-Hall, Inc., 1942

INDEX

INDEX